THE ROOTS OF FRENCH REPUBLICANISM

THE ROOTS
OF
FRENCH REPUBLICANISM

*THE EVOLUTION OF THE REPUBLICAN IDEAL
IN FRENCH-REVOLUTIONARY FRANCE
AND ITS CULMINATION IN THE CONSTITUTION OF 1793*

by

JAMES M. MOORE, PH. D.

THE AMERICAN PRESS   NEW YORK, N.Y.

AMERICAN PRESS PUBLICATIONS, Inc.
282-7th Ave. New York 1, N.Y.

CONTENTS

CONTENTS

To

All lovers of freedom and democratic constitutional government following the Franco-American tradition

and to

those family members and mentors who have been encouraging to me in the search for the roots of our common Franco-American heritage: my mother, Frances Maxwell Moore; my wife, Kenna McCarthy Moore; Lt. Commander Thomas A. Moore (U.S.N.R.); Frances Carol Moore; Brendan James Moore Jr.; Thomas Atherton Moore III; Professor Crane Brinton; Professor Franklin Palm; and Professor George Havens.

PREFACE

First the author of this monograph wishes to express his gratitude and indebtedness to the great specialists in the fields of French Revolutionary history and political theory who, either directly, through personal contact, or indirectly, through the written word, have aided him in its preparation. Professor Crane Brinton of the Society of Fellows, Harvard University, read the original draft and made valuable suggestions as to form and styling. Professor G. R. Havens, of Ohio State University, author of *The Age of Ideas*, also read the original draft and was especially helpful in the restyling of the first chapter, "Philosophy as an Important Factor in the Development of the Republican Ideal in France." Professor Franklin Palm, emeritus, of the University of California (Berkeley), first aroused the interest of the author in French Revolutionary studies when the author had the privilege of working under him as a graduate student. Moreover, he pointed out the immense value of contemporary French Revolutionary pamphlet literature — which the writer has continued to explore since his graduate days.

Finally, great appreciation must be expressed for those specialists, French and American, of the past and present, whose works have naturally been an inspiration and help. Their names are found in the bibliography. On this side of the ocean, just to mention a few names, in addition to those listed above, they are: Professors Richard Brace, D. Echeverria, Lucy Gidney, Leo Gershoy, R. K. Gooch, L. R. Gottschalk, Beatrice Hyslop, R. M. Palmer, Harold Parker,

J. Salwyn Schapiro, Roger Soltau, and John Hall Stewart — all of whom have made noteworthy contributions.

To the author, the research and writing about the roots of French republicanism has been a fascinating undertaking. Originally he made a study of France's first republican constitution — the Constitution of 1793 — as an isolated problem relating to partisan strife between the Jacobins and the Girondins. In the study of this great document — great for such innovations as the referendum, recall, petition, the right to work, the right to resist one's own government if it became oppressive and unrepresentative, and other unusual provisions — it was discovered that it was not only of considerable moment because of its intimate connection with the great political events of 1793, but that it was also significant as an integral part of the great democratic evolution going on in Europe and America during the eighteenth century. Recently Professor Palmer, in *The Age of the Democratic Revolution: A Political History of Europe and America,* 1760-1800, has pointed out the general significance of this movement in a splendid fashion. The author of the monograph has concentrated on the French scene, in the main. Of course, the men largely responsible for the constitutional work of 1793 — Condorcet (last of the *philosophes*), Tom Paine, Brissot, Robespierre, and others — were a product of the times and naturally were influenced by eighteenth-century philosophy and the republican example of the United States. Indeed, Tom Paine, a citizen of two worlds, was not only a founder of American republicanism. He was a founder of French republicanism as well.

France has had a number of constitutions since 1793. Perhaps none can compare in historical interest or in constitutional uniqueness to that of the First French Republic. France, today, still seems to have constitutional problems. In 1958 the French people adopted by referendum — even as in 1793 — the constitution of the Fifth French Republic. Showing customary concern regarding constitutional matters, perhaps, is the arrangement in the constitution for a Constitutional Council. This body is responsible for supervising all elections and referendums and must be consulted in all constitutional matters and before the President of the Republic assumes emergency powers. In 1793, on the grounds of a national emergency, the functioning of the first French republican constitution was postponed indefinitely. Yet today there are those who believe that the Constitution of 1793 represented the zenith of French democratic aspiration.

November, 1962
Norwich University
Northfield, Vermont

THE ROOTS OF FRENCH REPUBLICANISM

INTRODUCTION

Since the outbreak of the French Revolution in 1789, France's constitutional development has been characterized by rapid and, sometimes, spectacular changes. The period from May, 1789, to June, 1793, was one of such change. When the king, because of demands of reform, called the obsolete States-General[1] in May, 1789, France theoretically had one of the most absolute governments in Europe. The king was literally the state. Four years later France was to be without a king and was to have one of the most democratic constitutions of all time, a charter which, through a national *plebiscite*, had the approval of all the sovereign people. During this four-year interval there were rapid political transitions.

In June, 1789, the advisory States-General became the Constituent Assembly, with the bourgeoisie achieving dominance over the other two, more privileged classes — the clergy and the nobility. After working for over a year, the Constituents developed a Constitution, that of September, 1791, which provided for a limited monarchy partly checked by a single legislative body elected through restrictive suffrage. This frame of government was a distinct step forward from absolutism and apparently pleased the majority of all classes in France. However, there was a minority, a thinking and acting one, which seemed to be groping unconsciously for something more. This something more was a *republic*,

---

1. An advisory body which had not been called since 1614. It was made up of representatives of the clergy, nobles, and commons. These three orders had always deliberated and voted separately. When a measure was sanctioned by two of the groups, it was regarded by the king as being approved. Obviously, the two upper and more conservative orders would always have the preponderating influence under such an arrangement.

a word few dared utter before 1791. The minority represented the educated bourgeoisie and, sometimes, even nobles and clergymen; all had been steeped in republican ideas through their classical educations and their constant devotions to the works of the great philosophers. Events were to take place in such a way that the dream of a minority nearly became a lasting reality.

France's political history between September, 1791, and September, 1792, is the story of a shaky limited monarchy vainly endeavoring to maintain itself against the increasingly violent attacks of republicans both within and without the Legislative Assembly. The rising crescendo of republicanism finally resulted in the people's movement of August 10, 1792. An impotent and incompetent king was removed and a Convention was elected which declared France a republic on September 21, 1792.

The Convention had a turbulent existence of three years and yet managed to prepare two constitutions. It was the first, that of June, 1793, which was voted for by all the French people and embodied the democratic principles imbibed from the philosophers of the eighteenth century, plus the lessons learned from observing the government of the newly created United States of America. This constitution was really the result of the work of two constitutional committees. The first was largely made up of members of a Conventional faction, termed the Girondin. Condorcet, a famous philosopher, was the mainspring of the committee and did most of the work. Because of factional strife with another group in the Convention, termed the Mountain, this first committee, after preparing an unusual plan of constitution, had to give way to a new committee whose members represented the Mountain. These political opponents, borrowing generously from the first committee's scheme, quickly presented to a Convention shrunken by proscription the frame of government which has become known as the Constitution of 1793. It represents the zenith of French democratic aspirations in a constitutional way.

Chapter 1

Philosophy as an Important Factor in the Development of the Republican Ideal in France

Viewed in historical perspective, France's first republican constitution is not just another constitution — of which France has had a fair share since 1791. It is more than that. It represents the culmination of an ideal that had been germinating in the minds of a few individuals for years. From a historic standpoint, this liberal charter is not only significant because it incorporates unusually democratic procedures; it is also significant in representing a final phase of republicanism during the French Revolution.

The story of the constitution's evolution is largely the story of the men responsible for it, men who were outstanding Revolutionary leaders. When these leaders drew up their constitution in 1793, they made use of their past impressions, impressions gained from the peaceful contemplation of books as well as those gained from active participation in political affairs. Inasmuch as some of these leaders (above all Condorcet, probably the one man mostly responsible for the writing of the original plan) had devoted years of study to political institutions of the past, as well as those of their own time, the ideas they gained from study were, perhaps, more valuable than those they gained from political activities.

An eminent American authority on government once said that the tracing of modern constitutional tendencies could hardly begin much later than the second or third centuries B.C.[1] France's re-

1. McIlwain Charles H., "The Fundamental Law Behind the Constitution of the United States," *The Constitution Reconsidered* (Read, Conyears, ed., New York, 1938), p. 5.

publican charter of 1793 can, in an indirect fashion, be traced back to antiquity. The minds of the constitutional fathers of that year were filled with republican principles at least partly acquired by youthful training in the classics. This youthful training was later supplemented by a diligent study of the great French, English, and American philosophers or publicists, who often referred to the ancient republics in their writings.

Philosophy, as a dominant factor in the outbreak of the Revolution in France, and as a source of inspiration for the unfolding of the political ideals of its leaders, offers a splendid example of the effect of the written word on the minds of men. Most of the great leaders of the Revolution were well versed in the works of the French and English philosophers and constantly cited them in their political debates and pamphlets. A contemporary record[2] would confirm this influence. It declared that a revolution of opinions and events as important as that of 1789 could only be the result of a great and rapid diffusion of light, a light that a small number of philosophers had been endeavoring to spread for some time. Unfortunately, the record went on to say, most of these writings were too abstract or voluminous to be within the comprehension of most Frenchmen. A few men, however, helpfully took the concepts of the great political writers of the past and put them into language the common people could understand. Among the influential mentors of the people, such names as Condorcet, Robespierre, Paine, Siéyès, Brissot, and Marat would stand out.

There are two questions that have bothered scholars in the past and, perhaps, still bother them in the present. First, what was the precise degree of republicanism in France prior to the overthrow of the monarchy in August, 1792? Secondly, what part, if any, did the philosophers play in the spread of the republican doctrine? One scholar, an Indian, has devoted a book to answering these

2. *Le Moniteur universel* (*Journal officiel de l'Empire français*, 196 vols., Paris, 1789-1863), introduction to vol. I, p. 221. Hereafter this work will be cited simply as *Moniteur universel*.

two questions.[3] He expounded the thesis that there was no republican party in France before the Revolution. Furthermore,
he declared that the philosophers never favored a form of government other than that of a monarchy. No one would dispute
his first contention, and many would partly agree with his second.
Yet a statement of Wadia's to the effect that the philosophers were
not an important source of inspiration behind the momentous events
of the Revolution[4] would certainly call for some reservations.
These reservations were admirably delineated by the famous authority on the French Revolution, François Aulard. He asserted that
the political writers of the eighteenth century undermined royal
authority by discussing not only the so-called divine right of
kings but also the historical origins of sovereignty and its real
basis in the assent of men. The philosophers proved most embarrassing for the monarchy. Without actually favoring a republic,
they nevertheless placed republican ideas in vogue. Whoever read
and thought was impregnated with their philosophy.[5]

Of all the great minds influencing those of other men in the
eighteenth century and acting as motivating sources of energy in
the social upheaval of the end of this century, that of one man
stands out above all. The man was Rousseau, familiarly referred
to as "Jean Jacques" by the Revolutionaries.

Jean Jacques Rousseau (1712-1778), the celebrated Swiss-French
philosopher, whose personal life was sometimes bewilderingly at
odds with the sentiments expressed in his writings, was the author
of works embodying ideas which had an extremely great influence
on Revolutionary leaders. The number of times Rousseau's name
was mentioned in the debates of the various Revolutionary
assemblies, and the number of times it was written in the many

3. Wadia, P. A., *The Philosophers and the French Revolution*
   (London, 1904).
4. *Ibid.*, p. 18.
5. Aulard, François V. Alphonse, *Historie politique de la
   Révolution française: Origines et Développement de la Démocratie et de la République (1789-1804)* (Paris, 1901), pp. 7-8.

newspapers of the period, would prove what a familiar figure he had become.

As a sentimental novelist, Rousseau had been well known by the intellectuals since 1761, the year in which his novel *La Nouvelle Héloise (The New Héloise)* was published. This book, before 1800, was to go through thirty editions which were considered authentic. Counting pirated editions, the total number of editions for the same period would be around seventy.[6] In 1762 another work of Rousseau appeared, entitled *Émile*, a treatise on education which stressed the importance of following the dictums of nature in raising children. Nature, said Rousseau, produced innocence and virtue; civilization corrupted. *Émile* was immensely popular amongst the literate classes in France, bourgeoisie as well as nobles. The year of its publication, it sold for the high price of two louis.[7]

Before 1780, Rousseau's political writings apparently were not so well known as his novels. His chief political writing, *Du Contrat social (The Social Contract)*, appeared the same year as *Émile* but was not highly publicized before 1780.[8] However, between this date and the outbreak of the Revolution in 1789, it must have received the lion's share of publicity. Indeed, as demonstrated by the general familiarity of the Revolutionaries with Rousseau's principles of government, all the philosopher's political works were probably widely disseminated between 1780 and 1790. The

6. Mornet, Daniel, *Les Origines intellectuelles de la Révolution française, 1715-1787* (Paris, 1933), p. 134.
7. *Ibid.*, p. 132. Two louis in 1762, according to Mornet, would be equivalent to 600 francs in money of 1932.
8. An investigator of private library collections for the period 1750 to 1780 found that out of five hundred catalogues of the collections consulted, only one listed *The Social Contract*. Mornet, Daniel, "Les Enseignements des Bibliothèques privées—1750–1780," *Revue d'Histoire litteraire de la France,* 1910, p. 467.) Cited by Bonno, G., *La Constitution britannique devant l'Opinion française de Montesquieu à Bonaparte* (Paris, 1931), p. 35.

Bibliothèque de l'Homme public, reviewing, in 1790, a book on governments of the world by a Monsieur de la Croix, quoted this contemporary writer on the administration of states as saying that Rousseau's *Social Contract* was then the most frequently mentioned of all his works.[9] This would indicate that of the eighteen editions of the philosopher's works which had appeared before 1789,[10] some, at least, were appreciated because of the political essays they contained.[11] Aiding in the diffusion of Rousseau's principles were the newspapers. A French scholar who culled through newspapers for years 1778-1782 gathered more than five hundred pages concerning the philosopher and his political writings.[12]

There is no dearth of evidence showing the influence of Jean Jacques on men who were to be among the most active participants in the rapid political changes occurring after 1789. A contemporary of the Revolution, and one of the more conservative members of the Constituent Assembly, Mallet du Pan, made the startling claim that all the important Revolutionaries were disciples of Rousseau.[13] One of these men even had personal contact with him. Maximilien Robespierre, in the future to be a powerful leader at the Paris

9. *Bibliothèque de l'Homme public* (ed. by L. S. Balestrier de Canilhac, 128 vols. in 14, Paris, 1790–1792), III, 124. Hereafter the title of this work will be indicated simply by the initial B. D. H. P.

10. Mornet, *Origines intellectuelles . . .*, p. 135.

11. An important edition, containing his most important political writings, was one published in Amsterdam in 1769 by the publisher Marc Michel Rey. The full citation is Rousseau, J. J., *Oeuvres de J. J. Rousseau de Genève: Nouvelle Édition, Revue, corrigée et augmentée de plusieurs Morceaux qui n'avaient point encore paru* ((II vols., Amsterdam, 1769). This edition was used in the writing of the monograph.

12. Plon, P. P., "J. J. Rousseau raconté par les Gazettes de son Temps," *Mercure de France* (1912). As cited by Mornet, *Origines intellectuelles . . .*, p. 228.

13. As cited by Champion, Edme, *J. J. Rousseau et la Révolution française* (Paris, 1909), p. 3.

Jacobin Club and the supreme guide of France's destinies for
over a year, had visited Rousseau at his Ermenonville retreat in
1778.[14] At times during the Revolution, Robespierre was to express
opinions, some of which appeared academic, that bore a remarkable resemblance to parts of *The Social Contract.* Some of these
were: Any executive authority should always be regarded with
suspicion. The meeting place of legislators should be large enough
to admit great numbers of ordinary citizens as visitors. Thus, under
the watchful eye of the people, the representatives would be more
apt to pass worthwhile legislation. Economic inequality could be
reduced by decreasing useless luxury goods. A proper system of
taxation would be one that was based on individual income.[15]

Other outstanding men of the Revolution were also influenced by
Rousseau. Brissot, who was regarded as the nominal head of the
Girondin group in the Convention, had been deeply impressed by
the great philosopher. At one time he had even applied for the post
of nurse to Rousseau.[16] He said that he read Jean Jacques'
Confessions at least six times. Brissot flattered himself by saying
that many of Rousseau's traits, especially shyness, could be applied
to his own personality.[17] *The Confession of Faith of the Savoyard
Vicar,* in which Rousseau extolled a simple, natural religion without
ceremonial gaudery, removed all his religious prejudices, boasted
Brissot.[18] Condorcet, the principal author of the original draft of the
Constitution of 1793, and an eminent philosopher in his own right,
was thoroughly informed of the doctrines of the Franco-Swiss
philosopher. Some of these doctrines, such as the popular censure
of representatives, and the referendum, were to form part of his

14.   Schatz, Richard, *J. J. Rousseaus Einflusz auf Robespierre*
      (Leipzig, 1905), pp. 2-3.

15.   *Ibid.,* pp. 11, 14, 43, 42.

16.   *J. P. Brissot: Mémoires, 1754–1793* (ed. by Cl. Perroud,
      2 vols., Paris, 1911), 1, 147.

17.   *Ibid.,* 1, 18.

18.   *Ibid.,* 1, 38.

outstanding constitutional work.[19] Barère, a member of the first constitutional committee of 1793,[20] and often reporter of its proceedings, learned from reading Rousseau the nature of the authority of kings and the origin of the sovereignty of the people.[21]

Above all, it was during the period of debate in the Convention over the Constitution of 1793 that the author of *The Social Contract* was quoted as the supreme authority on democracy and the republican form of government. The Conventionals discovered in this work the evangelistic theory that they needed.[22]

A contemporary brochure writer, Barbet, said that the Convention, in its deification of Jean Jacques, had taken for a password "social contract."[23] During the course of debate at the Convention, and in the polemics of the press, there was competitive spirit to prove one's knowledge of Rousseau. Charles Lambert, deputy to the Convention from the department of Côte-d'Or, depicted him as the deputies' polar star in matters of legislation.[24] Durand-Maillane, deputy from Bouches-du-Rhone, pleaded for simplicity in manners and laws as a sign of virtue. He referred to

19. Alengry, Franck, *Condorcet: Guide de la Révolution française, Theoricien du Droit constitutionnel et Précurseur de la Science sociale* (Paris, 1904), pp. 820-821. Alengry is referring to Condorcet's constitutional work in 1793.

20. Refer to pp. 185-186.

21. Barère, Bertrand, *Montesquieu pein d'après ses Ouvrages* (Paris, 1796), p. 63.

22. Bonno, *op. cit.*, p. 35.

23. Barbet, —, —, *L'Ombre de Camille Desmoulins ou mon Opinion sur Le Gouvernement révolutionnaire.* This pamphlet does not give the place or time of publication. Internal evidence would indicate that it was published at Paris early in 1794.

24. *Archives parlementaires, 1787–1860: Recueil complet des Débats des Chambres françaises* (ed. by Mavidal, Jerome; Laurent, Émile, and others; series I, 1787-1799, 82 vols., Paris, 1879-1913; series II, 1800-1860, 137 vols., Paris, 1862-1913), series I, vol. LXII, p. 470.

definite chapter and book in *The Social Contract* to impress his point.[25] Durand-Maillane said he was happy to quote Rousseau because the time had now come (after the abolition of royalty) to freely reveal, and apply, the wonderful principles of a great philosopher. It was from the Genevan sage, and him alone, that they had first learned about liberty and the contract theory of government. The explicit moral right for the then-existent French Republic was "incontestably" found in *The Social Contract*.[26] Armand Guffroy, the representative of Pas-de-Calais, speaking figuratively, said that they should always have before their eyes the pact traced by Jean Jacques.[27] Buzot, a Girondin leader and deputy from L'Eure, in commenting on the disorder which was then rather prevalent in Paris, referred to a phrase in *The Social Contract* which stated that liberty could not long exist in a state where a mass of men devoured and dominated all those around them.[28]

To further refresh the minds of the deputies to the Convention regarding their debt to Rousseau, Paris, the great metropolis, was the seat of a Jean Jacques Rousseau society. This society published a manifesto saying that its purpose was "to propagate, follow, and prove the moral virtues of the great man they had taken for patron."[29]

25. *Ibid.*, LXII, 375.
26. *Ibid.*, LXII, 377.
27. *Moniteur universel*, May 24, 1793.
28. *Loc. cit.*
29. Buffenoir, Hippolyte, "L'Image de Jean Jacques Rousseau dans les Sociétés de la Révolution à Paris," *La Révolution française* (November-December, 1917), LXX, 16. According to Buffenoir, it is by studying the origin and function of the many societies of the Revolution that one will learn of the prodigious influence of Rousseau (*ibid.*, p. 504). At the Jacobin Society of Paris, the greatest of the political clubs, there was constant reference to Rousseau even before the fall of the monarchy. Speaking at the club's meeting, in December, 1791, a member proposed that a bust of Jean

An analysis of Rousseau's famous writing describing the contract theory of society will reveal why it was regarded as a republican handbook by members of the Convention. It not only contained sentiments destructive of the idea of monarchy, or any other form of one-man government, but it also offered constructive suggestions as to how a republic might function. This account furnished Revolutionary leaders with arguments against the institution of monarchy, and was an important factor in causing discontent with divine-right rule.

The Social Contract began with the statement that man was born free and everywhere was found in chains.[30] In it the question was raised by Rousseau as to whether or not a people could alienate themselves to a king. The answer, filled with irony, was: "A man might sell himself as a slave for subsistence, but a whole people cannot alienate themselves to a king for such subsistence, for it is the case that they feed him, rather than that he feeds them."[31] In answer to any argument about kings' bringing tranquility and order, Rousseau answered that they brought wars and disorders.[32]

Jacques be placed in their assembly hall. It was Rousseau, said the member, who "first wrote so that the people might learn the imprescriptible rights they had to sovereignty and liberty." Aulard, François V. Alphonse, ed. *La Société des Jacobins: Recueil de Documents pour l'Histoire du Club des Jacobins de Paris* (6 vols., Paris 1891-92), III, 291. The newspaper *Révolutions de France et Brabant*, for March 15, 1790, in its list of new books mentions three by Rousseau. These three head the list. There is also a book listed about Rousseau bearing the interesting title *Jean Jacques Rousseau à l'Assemblée nationale* (Constituent). Thus, even at the time of the debates over France's first constitution, that of a limited monarchy, Rousseau's doctrines interested the public.

30. Rousseau, Jean Jacques, *Du Contrat social*, in *Oeuvres*, II, 2.
31. *Ibid.*, II, 8.
32. *Ibid.*, II, 9.

Despite his statement that monarchy was more suitable for a large state,[33] Rousseau nevertheless proceeded to figuratively tear down monarchies and to exalt the virtues of republics. It was in republics alone, said he, that the public interest governed and the public weal counted for something. Every legitimate government was republican.[34] The great difference between a republic and a monarchy, commented the philosopher, was that in the former men succeeded because of their talents. In the latter they succeeded because of their flattery and intrigues.[35] Kings tended to become absolute in a monarchical form of government. They preferred to win this absolutism through popularity with the people. However, cynically remarked Rousseau, their love for absolute power made them dispense with popularity if necessary.[36]

In his remarks as to what constituted good government, Rousseau, in detail, described the justice of republicanism. The essence of the social pact was that sovereignty resided with the people, or general will. Sovereignty should never be alienated, even by the people themselves.[37] It was the duty of society to provide a government that would not only guarantee this, but would also protect, with all the common force, the person and goods of each of society's members.[38] According to the social pact, each individual placed

33. *Ibid.*, II, 103. At the same time he said there were few princes capable of managing a large state. "With an adequate lever, with one finger one can crush the world, but in order to sustain it, the shoulders of Hercules are necessary" (*Ibid.*, II, 98).
34. Rousseau, *Du Contrat social*, in *Oeuvres*, II, 90.
35. *Ibid.*, II, 95.
36. *Ibid.*, II, 93.
37. *Ibid.*, II, 29. Rousseau had an example from antiquity in mind. When the Roman people, in times of crisis, felt that an extreme emergency justified such a step, they handed over their natural rights of sovereignty to one individual — a dictator.
38. *Ibid.*, II, 16.

his person and all his goods under the supreme protection of the general will. Each individual formed an indivisible part of this general will.[39] By the union of individual wills a public person was formed, called a *republic*.[40]

Rousseau was not so concerned with the terminology applied to a government as he was with the guarantee of the citizen's rights under a particular form of administration.[41] All the citizens should exist on a plane of equality and enjoy the same rights.[42] The principal function of the legislative power was to see that citizens were protected in their rights of liberty and equality.[43]

Although Rousseau distrusted a purely democratic government as one being subject to civil wars and intestine agitations,[44] he, nevertheless, favored some of its practices; above all, those which guaranteed the preservation of people's rights. In a truly free

39. *Ibid.*, II, 16.
40. *Ibid.*, II, 19. Rousseau said that a monarchy could be a republic. *Ibid.*, II, p. 46, footnote i. Explaining this apparent confusion of terms, he said that a monarch could be subject to the will of the people, where true sovereignty lay. Furthermore, said Rousseau, a monarch might just as well be called a president or executive, as his will could only be that of the general will, expressly granted to him by the whole people. As soon as he attempted to change the public will to his own private will, the social union would vanish and the political body would be dissolved. This meant that the people could take back their delegated authority. *Ibid.*, II, 78.
41. Perhaps this is shown by Rousseau's somewhat confusing use of terms. It appears that the philosopher had no faith in terms as such. The important thing was for the rights of all people to be guaranteed by a collective pact, representing the rights and duties of all. The ideal form of government, as described in *The Social Contract*, although rarely named, was a republic.
42. Rousseau, *Du Contract social*, in *Oeuvres*, II, 38.
43. *Ibid.*, II, 65.
44. *Ibid.*, II, 88.

state, he said, the citizens participated in government themselves and did not pay individuals to represent them.[45] The deputies of the people could not be their representatives, actually. Therefore, they could not pass any law definitively. Laws were to be ratified by the collective citizenry.[46]

While the people could not be represented in their legislative rights, they could, and ought to be, represented in the executive power, which was only force applied to law.[47] However, the depositories of the executive power were by no means the masters of the people. They were only their servants, and the people could make or remove them as they pleased.[48] If a citizen was charged with an executive post, he was being asked solely to fulfill one of his duties as a citizen. To prevent usurpation by any magistrate, periodic assemblies of the people should be provided for; their convocation should be automatic, not depending on the will of any individual or body.[49]

There were other principles proclaimed in Rousseau's epochal political writing which were to be announced endlessly by many of the Conventionals in 1793: It was dangerous for any one city to have too much power. Instead of having one capital, the government should sit alternately in different localities.[50] In their debates with the Jacobins in 1793 over the issue of a capital, the Girondins were to use a similar argument.[51] In voting, said Rousseau in *The Social Contract*, the voice of the greater number

45. *Ibid.*, II, 123-124.
46. *Ibid.*, II, 51, 125. This principle was adopted by the Conventionals as one of the outstanding features of the Constitution of 1793.
47. *Ibid.*, II, 127.
48. *Ibid.*, 73, 133.
49. Rousseau, *Du Contrat social*, in *Oeuvres* II, 134-135. This principle would be much acclaimed in the constitutional debates of 1793.
50. *Ibid.*, II, 122.
51. Refer to pp. 283-284.

should always obligate the minority.[52] Condorcet was a constant exponent of majority rule. The idea of a tribunate between the government and the people, to safeguard the people's rights, was a concept of *The Social Contract*.[53] The same principle will be found in some of the constitutional plans presented to the Convention. Periodic reviews of the constitution to keep it in tune with natural progress was another concept. For a government to be legitimate, said Rousseau, the people in each generation should have the right to sanction or reject it.[54] Finally, in a proper system of administration there should be rigorous separation of powers. The executive and legislative branches should be carefully separated, and any encroachment of the executive over the legislature should be prevented.[55]

Two other works by Rousseau contained revolutionary opinions for the time. In the *Discours sur l'Origine et les Fondements de l'Inégalité parmi les Hommes (Discourse on the Origin and Foundation of Inequality Amongst Men)*[56] he reiterated that the people were sovereign. The only reason that they ever gave themselves chiefs was in order to defend their liberty and thus to keep from becoming slaves. In this discourse on the origin of inequality, Rousseau sanctioned insurrection as a rightful and natural act to be directed against any attempted usurpation by the people's authorities. His *Discours sur l'Économie politique (Discourse on Political Economy)*[57] also contained maxims which were popular in 1792 and 1793. The first and most important maxim was that the general will of the people ought to be followed in all matters.[58] Other axioms

52. Rousseau, *Du Contrat social*, in *Oeuvres*, II, 141.
53. *Ibid.*, II, 163.
54. *Ibid.*, II, 9.
55. *Ibid.*, II, 50.
56. Rousseau, *Discours sur l'Origine et les Fondements sur l'Origine de l'Inégalité parmi les Hommes*, in *Oeuvres*, II, 1-162.
57. Rousseau, *Discours sur l'Économie politique*, in *Oeuvres*, II, 1-64.
58. *Ibid.*, II, 12.

were: Every state should have a public system of education in which patriotism would be stimulated.[59] The right of property was the most sacred of the citizen's rights and the foundation of the social pact.[60] Taxes should be proportional to income and should be levied only with the consent of the people.[61]

Rousseau's influence and importance can best be summed up in the words of authorities on the spirit behind the Revolution. Buffenoir, citing as reference an article appearing in the *Revue des Deux Mondes* for November, 1831, said there never was a philosopher who obtained so complete an execution of his maxims. If he were removed from the eighteenth century, the Revolutionaries' insurrection of minds, their ardor for liberty, and their enthusiasm, coupled with faith, would not be explicable.[62] According to Mornet, the philosopher prepared a revolutionary spirit which was unexpected. His works cultivated the spirit of exaltation and enthusiasm, a spirit which characterized the Revolution.[63] Wadia and Champion both agreed that *The Social Contract* contained many doctrines which inspired the Constitution of 1793.[64] In the opinion of Aulard, Rousseau prepared the ruin of the monarchical system by his assertion that the two principal objects of every system of legislation ought to be liberty and equality; he substituted the republican idea of fraternity for the mystical idea of charity and humility.[65]

Ranking second to Rousseau as a precursor of the French Revolution, and outdistancing him as a liberal philosopher in many respects, was Abbé Mably (1715–1789). The writings of this proponent of many extreme republican ideas were widely read in the years prior to 1789.[66] They had thoroughly penetrated the minds

59. *Ibid.*, II, 34.
60. *Ibid*, II, 38, 49-50.
61. *Ibid.*, II, 52.
62. Buffenoir, *op. cit.*, p. 509.
63. Mornet, *Origines intellectuelles*, p. 229.
64. Wadia, *op. cit.*, p. 125; Champion, *op. cit.*, p. 16.
65. Aulard, *Histoire politique*, pp. 3-4.
66. Champion, *op. cit.*, p. 25.

of many men.[67] During the stormy years of the Revolution itself, this liberal philosopher was constantly cited as an authority on politics.[68] Mably's name, like Rousseau's, figured often in the Revolutionary journals as well as in the speeches before the national assemblies.[69] The following statement taken from the *Moniteur universel* for December 25, 1789, will show how important Mably was in the eyes of some of the Revolutionaries: "Most of the pamphlet writers have copied from them [Mably's works] without giving the reference."[70] There is no doubt that the *cahier* writers drew heavily on Mably. The list of grievances submitted to the king in 1789 showed many traces of his influence.[71]

Of all the phases of the French Revolution, it was probably during that of the Convention that the influence of Mably was most evident. Many Conventionals, especially those belonging to the Girondin group, were conversant with the principles of his books. There was, incidentally, an ever increasing demand for his books. Between 1790 and 1797 there appeared four editions of his collected works, besides a number of reprints and pirated copies.[72]

Acknowledgment was made by the Conventionals of their debt to Mably. During the last days of the Convention, one of the executors of Mably's estate presented a complete edition of his works to the constituent body.[73] He referred to Mably as a torch

67. Aulard, *Histoire politique,* pp. 3-4.
68. Whitefield, Ernest A., *Gabriel Bonnet de Mably* (London, 1930), p. 3.
69. Guerrier, M. W., *L'Abbé de Mably, Moraliste et Politique: Étude sur la Doctrine morale du Jacobinisme puritan et sur le Développement de l'Ésprit républicain au dix-huitième Siècle* (Paris, 1886), p. 5.
70. *Moniteur universel,* December 25, 1789.
71. Guerrier, *op. cit.,* p. 5.
72. Whitefield, *op. cit.,* p. 28.
73. The twelve-volume edition of 1795. It was this edition, edited by Charles Desbrière, that was consulted in the preparation of this book.

in the path of the Revolution. Jean Dusaulx, deputy from the department of Haute-Loire, thanked the executor and made a motion that Mably's body be carried to the Pantheon. This would be a fitting honor for "one of the greatest teachers of true liberty that the world had ever produced."[74] A pamphleteer, writing in 1794, said that all the men of talent owed their genius to Mably as well as Rousseau.[75]

In some of the constitutional plans suggested in 1793, the liberal churchman's viewpoints were noticeable. He was, above all, favored by the Conventionals because of his many convenient allusions to the republics of ancient Greece and Rome.[76] By borrowing these handy allusions, it was possible for certain public men to parade their knowledge of ancient history without having recourse to burdensome Greek and Latin texts. Antoine Wandelaincourt, deputy to the Convention from Haute-Marne, in his observations as to what could best be borrowed from antiquity, repeatedly cited the abbé as the authority for his comments about the institutions of Republican Rome.[77]

Mably's political system, as revealed by his writings, was one permeated with republican ideals. Principles of equality and liberty were dominant.[78] This opinion, expressed by one authority on eighteenth-century France, might be qualified, however.

In one of his earlier works, appearing in 1763, *Entretiens de Phocion sur le Rapport de la Morale avec la Politique (Conver-*

74. Guerrier, *op. cit.*, p. 7.
75. Barbet, *op. cit.*, p. 1.
76. Mably had been greatly inspired when he read in the classics about the republics of Greece and Rome. Whitefield, *op. cit.*, pp. 6-7, 19. He always remained faithful to the ideal of the ancient republics. Mornet, *Origines intellectuelles*, pp. 231-232.
77. Wandelaincourt, Antoine, *Observations sur le Plan de Constitution* (the place and time of publication were not indicated), pp. 1-18.
78. See, Henri, "La Doctrine politique et sociale de Mably," *Annales historiques de la Révolution française* (March-April, 1924), I, 148.

sations of Phocion Concerning the Connection between Morals and Politics), Mably apparently, like Rousseau, was distrustful of too much democracy. He believed that the mass of people were not in a position to govern properly. The majority not only lacked educational requirements; in the time-consuming business of making a living, they also lacked the leisure for government.[79] The decline of Athens after the death of Pericles was attributed by Mably to the increased suffrage.[80] In this connection the abbé said: "In democracies the multitude, which is sovereign, is inconstant, prideful, flighty, and vindictive."[81]

An imaginary dialogue was carried on in the *Conversations of Phocion*. When one of the conversationalists made an anti-democratic statement, the effect of his remark was counterbalanced by one from the other, which was democratic. This, doubtless, was to keep from arousing the suspicion of the king's authorities, who clamped a heavy censorship on all books which appeared to subvert the monarchy. The dialogues, while formulating the opinion that only those having land should vote,[82] at the same time mitigated this seeming unfairness by condemning those excessive fortunes which caused a crowd of unfortunates to languish in indigence.[83] Mably's ideal, which would be that of many of the Girondins in 1793, was some form of republic offering the opportunity for all to have small landholdings, with the contingent right of participating in the government. The reason for the land-property qualification was to prevent those who had no stake in

79. Mably, Abbé, *Entretiens de Phocion sur le Rapport de la Morale avec la Politique*, in *Oeuvres* (ed. by Charles Desbrière, 15 vols., Paris, 1794-1795), X, 122. Rousseau said the best and most natural order was that in which the wiser govern the multitude. Rousseau, *Du Contrat social*, in *Oeuvres*, II, 90.

80. Mably, *Entretiens de Phocion*, in *Oeuvres*, X, 121.

81. *Ibid.*, X, 148.

82. *Ibid.*, X, 121, footnote 1.

83. *Ibid.*, X, 193-194.

real republican government from possibly being influenced by those who would establish some form of tyranny. Men with property which they valued, thought Mably, would be sure to uphold and to stabilize a government which protected them and their interests. The greater the number of landholders, the greater the number of those desiring a sound and stable government.

A book written earlier than *Conversations of Phocion* but not published until 1789 was *Des Droits et des Devoirs du Citoyen (Concerning the Rights and Duties of the Citizen)*.[84] Because of its statements Mably never had the courage to publish it during his lifetime. It has been aptly described by a biographer of Mably as the abbé's most interesting writing.[85] In this work was predicted the Revolution, the calling of the States-General, and the formation of the Constituent and Legislative Assemblies. Moreover, practically all the principles regarding government found within it were to be voiced by the Revolutionaries.

Proceeding from the postulate that men had emerged from the hands of nature perfectly equal and unburdened by a hierarchy of kings, magistrates, or subjects, Mably asserted that the belief in any divine and hereditary right of rule was absurd and contrary to nature.[86] It was only by the abuse of rights of others that such a system, opposed to the best interests of society, could be established.[87] Mably enumerated some of the things regarding rulers that the people should always keep in mind: In all periods of history, said the abbé, it was the hereditary ruler who turned into a despot.[88] The handling of public funds by a single magistrate or ruler might be conducive to corruption. The right to declare war or to make peace, in a just government, must never be within

---

84. Written in 1758, it antedated Rousseau's *Social Contract* by four years.
85. Whitefield, *op. cit.*, p. 9.
86. Mably, *Des Droits et des Devoirs du Citoyen*, in *Oeuvres*, XI, 281.
87. *Ibid.*, XI, 287.
88. *Ibid.*, XI, 292.

the jurisdiction of only one man; neither should the right to convoke or disband a legislative body be entrusted to the judgment of a single individual. Rulers should not be the sole source of law. It was the duty of the people to legislate for themselves. If the people did not make their own laws, they were in danger of losing their liberty: "Despotism necessarily commences where liberty leaves off." Mably concluded his list of warnings by advising the people to be continually on guard against their rulers, even the most amiable. It was by surprise, skill and ambition that the French kings took possession of the legislative power.[89]

Mably was a staunch advocate of the evolutionary principle of government, when this was possible, as the only way to prevent government from becoming static and arbitrary. It was the business of enlightened ones to inform others as to what was lacking in a government, and to point the way to reform.[90] If people developed a lazy state of mind and preferred the false repose of unquestioning accession to authority, rather than the uncertainties due to change, they were on the their way to being the victims of despotism. If the people of the Roman Republic had preferred repose above everything else, they would have been the slaves of the nobility.[91] The sacred principle of insurrection, when peaceful parleying failed, was legitimate against arbitrary authority. Arms should be taken up against an oppressor who violated or abused laws.[92] The people, in whom sovereignty resided, had the eternal right of modifying or annulling their government.[93]

Sentiments deprecatory of monarchies are numerous in *The Rights and Duties of the Citizen*. Such a writing, appearing as it did early in 1789, did not help the cause of a tottering monarchy.

89. *Ibid.*, XI, 307-310.
90. Mably, *Des Droits et des Devoirs du Citoyen* in *Oeuvres*, XI, 316.
91. *Ibid.*, XI, 321.
92. *Ibid.*, XI, 334. The sacred right of insurrection is one of the important features of the Constitution of 1793.
93. *Ibid.*, XI, 341.

Mably boldly affirmed that it was ridiculous to expect in a monarchy — or any form of aristocratic form of government, for that matter — just and reasonable laws.[94] Monarchs, or disdainful patricians, were not capable of enjoying legislative power. Their passions would cause them to make laws advancing their own evil ends.[95] The only wise and reasonable laws were those made by the people themselves.[96] As for the authority of the king, it was based on a few ancient charters, monuments of tyranny and the enslavement of the people.[97] To prevent further tyranny, Mably asked for the immediate convocation of the States-General. It should be remembered that the abbé was writing some years before the Revolution. The States-General would not be summoned until May of the year 1789. Once it was convoked, said Mably, it should pass a fundamental law stipulating that henceforth it would meet every year without fail.[98] This former advisory body, becoming an authoritative legislative assembly, could, in time, remove all the king's power. As a starter, it might handle all financial matters.[99] To prevent any further usurpation by the executive, it could make arrangements for several classes of magistrates. By all means the States-General should declare that in the future the right of declaring war was to belong to the people.[100]

De la Législation ou Principes des Loix (Concerning Legislation or Principles of law) was Mably's greatest work as far as the Revolution was concerned.[101] In this book, appearing in 1776, Mably, in his political enunciations, went far beyond anything he ever wrote before or after this date. It is rather hard to define the type of state described in this unusual work. Perhaps it was

94. Ibid., XI, 372.
95. Loc. cit.
96. Loc. cit.
97. Ibid., XI, 399.
98. Ibid., XI, 451-452.
99. Ibid., XI, 488.
100. Ibid., XI, 490.
101. Whitefield, Mably, p. 13.

utopian. Nevertheless, the doctrines proclaimed in this writing were to strike a chord of sympathy in the hearts of many of the constitution-makers of 1793. The legislator's primary duty, said Mably in his *Concerning Legislation or Principles of Law,* was to establish equality in the fortune and status of citizens.[102] It was inequality of fortune that decomposed and altered sentiments in the hearts of men.[103] As soon as riches were respected, it followed that the rich tried to take over public authority.[104] Property was the first cause of inequality in fortunes. Mably praised Lycurgus of Sparta, who allegedly prepared a constitution providing for community of goods. It was this arrangement, said Mably, that stopped all wrangles over the rights of property.[105]

Oddly, Mably's views on property as expressed in *Concerning Legislation or Principles of Law* had changed somewhat from the opinions expressed in his earlier work, *Conversations of Phocion.*

There were other interesting ideas presented in *Concerning Legislation or Principles of Law*: All laws tending to increase the needs of a state or its administrators were by their very nature a vice. Every law which diminished the state's needs was a wise law; the art of the legislator consisted in making laws to this end.[106] Moreover, legislators should pass not only legislation which prevented excessive inheritances, but also laws permitting those who had the smallest incomes to pay the least taxes.[107] Provision should be made to preserve all the authority of the legislative body.

102. Mably, *De la Législation ou Principes des Loix,* in *Oeuvres,* XI, 44.
103. *Ibid.,* XI, 45.
104. *Ibid.,* XI, 48-49.
105. Mably's approach was now the very antithesis of the one he took in writing *Conversations of Phocion,* Refer to pp. 31-33.
106. Mably, *De la Législation ou Principes des Loix,* in *Oeuvres,* XI, 119-120.
107. *Ibid.,* XI, 141-143, 122. Both these doctrines would be reiterated in 1793; the latter would be a provision of the constitution of that year.

This authority could never be safely entrusted to magistrates.[108] As force was used only by animals, and peace was the natural state of man, the legislature should be expressly forbidden from undertaking wars of conquest.[109]

The philosophical abbé made thought-provoking remarks in another early work. In *Doutes proposés aux Philosophes-Économistes sur l'Ordre natural et essential des Sociétés politiques (Doubts Proposed to Philosopher-Economists on the Natural and Essential Order of Political Societies)*, he accused all existing governments of having been turned aside from their fundamental duty (to administer for all the people). They now favored the interests of the rich and ambitious and really represented these interests.[110] He asked why philosophers had not disclosed this unhappy condition in their writings. Why, indeed, had some philosophers tried to justify such a state?[111]

Concepts, sometimes historically inaccurate but popular in 1792 and 1793, were found in *Doubts Proposed to Philosopher-Economists.* Some of these concepts were: Republics had always produced the best laws; that was why Sparta and Rome were such strong states.[112] The most crushing tyranny was to be found in states where the legislative and executive power were one.[113] Magistrates should not be in office too long and should revert to the rank of simple citizens once their terms of office were over.[114] Despotism of the executive power could be prevented by splitting it into several branches.[115] Referring to the writers of antiquity as authorities, it

108. *Ibid.,* XI, 305.
109. *Ibid.,* XI, 190-191.
110. Mably, *Doutes proposés aux philosophes,* in *Oeuvres,* IX, 19.
111. *Ibid.,* IX, 19.
112. Mably, *Doutes proposés aux Philosophes,* in *Oeuvres,* IX, 72-73. Rome was strongest under the early Caesars.
113. *Ibid.,* IX, 139.
114. *Ibid.* IX, 19.
115. *Ibid.,* IX, 152.

was held that the more the people participated in lawmaking, the more often the laws were fair and impartial.[116]

At the invitation of the Polish government, Mably visited Poland in 1770. He remained there a year, thoroughly studying Polish institutions. The outcome of the year's study was *Du Gouvernment et des Lois de la Pologne (Regarding the Government and Laws of Poland)*. In this work he advised the Poles to form a government in which the legislative power would be supreme; the legislative power was the soul of society.[117] Deputies to the legislature should be thirty years of age, possess a certain amount of land, and exercise no domestic employment. Their persons must be sacred.[118] In the system Mably recommended to the Poles, the supreme law-making body would be the legislative branch; the king and his ministers would not be able to oppose its will.[119] War could be declared only by the legislature, and all treaties must have its ratification.[120]

In his advice to the Poles, Mably showed his usual distrust of kings or any other form of executive:[121] "The executive power has been, and will be, eternally the enemy of the legislative power."[122] To prevent a ruler from over-stepping his authority, it was best for him to have but a short term of rule.[123] Mably believed that all kings inevitably strove for absolute power.[124]

---

116. *Ibid.*, IX, 173-179.
117. Mably, *Du Gouvernement et des Lois de Pologne*, in *Oeuvres*, VIII, 46.
118. *Ibid.*, VIII, 20-21.
119. *Ibid.*, VIII, 16-17.
120. *Ibid.*, VIII, 184.
121. The Conventional debates of 1793 revealed a suspicion of all executive authority by many of the delegates.
122. Mably, *Du Gouvernment et des Lois de Pologne*, in *Oeuvres*, VIII, 60.
123. *Ibid.*, VIII, 54. Mably is speaking here of an elective monarch.
124. *Ibid.*, VIII, 63.

Excessive revenue aided them in their strife for this power. As a case in point, he described the condition of the king of England, George III, who used his extreme wealth to bribe Parliament.[125]

At the invitation of John Adams,[126] who a few years later was to be the second President of the United States, Abbé Mably wrote *Observations sur le Gouvernement et les Lois des États-Unis d'Amérique (Observations on the Government and Laws of the United States of America)*. Written in 1783, this was to be Mably's last book published in his lifetime. It was written at a time when the United States aroused the sympathy and admiration of almost all France for having broken away from the mighty British Empire, France's mortal enemy. There were more than a few Frenchmen who admired the United States for having dared to initiate a republican form of government. Mably's book was one of many describing the republican United States and its constitutions, both federal and state; numerous such books appeared in France during the next ten years. The style adopted in this work was that of a series of letters written by Abbé Mably to John Adams, the latter then being minister plenipotentiary to Holland. In these letters was found a careful analysis of the various constitutions of the new republic.

Comparing the conditions of the citizens of the United States with those of most people in Europe, Mably said the former lived under constitutional principles derived from philosophy, while the latter, ignorant of constitutional principles, lived as beasts of burden governed for the private advantage of proprietors.[127] The various states of the United States proved their unshakable belief in liberty when they gave themselves constitutions that established, as a definite axiom, the principle that all authority lay with the people. These constitutions also gave the people the inalienable right to

125. *Ibid.*, VIII, 68. This was during the early years of the reign of George III (1738–1820).
126. Whitefield, *Mably*, 15.
127. Mably, *Observations sur le Gouvernement et les Lois des États-Unis d'Amérique*, in *Oeuvres*, VIII, 340.

make or to annul laws.[128] The abbé praised the representative system as being suitable for a large country. It was splendid, thought he, that the representatives were held answerable to public opinion and that they had to answer to their constituents for any faulty actions.[129] The jury system, establishing equality between strong and weak, also merited Mably's praise.[130]

When Mably spoke of the right of the people to govern themselves, he was not generally referring to *all* the people, irrespective of their age, education, or property-holding status. His works sometimes reveal inconsistencies in his approach to pure democracy. In his discussion of the United States, for example, he shows some distrust for absolute democracy. Such an ideology was to be applied with extreme precaution.[131] A degraded multitude had neither the means nor the time to elevate itself, through study, to an understanding of wise governmental principles.[132] Pure democracy could exist only in republics such as those of ancient Greece, remarked Mably without proper qualification. He cited Plato and Aristotle as authorities.[133] The reason Mably feared democracy of the purer variety was that he felt it might be subverted to selfish ends by the wealthy or ambitious. He was also against freedom of the press because it invited disorder by allowing any malevolent person to attack, with impunity, fundamental principles of organized society.[134]

Pennsylvania's constitution interested Mably in much the same way that it was to interest Condorcet later. However, there were parts of it that he did not favor. For one thing, the secret-ballot system incurred his criticism. Voting aloud, he believed, would

128. *Ibid.*, VIII, 342.
129. *Ibid.*, VIII, 348.
130. *Ibid.*, VIII, 349.
131. *Ibid.*, VIII, 353.
132. *Ibid.*, VIII, 354.
133. *Ibid.*, VIII. 366.
134. *Ibid.*, VIII, 416-417.

insure the honesty of those voting.[135] Moreover he thought the two-year residence requirement demanded before one could become a deputy was too short. A somewhat longer residence was necessary. Furthermore, Mably was of the opinion that all representatives should be required to hold some other office before being eligible to be deputies. He agreed, however, that only those who paid taxes should be permitted to hold office or to be electors.[136]

There were two features of Pennsylvania's constitution that Mably strongly disliked. One was the provision that prohibited any change in the constitution.[137] The other was the arrangement for a single-house legislature. A system of two houses was more conducive to proper legislation, he stated. In discussing the provision in Pennsylvania's constitution for an executive council of twelve members, Mably, while favoring such a council, argued that its members should be selected by the legislature rather than by the voting populace.[138] The final version of the Constitution of 1793, adopted by the French people in plebiscite, provided for the selection of the executive council in somewhat this manner. Members of the executive council, however, were elected by the legislative assembly from candidates (one per department) chosen by the electoral assemblies of each department.

While praising America for having adopted the republican form of government, Mably was not completely optimistic about her future. He believed America would be pushed into aristocracy by some superior force, unless she placed barriers to the accumulation of large fortunes. If laws were not passed to check abuses by the rich, another revolution was not an impossibility: "The poor will become too proud of the equality given them," said Mably rather ambiguously.[139] Apparently he thought that the populace,

135. Mably, *Observations sur le Gouvernement et les Lois des États-Unis d'Amérique* in *Oeuvres*, VIII, 361-362.
136. *Ibid.*, VIII, 363.
137. *Ibid.*, VIII, 369.
138. *Ibid.*, VIII, 375-376.
139. *Ibid.*, VIII, 356-357.

becoming too ambitious through political equality, might have illusions of attaining economic equality as well.

Two other books written by the rather unorthodox French cleric which were to furnish the Revolutionaries with suitable examples of republicanism to be found in history were *Observations on the History of the Greeks and Romans* and *The History of France*. The first, while it related the whole history of Greece and Rome, gave great prominence to the republican ideas of the ancients. The second found in the history of France proof that this great nation formerly had had legislative assemblies. It claimed that the kings had been mere executors of laws. It even affirmed that a constituent assembly had met in Charlemagne's time.

Rousseau and Mably, because of the many republican doctrines found in their writings, were the two most popular of the political philosophers in 1793. There were others, however, whose influence, prior to the Revolution, was considerable in pointing out the weaknesses of the monarchy and the need for governmental reform.

Montesquieu (1689–1755), although he favored a monarchy himself and enjoyed all the prerogatives of a noble in a monarchical system, was, nevertheless enough of an objective scholar to reveal the shortcomings of government by an absolute king.[140] His greatest work, *L'Esprit des Lois* (*The Spirit of Laws*), appearing in 1748, was considered by the Revolutionary leaders as the first real attack on the institution of monarchy. It was revered as the first important writing of the century to dare to examine critically the origin and justice of one-man rule. Appearing at a time when the French monarchy was a glaring example of corruption and inefficiency, it caused many an intellectual to take stock of conditions around him. Moreover, within it the separation-of-powers doctrine, where-

140.   Study was the chief joy of Montesquieu. "Study has been for me the sovereign remedy against the vexations of life," he writes. "I have never suffered anything that an hour of reading could not cause me to forget." *Pensées diverses;* as quoted in *Histoire illustrée de la Litterature française* (ed. by Abry and others, Paris, 1924), p. 343.

by the legislative, executive, and judicial branches are separate and have distinct functions, was recommended for sound government.

Barère, a member of the constitutional committees of 1793, in a book in praise of Montesquieu, said that no philosopher before him had attempted to examine the authority of monarchs, the power of legislation, and the origin of the sovereignty of the people: *"The Social Contract* had not yet enlightened the political horizon; Mably was yet to write his magnificent works about the morals of states, the philosophy of history, and the duties of citizens."[141]

The Spirit of Laws was first printed at Geneva in November, 1748. Montesquieu, for fear of consequences, had published the volume anonymously. Although the royal government, at the time, did not grant permission for its circulation in France, the book nevertheless was soon found in the libraries of French intellectuals. Enlightened Paris received the book with enthusiasm. People recognized the style of Montesquieu at once. All the literate classes of the metropolis eagerly read this thought-provoking work, and it was not long before it was found on the dressers of ladies and dandies as well as in the studies of scholars.[143] Within eighteen months of its first appearance, there were thirteen editions published. When the French government finally took the decision to grant official permission for the book to appear in France, all the chief libraries were already furnished with the work.[144] Between 1748 and the outbreak of the Revolution, it was to enjoy a wide dissemination. Ten more editions were printed during the interval 1751 to 1789.

Proof of the popularity of Montesquieu's outstanding work was thus found in the many editions that appeared before 1789. Evidence of its influence on Revolutionary leaders was to be found

141. Barère, Bertrand, *Montesquieu peint d'après ses Ouvrages* (London, 1797), p. 63.
142. *Ibid.*, p. 14.
143. Bonno, *op. cit.*, p. 7.
144. *Ibid.*, pp. 7-8.

in their own written statements. They found within its pages, authoritatively written by a scholar recognized by all literate classes, political arguments which coincided with and obviously strengthened their own. Barère was so taken with this work that he wrote a book analyzing all of the writings of Montesquieu. The purpose of the book, said Barère, was to serve as an abridged edition of Montesquieu's works for the use of republicans.[145] It was this great scholar, said he, who had first made him hope for the triumph of republicanism.[146] The author of *The Spirit of Laws*, continued Barère, was the first to show that all monarchies slip into despotism just as inevitably as rivers flow into the sea.[147] Montesquieu was always the defender of humanity, the enemy of despotism, and a man of liberty.[148] Barère wound up his eulogy with the somewhat exaggerated statement that the French Revolution was born from the very works of the liberal baron.[149]

Volume V of the annual *Bibliothèque de l'Homme public*[150] (for the year 1790) favorably reviewed *The Spirit of Laws* and pointed out its significance. Although the reviewing article was unsigned, the style of the article would indicate that the author might have been the celebrated philosopher Condorcet, last of the *philosophes*, and prime constitution-maker in 1793. The review emphasized the intelligent criticism of the weaknesses of monarchies, as pointed out by Montesquieu, compared with the many advantages

145. Barère, *op. cit.*, p. 6.
146. *Ibid.*, pp. 6-7.
147. *Ibid.*, pp. 64-65.
148. *Ibid.*, p. 73.
149. *Ibid.*, p. 143.
150. *Le Bibliothèque de l'Homme public (Library of a Public Man)* was a series of books that, beginning in 1790, appeared yearly. These books analyzed some of the greatest political works of all time. Their purpose was to educate public opinion along democratic lines. Condorcet was one of the main contributors, and many of the articles were written by him. The publication of this set continued for only a few years, however.

to be had in a republic. By reading this great work, the author of
the review remarked, one could have foreseen the Revolution.[151]
In another article in the *Bibliothèque de l'Homme public*, presumably by the same author, the comment was made that Montesquieu was the leading inspirer of the changes now (1790)
promised to France.[152]

Citations from Montequieu in the legislative and press debates
of 1793 were not as numerous as those from Rousseau and Mably.
Still, they were to be found, and significantly enough, the author
of *The Spirit of Laws* was recalled for his comments on republics.
In the *Chronique de Paris* for January 3, 1793, Rabaut Saint-
Étienne, deputy to the Convention for the department of Aube
(who had also been a member of the Constituent Assembly's constitutional committee from 1789 to 1790),[153] had the following praise
for Montesquieu: "Montesquieu thoroughly understood the spirit
of various governments and that of a republic in particular. It is
from his book [*The Spirit of Laws*] that legislators may draw the
rules for a sound democracy and the institutions that democracy
needs in order to be durable."[154] Antoine Wandelaincourt, Conventional deputy from Haute-Marne, in the constitutional project
he presented to the Convention, quoted from Montesquieu as
well as Rousseau and Mably.[155] In the constitutional debates of
1793, mention is often made of Montesquieu.[156]

151. "L'Ésprit des Lois de Montesquieu," in *B. D. H. P.*, V, 7.
152. "De l'Autorité de Montesquieu dans la Révolution présente,"
      in B. D. H. P., VII, 6.
153. It is interesting to note that, as a member of this committee,
      Rabaut was firmly monarchist. In September, 1789, he made
      the following remark: "It is impossible to believe that anyone
      in this Assembly (Constituent) might have conceived the
      ridiculous idea of converting the kingdom into a republic."
154. *Chronique de Paris* (January 3, 1793).
155. Wandelaincourt, *op. cit., passim*.
156. *Moniteur universel*, May 11, 1793; *Moniteur universel*, May
      29, 1793; *Archives parlementaires*, LXII, 378; *Archives
      parlementaires*, LXII.

Rather than analyze all of Montesquieu's works afresh, it might be better to continue enlarging upon the Revolutionaries' own opinions of these writings. The principles they discovered, or thought they discovered in them, were those which helped to guide them after 1789. It is superfluous to point out that, of all the philosopher's works, *The Spirit of Laws* was the one they usually mentioned.

A review of this essay on laws in the *Bibliothèque de l'Homme public* stressed the democratic ideas to be learned by reading Montesquieu. In its analysis of his most important work, it found that he described democratic government as one in which the people did all they could for themselves and left the rest to ministers. In a democratic government the people named their own magistrates and subjected them, if necessary, to criticism when their terms of office were ended.[157] According to Montesquieu, said the review, all magistracies should be of short duration. Moreover, as in Athens and Rome, the decrees of the legislature should have force for but a single year, becoming perpetual only when the people so willed.[158]

In its comments on Montesquieu's comparison between republics and monarchies, the review held that he favored a republic.[159] Virtue was the characteristic of democracies, and luxury that of monarchies.[160] The love for a republic in a democratic society was the love for democracy itself, and therefore the love of equality and frugality.[161] There could not be luxuries in a real democracy, in

157. "L'Ésprit des Lois de Montesquieu," in *B. D. H. P.*, V, 12-13.
158. *Ibid.*, V, 13-15.
159. The review was mistaken. Although he recognized the virtues of republics, Montesquieu felt this form of government to be impractical for large states. He even had some doubts about its practicability for small states. In spite of a republican government, small states might be invaded by a larger, despotic state.
160. "L'Ésprit des Lois de Montesquieu," in *B. D. H. P.*, first year, V, 16-17.
161. *Ibid.*, V, 22-23.

which the wealth was shared equally.[162] The following principles, dear to the hearts of the men of 1793, were found by the reviewer in *The Spirit of Laws*: physical necessities should not be taxed; the useful might be taxed, but less than the superfluous;[163] liberty signified permission to do all that was not contrary to law.[164]

Barère had no doubt that the author of *The Spirit of Laws* was republican. The only reason Montesquieu was careful in the way he wrote about the French monarchy, said Barère, was that he was subject to its jurisdiction. Barère discovered that *The Spirit of Laws* was filled with ironic comments about monarchies which the superficial reader might not see.[165] For example, he referred to a statement in this book in regard to education in a kingdom. Even a superficial reader, thought Barère, would see that this was a criticism of monarchies. Education, when it existed, said Montesquieu, was reduced to placing fear in children's hearts and teaching them a few simple religious principles. Far too often education did not exist at all in a royalist society.[166]

Montesquieu, simply with a flourish of his pen, said Barère, traced a system based on the sovereignty of the people. The people ruled through their duly elected representatives.[167] Barère finished his eulogy by saying he was sick and tired of hearing that Montesquieu had claimed that republics could endure only in small states. This was the argument of aristocrats.[168] The representative system, recommended by the philosopher, was a means of organizing the sovereignty of the people even in large republics.[169]

162. *Ibid.*, V, 41-42. Montesquieu, however, warned against that spirit of extreme democracy in which everyone wished to be equal to those who commanded. *Ibid.*, V, 49.
163. *Ibid.*, V, 83.
164. *Ibid.*, V, 72.
165. Barère, *op. cit.*, pp. 82 and 83, footnote (unnumbered).
166. *Ibid.*, 86.
167. *Ibid.*, p. 77.
168. *Ibid.*, p. 99.
169. *Ibid.*, p. 101-102.

Montesquieu's influence on the Revolution was acknowledged in the article "De l'Autorité de Montesquieu dans la Révolution présente."[170] However, it criticized him for showing that monarchies had some advantages. It also criticized him for offering a plan of monarchical government which gave privileges to a few.[171] Finally, it said, he made a mistake in not recognizing the great middle class. The middle class, through the constructive pursuits of commerce, industry, and manufactures, brought prosperity as well as law and order.[172]

Thus, even though some Revolutionaries might not agree that Montesquieu was a republican, they did agree that his ideas in this direction had a weighty part in shaping their own preferences for republics. His criticisms of monarchy increased their own odium for this type of government. On the other hand, his suggestions as to the best points to be discovered in a republican administration made them appreciate the advantage of representative government.

Another name which has attained wide notability in the world as a precursor of the French Revolution is that of François Marie Arouet de Voltaire (1694–1778). Doubtless, his writings were of importance in adding fuel to the evergrowing fire of discontent manifest in France at the end of the eighteenth century. However, there was little in his literary masterpieces favorable to republicanism; he wrote nothing that adequately described the workings of representative government. In this respect his works differ from those of Rousseau, Mably, or Montesquieu. Hence, after 1790, when the republican spirit became strong in France, it was from the works of the latter three that one quoted, rather than from those of Voltaire.

Voltaire did, however, vigorously attack the church. In that the

170. *B. D. H. P.*, VII, 1-85.
171. "De l'Autorité de Montesquieu dans la Révolution présente," in *B. D. H. P.*, VII, 75, 85.
172. "De l'Autorité de Montesquieu dans la Révolution présente," in *B. D. H. P.*, VII, 64-65.

church was closely connected with the monarchy, it might be said that indirectly, at least, Voltaire helped to undermine the institution of kingship.[173] Yet if Voltaire undermined the throne, he did this unwillingly. He never was a revolutionary democrat or liberal in a political way. He never demanded that the social system be changed or that there be a leveling of all classes.[174] Voltaire was chiefly interested in being able to write, speak, and move in complete independence.[175] When the society of his time denied him this, he replied by his pen more in the spirit of personal revenge than in the spirit of reform.

The opinion of Voltaire in regard to representative government was not very high. He thought it founded on the ambitions of others. Laws might maintain a form of equality as long as possible, but in the end a voracious and vigorous man would come along and assume full control.[176] Men were not capable of governing themselves, said Voltaire.[177] Yet he recognized the worth of republicanism as a pure ideal. It was all right to talk about its good points in a theoretical way, but in actual practice these would degenerate into the wrongs of most governments. The ideal of a government might be perfect but certainly the men manipulating its agencies would not always be perfect. An uneven distribution of talents would prevent this. And an uneven division of talents would always result in two classes: those of the rich, who would command, whatever the form of government; and those of the poor, who would serve.[178]

Voltaire's literary output was voluminous. The number of editions

173.   Aulard, *Histoire politique*, p. 10.
174.   Michel, Henry, *L'Idée de l'État: Essai critique sur l'Histoire des Théories sociales et politiques en France depuis la Révolution* (2d. ed., Paris, 1896), p. 13.
175.   *Loc. cit.*
176.   Aulard, *Histoire politique*, p. 9.
177.   Fabre, Joseph, *Les Pères de la Révolution de Bayle à Condorcet* (Paris, 1910), p. 233.
178.   Fabre, *op. cit.*, p. 236.

of his works was large. In 1747 there were extant at least eleven editions of his general works. Ten more appeared between 1748 and 1770, and five from 1771 to 1789. His main writings, such as *Candide* and *Lettres philosophiques,* ran into some forty editions. The majority of the Revolutionary leaders thus had plenty of opportunity to familiarize themselves with Voltaire through his writings.[179] If they found no helpful suggestions for a better form of government, at least they came to realize that their own monarchical system was far from perfect.

Besides the four great philosophers already mentioned, there were other men, perhaps of lesser fame, who had some bearing on the evolution of republican beliefs in France before the Revolution. It may be that these lesser lights did not achieve the reputation of a Rousseau or Voltaire. They were, nevertheless, important for the sway their precepts had over the leaders of political thought just before and immediately after 1789. They had taught, moreover, a few educated men to think about political and social questions and caused doubts to be raised in these educated minds over existing conditions.

The political works of John Locke (1632–1704), the English philosopher, were doubtless known to most of the leaders of the French Revolution. Probably the majority of French intellectuals were as familiar with Locke as they were with their own philoso-

179. Brissot de Warville, important constitutional leader in 1793, had an interesting experience in connection with Voltaire. As a young man, Brissot was highly embarrassed when he witnessed a case in which the identity of the great philosopher was not recognized. A lawyer, at whose office Brissot happened to be on business, failed to recognize Voltaire when the world-famous philosopher entered his office. To the consternation of young Brissot, the legal gentleman asked the elderly, somewhat eccentrically dressed philosopher what his occupation might be. "To enlighten the world," answered Voltaire ironically. *J. P. Brissot: Mémoires* (ed. by C. Perroud), I, 146.

phers. If, by chance, there were a few that were not, even these few, through the writings of Rousseau, knew something of Locke's ideas. Fabre says that in over a hundred places the body of Rousseau's discourses was borrowed from Locke.[180] Locke spoke a great deal of the state of nature, as did Rousseau.

The state of nature, said the English philosopher, was that of equality. It was not a condition in which certain ones were destined to all the power and others to slavery.[181] As regards political power, Locke said that all powers and jurisdiction were reciprocal, no one person having more than another. Creatures of the same species, all born to the same advantages of nature and the same use of faculties, should be equal amongst one another, without subordination or subjection.[182] Absolute power, or the placing of one man above many, was inconsistent with civil society, stated Locke.[183]

The theme of equality, so reiterated by Rousseau, was probably

180. Fabre, *op. cit.*, p. 39. The seventh French edition of Locke's *Du Gouvernement civil (Concerning Civil Government)* appeared at Paris in 1795. The first French edition, translated by David Mazel, was published at Geneva in 1724. Aulard says that this work was one of the most widely read political works in eighteenth-century France and had a great influence on the precursors of the French Revolution. Rousseau owed both his theory of the state of nature and that of the civil state to Locke. According to Aulard, Locke's influence was reflected in the United States Constitution, which in turn influenced the French Constitutions of 1790 and 1793. Locke was the common godfather of the American and French Revolutions. Aulard, Francois V. Aphonse, "La Révolution américaine et la Révolution française; William Penn et Locke," in *La Révolution française* (January-February, 1918), LXXXI, 37.
181. Locke, John, *Two Treatises on Civil Government* (London, 1884), pp. 141-148.
182. *Ibid.*, p. 193.
183. *Ibid.*, p. 236.

not the only doctrine which was at least partially derived by the Genevan sage from Locke. It might be, too, that he borrowed from the English philosopher the concept that an oppressed people had the right of insurrection. According to the principle fixed by Locke, the right of insurrection should pre-exist in every constitution. The people, as the true sovereign, had the right to protect themselves against any unjust encroachments by the governmental branches, even against those of the legislature, in virtue of natural law. They were able, for lack of a possible appeal on earth, to place their fate in the hands of God and have recourse to revolution. Without the great social right of revolt, the human species would lose all dignity, as well as honor.[184]

Locke also sketched the separation-of-powers idea before Montesquieu did[185] and firmly expressed, before Voltaire, the desire that church and state should be separated. A government should concern itself with its own world, and not with the world beyond, said he.[186]

A contemporary of Locke, and as famous in France as Locke was in England, was Pierre Bayle (1647–1706). Bayle was considered one of the great philosophers of his day. His publications, however, deemed quite radical for his time, caused him considerable trouble. Because of them he lost teaching positions both in France and in Holland. It might have been possible to ostracize the person of Bayle, but not his ideas. Famous in his own lifetime, these ideas became even more so after his death. Emphasizing the renown and ascendancy of this seventeenth-century liberal, a modern historian once said that the Revolution was prepared in the seventeenth century by the European publicity of Bayle's writings, printed several times during the course of his life.[187]

184. As cited by Fabre, *op. cit.*, p. 44.
185. *Ibid.*, p. 43.
186. Fabre, *op. cit.*, pp. 47-48.
187. Souquet, Paul, "Pierre Bayle, Libre-Penseur et Politique (1647–1706)," in *La Révolution française* (February, 1890), XVIII, 97.

Voltaire called him *"mon père"* and carried over many of his ideas.[188]

The chief contribution of Bayle in the realm of governmental science was his doctrine that the individual, whether in politics or religion, was worth something. He approached anarchy in his *Continuation des Pensées diverses (Continuation of Sundry Thoughts)* when he asked the questions "whether societies are absolutely necessary in order to preserve the human species" and "whether religion is absolutely necessary in order to conserve societies."[189] Following Bayle, the individual should have the inalienable right of professing his own religious beliefs. He should have the right of spreading these beliefs by all honest means.[190] To procure civil peace, the prince or magistrate should respect the freedom of conscience of all men.[191] Bayle foresaw the final separation of church and state as an outcome of individualism. The state, then, would not be able to dictate the religious views of its citizens.

A contemporary of Bayle, but not quite so well known, was the Abbé de Saint-Pierre (1658–1743). The far-sighted views of this man of letters, however, gave him the right to be remembered by the Revolutionaries, especially by the liberal scholar and constitution-maker of 1793, Condorcet. Saint-Pierre was far ahead of his times when he advocated a league of nations to maintain perpetual peace. He was a forerunner of Condorcet in the belief that all philosophy which did not lead to the amelioration of certain unfavorable conditions of life was pure vanity. He argued for the eradication of mendicity, a progressive tax on revenues, suppression of the right of primogeniture, and universal education.[192]

One of the best sources for the political and social conditions of France in the first half of the eighteenth century is the memoirs

188. *Loc. cit.*
189. Souquet, *op. cit.*, p. 110.
190. *Loc. cit.*
191. *Ibid.*, p. 224.
192. Fabre, *op. cit.*, pp. 72-73.

of the Marquis d'Argenson. The marquis was a shrewd political observer and believed that he saw a rising tide of revolution in France. Apparently he had nothing but contempt for the decadent monarchy of his own time, as exemplified in the bored and enervated Louis XV. Writing in April, 1754, d'Argenson stated that a treatise in which Locke had decided that kings could be deposed had caused much discussion in France.[193] Some time before the appearance of this treatise, D'Argenson had written that a study of monarchical rule and its consequence for society would persuade one that it was the worst possible form of government.[194] As early as 1743 he predicted revolution and was certain that France would soon have some other type of administration.[195] As time went on, he said, republicanism would win over more philosophical minds every day.[196]

The names Diderot (1713-1784) and D'Alembert (1717-1783) are usually associated together as co-editors of the *Encyclopédie (Encyclopedia)*. These two outstanding scholars compiled a vast work of some seventeen volumes of text and ten of plates, which contained articles contributed by all the representative writers and eminent men of the eighteenth century. Some of those who contributed were Montesquieu, Rousseau, Voltaire, Turgot, Raynal, and Condorcet. The broad aim of the *Encyclopedia* was the advancement of human happiness by means of knowledge. In searching articles it exposed the shortcomings of the French monarchy and traced the rise and fall of various other forms of government. Although it contained many articles on the physical sciences, the *Encyclopedia's* greatest worth was its thought-provoking articles concerning the social sciences. It gathered, as in a fasces, the new ideas of the eighteenth century and made them available to the public[197] in a convenient form.[198]

193. Champion, *op. cit.*, p. 19, footnote 1.
194. *Ibid.*, p. 20.
195. *Loc. cit.*
196. Aulard, *Histoire politique*, p. 13.
197. Fabre, *op. cit.*, pp. 459-60.
198. *Ibid.*, p. 480.

Diderot and D'Alembert were both opponents of absolute government. The first said that all arbitrary government was bad, even though the master might be excellent. Scolding against privilege, he asserted that those who enjoyed most of the prerogatives in society contributed least to its expense.[199] It was the consent of the people, declared D'Alembert, that gave all chiefs their authority. D'Alembert's ideal government would be a limited monarchy in which the king would be prevented by the people from becoming absolute. In his political system there would be no hereditary prerogatives.[200]

Georges Louis Leclerc de Buffon (1707–1788), perhaps the most widely read man of the century, had some influence on the republican constitutional leaders of 1793.[201] Writing almost entirely about natural science, he still managed to place certain social concepts into his publications. He praised the idyllic life of wild animals and savages; they, said he, had love, liberty, and equality. He believed in the unity of all races and strongly opposed slavery. He bemoaned the fact that man seemed more interested in research on wrongs than in research on rights. No arts had progressed as much as those of war, deplored Buffon;[202] it was his prayer to God that the names of all military heroes might be buried in forgetfulness.[203] Condorcet adopted many of Buffon's principles. Two of these, faith in human progress and the belief in a natural evolution towards a better way of life, were pet principles of the future constitution-maker.

D'Holbach (1723–1789) was another pre-Revolutionary philosopher who did much to shape the thinking of Condorcet.[204] Some

199.   *Ibid.*, pp. 459-60.
200.   *Ibid.*, p. 480.
201.   Condorcet wrote a flattering account of Buffon. Condorcet, Marquis de, *Éloge de M. le Comte de Buffon*, in *Oeuvres complètes*.
202.   Fabre, *op. cit.*, p. 209.
203.   *Ibid.*, p. 240.
204.   D'Holbach was a close friend of Condorcet; they spent a

of the principles of the Constitution of 1793 compare with the opinions found in Holbach's essays.

As an unshakable adversary of despotism, D'Holbach wished a government based on natural laws respecting the rights of the nation.[205] He admitted no other justification for authority than that founded on explicit or tacit consent between the nation and the ruler. Society was always the mistress of sovereignty. "The power of the monarch always remains subordinate to that of the representatives of the people; these representatives always depend on the will of their constituents."[206] Although sanctioning violence only when absolutely necessary, D'Holbach averred that the people could claim their rights by a legitimate revolt if necessary.[207] "Passing troubles are more advantageous than an eternal languishment under continual tyranny."[208]

Complete equality was a chimera, thought D'Holbach. It was an ideal which could be approached but never reached. By way of approaching it, however, there were certain acts which the government could perform. Minds could be elevated and placed on a more nearly common plane by increased educational opportunities.[209] Education could be taken away from the church and placed in less biased hands. There could be equality of taxation, with no unjust exemptions.[210] Excessive differences in wealth might be

great deal of time together. Both were very progressive in their ideas and hoped for a better order in France. When d'Holbach died he made the Marquis de Condorcet his heir. Fabre, *op. cit.*, p. 488.

205. Lion, Henri, "Les Idées politiques et morales de d'Holbach," in *Annales historiques de la Révolution française* (July-August, 1924), I, 358.

206. Mornet, *Origines intellectuelles*, p. 103.

207. Lion, *op. cit.*, p. 359.

208. As quoted by Mornet, *Origines intellectuelles*, p. 103.

209. Lion, *op. cit.*, p. 361.

210. *Ibid.*, p. 365.

mitigated; extreme wealth was the main cause for the disintegration of states.[211]

Probably the publicist most violently anti-monarchical, in the years just prior to 1789, was Abbé Raynal (1713–1796). His *Histoire philosophique et politique des Établissements et du Commerce européen dans les deux Indies (Philosophical and Political History of the European Colonies and Commerce in Both Indies)*, first published in 1770, became famous. Never was such insulting language used openly against kings. By looking around, said Raynal, one would see the unbelievable sight of millions of men led by a dozen individuals called "kings." Scolding people for their passiveness, Raynal almost literally shouted the words: "Cowardly people! Imbecile flock! You are content to groan when you ought to bellow."[212] Raynal declared that it was not proper for an intelligent people to undergo a master, whatever the master's talents.[213] After all, there was no other authority than that held from the citizens.[214]

Freedom of speech, press, and religion, and equality before the law, plus the right to a means of livelihood through work, were all legitimate rights of the people, said Raynal. These principles found great favor with most of the republican-inclined French Revolutionaries, of course. Many of the leading Girondins claimed that the opinions of Raynal coincided with their own.[215] These

211. *Ibid.*, p. 364.
212. As quoted by Fabre, *op. cit.*, p. 514.
213. *Ibid.*, p. 523.
214. *Ibid.*, p. 524.
215. *Ibid.*, p. 530. An authority on Raynal, Anatole Feugère, said that his *Philosophical and Political History of the European Colonies and Commerce in Both Indies* (which was burned, incidentally, at the hands of the public executioner in 1781) became the breviary of the generation which carried out the French Revolution. Feugère, Anatole, *Un Precurseur de la Révolution: L'Abbé Raynal, 1713–1796* (Angoulême, 1922), Introduction, p. IV. He added that during his lifetime

opinions would constantly reappear in the constitutional debates of 1793.

If there was one man who might have prevented the French Revolution, that man was Turgot (1727–1781), controller-general of France from 1774 to 1776. His economic and political plans were such that, had they been put into operation, the increasing discontent with the monarchy might have been checked. Unfortunately for the monarchy, the selfish advisers surrounding Louis XVI persuaded this lackadaisical ruler to get rid of his one enlightened minister. Proceeding along the path of its old absolute ways, it was not long before the monarchy reached the point of dissolution.

Although Turgot's ideas had no visible effect before 1789, they did make an impression on future leaders: amongst others, Condorcet, friend and biographer[216] of the displaced minister. Turgot was less occupied with the form of the French government than he was with practical reforms that he considered necessary for the welfare of the state and the happiness of its citizens. His concept of individualism carried with it all the thought of the century. His state of mind was very similar to that of the men who were going to accomplish the revolution in 1789.[217]

Turgot believed that society was made for the individual and instituted only to protect his rights.[218] Any hindrance to the rights of one of society's members was an injustice. Religious and economic freedom was defended by Turgot on the grounds of individual rights. The king had no authority over the consciences of the inhabitants of his kingdom.[219] No more did a government

Raynal was admired as much as Voltaire and Rousseau. The Constituent Assembly wished to honor him as a benefactor of humanity. *Ibid.*, Introduction, p. vi.

216. Condorcet, Marquis de, *Vie de M. Turgot*, vol. V. of *Oeuvres complètes*.

217. See, Henri, "La Doctrine politique et sociale de Turgot," in *Annales historiques de la Révolution française* (September-October, 1924), I, 413.

218. See, *op. cit.*, p. 414.

219. *Ibid.*, p. 415.

have a right to interfere with the free trade of its citizens.[220] The only restrictions Turgot would apply to a policy of economic individualism, or *laissez-faire*, would be those which were necessary to preserve the economic and political rights of the humble against infringement by the more economically fortunate. Turgot made the right to work the "most sacred and imprescriptible" of all rights.[221] The fiscal privileges granted the nobles were outrageous, said Turgot. All should contribute taxes whether they possessed a title or not.

Louis XVI's controller-general outlined a system of municipal government containing a few features that impressed Condorcet. This system was one whereby the monarchy would depend for its main support on a large number of self-governing municipalities. By allowing the municipalities to govern themselves, the king would gain the advantage of a favorable public opinion.[222] At the apex of the municipal structure would be a national assembly to supplement the authority of the king. Turgot's liberal municipal plan, tending away from absolutism and privilege, was, however, foolishly brushed aside by the court of Louis XVI.

The last great French philosopher of the eighteenth century was the Marquis de Condorcet. Although he will be treated fully in other chapters, it is well at this point to indicate something of his significance as a philosopher, and to summarize the importance of his connection with eighteenth-century philosophy. Condorcet was important, for one thing, in that he synthesized the best of past philosophy with his own enlightened concepts. Having the advantage of being alive when the Revolution broke out, he had the wonderful opportunity of being in a position to put the theories of political philosophy to practical use. Courageously, but perhaps unrealistically, he endeavored to establish a system of government based on his philosophical reflections in the study and his per-

220. *Loc. cit.*
221. *Ibid.*, p. 417. The right to work was one of the notable social clauses of the Constitution of 1793.
222. *Ibid.*, p. 424.

sonal experience in the stormy arena of Revolutionary politics. Condorcet's ideas, even as those of other intellectuals in politics since, hardly received proper consideration, it would seem.

All of Condorcet's study of political institutions proved to him that the best form of government was one in which the people ruled themselves to the greatest possible degree. The Constitution of 1793 was to provide such a form of government. Condorcet, with the help of a few other Revolutionary leaders, coordinated the republican doctrines of the philosophers with the lessons to be learned from an observation of the institutions found in the republican United States. The result of their work was the most democratic constitution that France ever produced.

In the evolution of republican ideas in France, the philosophers played a major part. Their writings educated the Revolutionary leaders in political principles which were directly contrary to those of authoritarian rule. The political, social, and economic upheaval in 1789 was not a sudden, impetuous movement. It resulted partly from ideals that, since the beginning of the eighteenth century, a few dominant minds had been putting into print. As R. M. McIver aptly stated: "Whatever may be the eruptive forces that precipitate the grand events of history, it can scarcely be denied that the particular contours of these events are molded by the thoughts of dominant minds."[223]

The philosophers and publicists, by their writings describing the virtues of republican principles, had enhanced, in the eyes of the revolutionaries, a republicanism they had already learned to idealize through their early training in the classics.[224] The revolution in

223. MacIver, R. M. "European Doctrines and the Constitution," in *The Constitution Reconsidered*, op. cit., p. 5.
224. The influence of antiquity on Revolutionary leaders is an interesting sidelight. Most of the outstanding leaders of the Revolution had received a fairly good classical education. The schools of the Old Regime stressed the classics as the main part of the curriculum. In the *collèges*, Cicero, Livy, and Plutarch were all studied by the students. It was these

America, with the resultant creation of the Republic of the United States, was to offer a practical contemporary proof that many of the democratic ideals described by the philosophers actually worked.

ancients who wrote about republican institutions and the virtues of citizens in a republic. Parker, Harold. *The Cult of Antiquity and the French Revolutionaries: A Study in the Development of the Revolutionary Spirit* (Chicago, 1937), p. 3. Camille Desmoulins, one of the first actively agitating republicans of the Revolution, and upon whom antiquity exerted a decisive influence, attributed the desire for political change, so prevalent amongst Revolutionary leaders, to their *collège* instruction. He also attributed the rise of a republican movement during the Constituent Assembly (1789–1791) to the classical training of a few leaders. (*Archives parlementaires*, LXXV, 622.) Robespierre, in the course of debate over the Constitution of 1793, wanted provision made for a system of public schools. He recalled that the *collèges* of the Old Regime had been the nursery of republicans. (*Moniteur universel*, June 21, 1793.) Condorcet and Brissot had excellent educations as youths; even in later years they enjoyed reading classical literature. (Parker, *op. cit.*, 16.) Brissot, as a member of the Legislative Assembly, displayed his classical training in debates. He took second place after Desmoulins, also a representative in the Legislative Assembly, in the number of references made to antiquity. (*Ibid.*, p. 15.) Saint-Just, prominent member of the Montagnard group in the Convention, and close associate of Robespierre, was so enamoured with what he had learned from reading about the ancient Greeks and Romans that he uttered scarcely a phrase that did not include some analogy with an event of antiquity. Madame Roland, a respected adviser of the Girondin faction, at whose house its leaders often met, said that at the age of eight she carried Plutarch's *Lives* to church instead of her prayer book. (*Mémoires de Madame Roland* [ed. by Cl. Perroud, 2 vols., Paris, 1905], I, 37.) Madame Roland once told Brissot that the man who read Plutarch when he was fifteen and then again when he was sixty was certain to be at all times a good man and citizen. (J. P. Brissot: *Mémoires* [ed. by Cl. Perroud], I, 4-5.) The reason for the numerous compliments paid to Rome was that in their school training the Revolutionary leaders had been mainly exposed to the short period of Roman history between 80 B.C. and 120 A.D. This, according to Parker, was the period when the Roman Republic saw its greatest days. (Parker, *op. cit.*, p. 22.) After leaving school, by reading the works of the philosophers such as Montesquieu, Rousseau, and Mably, the Revolutionaries learned still more about the republican virtues of ancient Rome.

Chapter II

American Republicanism and French Thought

The transition of Great Britain's thirteen original colonies into the Republic of the United State had a distinct relationship to the growth of republican principles in France between 1776 and the French Revolution. Much of the success of this evolution — or, better, revolution — in the New World could be attributed to the generous, unstinting aid of the French monarchy, which saw its chance to have revenge against Great Britain for the loss of French colonies in 1763. Little did the French monarchy foresee that it was helping to prepare its own extinction by aiding in the creation of a type of government of which many of its philosophers, some still alive in 1789, had extolled the virtues. Philosophers and publicists with inclinations towards self-government could now point to the United States as a practical proof of principles they had described in their writings as ideals. They could draw parallels between the new democratic republic and absolute France, with unfavorable results for the latter.

It was not only a hatred for England that gave Frenchmen so much enthusiasm for the cause of American independence. It was also a hatred for despotism[1] in general, a hatred which philosophers had been encouraging since the beginning of the eighteenth century. Condorcet, as a philosopher himself, realized

1. Aulard, François V. Alphonse, *Histoire politique de la Révolution française: Origines et Développement de la Démocratie et de la République (1789–1804)* (Paris, 1901), p. 20.

this. Discussing the effect of the American Revolution on France he said:

> "Men whom the reading of philosophic books had secretly disposed to love liberty were filled with passion over that of a foreign people. They were only waiting until they could occupy themselves with the recovery of their own freedom. They seized with joy this occasion [the American Revolution] to publicly confess sentiments that prudence had obliged them to maintain in silence."[2]

The influence of the American Revolution on France can well be told in the activities and interrelationships of a small group of liberally minded men, Frenchmen and Americans. These men were often, when not personally acquainted with one another, at least familiar with each other through their writings. Significantly, the men most active in France in heralding the advent of a new republic and its institutions, and those giving it the most publicity in their works, were men who would later be strong proponents of republicanism in their own country. In fact, two of these men, the philosopher Condorcet and the publicist and future factional leader Brissot, would serve on the first republican constitutional committee in 1793. Their works and those of other prominent and like-minded Frenchmen, describing the United States and its leaders, enjoyed wide circulation amongst French intellectuals. Encouraging the publicists in their vivid accounts about the great

---

2. Condorcet, Marquis de, *Éloge de Franklin* in *Oeuvres complètes* (21 vols., Paris, 1801–1804), IV, 1414. This passage is an excellent statement of Condorcet's own feeling.

political revolution across the ocean was an American who had all the philosophic appeal of Rousseau's natural man.[3]

Benjamin Franklin (1706–1790), American patriot, whose shrewd common sense and charming personality were to prove helpful traits in winning French aid for the revolting British colonies, arrived in France in December, 1776.[4] He came to the court of the French monarch as the colonies' chief emissary. He was the only man of America who then had a famous reputation in Europe.[5] French scientists respected him for his experiments in the field of electricity. The philosophers knew Franklin to be an advanced political thinker and a believer in representative government. He was all the more respected by French intellectuals for being a self-made man, educated according to the best tenets of *Émile*, Rousseau's treatise on education. Even the less intellectual knew Franklin through his *Science du bonhomme Richard (Poor Richard's Almanac)*, first translated into French in 1773. This book, with its witty homespun philosophy, delighted the French public and was to reappear in at least eight editions in the next three years.[6] Thus, Franklin was far from a stranger to Frenchmen when he disembarked at a French seaport in the winter of 1776.

Franklin's sojourn in France from 1776 to 1785 had an im-

3. Brissot even compared Franklin with Rousseau. (Brissot, J. P., *New Travels in the United States of America* [tr. from the French, translator unnamed, Dublin, 1792], pp. 219-220.)

4. Franklin was already well known, having previously visited France in 1767 and 1769.

5. Condorcet, *Éloge de Franklin* in *Oeuvres complètes*, IV, 104. In 1772 Franklin had been made a member of the French Academy of Sciences. (Hale, Edward E., and Hale, Edward E., Jr., *Franklin in France* [2 vols., Boston, 1887], I, 169.) Voltaire and Condorcet were also members of this illustrious body.

6. Mornet, Daniel, *Les Origines intellectuelles de la Révolution française, 1715—1787* (Paris, 1933), pp. 393-394.

portant bearing on the development of republicanism in both France and America. Franklin was the means by which the American colonies secured French aid. Without this aid it is doubtful that they would have won their independence; without independence they could not have set up a representative form of government very easily, considering the rather absolute nature of British rule at the time. As far as French republicanism is concerned, Franklin was an important factor in causing the contagion of representative government to spread from America to France.[7]

Shortly after Franklin's arrival, extracts from the American Declaration of Independence began to circulate. All the journals spoke of this Declaration as a grand and sublime piece of writing. The *Gazette de France* described the exaltation that carried away American troops when the Declaration was read to them. Long details were given by this journal relating to the ceremonies celebrated at Philadelphia and Boston in order to commemorate July 4, 1776. It told of the "enthusiasm that liberty inspires in republican souls."[8] In 1777 the *Courrier de l'Europe*, a liberal newspaper with a wide European circulation, printed in England and secretly subsidized by the French government,[9] gave the com-

7. The historian Faÿ believes it was Franklin's diplomatic astuteness that caused the American Revolution to terminate successfully for the colonists. Moreover, says Faÿ, the greater part of the visions and hopes prevalent amongst French Revolutionary leaders was due to the influence of Franklin's long sojourn in their country. Faÿ, Bernard, *L'Esprit révolutionnaire en France et aux États-Unis a la Fin du XVIII*e *Siècle* (Paris, 1924), pp. 94-95.

8. *Ibid.*, pp. 55-56.

9. The position of the French monarchy before 1778 was unique. An absolute government, it could not openly express sympathy for a republican cause. Still, it did all it could to promote enthusiasm for American independence by allowing newspapers to print material favorable to the Americans. It even

plete text.[10] Practically all Frenchmen, on reading this American declaration of freedom, were swept by an emotionalism almost religious in its intensity.[11] Franklin, as a signer of the Declaration of Independence, was all the more revered.[12] He capitalized on

subsidized some newspapers. Brissot, the future Girondin leader, said the *Courrier de l'Europe* was started in order to keep France informed about the American Revolution. By arousing the sympathy of all France (a sympathy made practical when the French government shipped arms and men to America), this journal contributed, he said, to the success of the American war and consequently in an indirect way (by causing some Frenchmen to be discontent with their own government) to that of the French Revolution. (*J. P. Brissot: Mémoires, 1754–1793* [ed. by Perroud, Cl., 2 vols., Paris, 1911], I, 305.) The newspaper had a large circulation for those days. According to Brissot, there were more than 100,000 subscribers. (*Ibid.*, I, 307.)

10. Faÿ, *op. cit.*, p. 57. Brissot later became a reporter on this newspaper. In his *Mémoires* he related how gratefully he accepted this position when it was offered by Swinton, the English publisher. Brissot, whose pecuniary position was none too good, was living with a friend in Paris at the time of the offer, and, somewhat unprofitably to himself, vainly trying to carry on a literary career. He was glad to obtain a position which made him more financially secure. Still, he hated to leave Paris, which he referred to as being a fascinating place at that time. It was near the end of Franklin's sojourn in France. Brissot said that everyone patterned himself after the American envoy and even followed him to his retreat at Chaillot. (*J. P. Brissot: Mémoires* [ed. by Perroud, Cl.], I, 140-141.)

11. Faÿ, *op. cit.*, p. 57.

12. Hale and Hale, *op. cit.*, I, 69-70. From 1778 to 1783 three editions of the Declaration of Independence were to be published in France with the tacit consent of the government. (Mornet, *op. cit.*, p. 395.) This historic document in the

his popularity by doing all he could to enlighten the French people on events in America.

Besides the Declaration of Independence, there was another American writing that caused quite a stir in France. Franklin, who was the principal editor of the journal *Les Affaires de l'Angleterre et de l'Amerique* (*English and American Relations*), had large sections of Tom Paine's *Common Sense* printed in his newspaper.[13] Paine's revolutionary pamphlet, written in 1776, extolled the American cause as being one in which the people were only trying to win their just right to govern themselves. It was also a strong indictment of the corrupt British monarchy of that time and could be taken as a criticism of monarchies in general. Doubtless many French intellectuals viewed it as such.[14]

evolution of man's freedom, written largely by Thomas Jefferson, contains much of the philosophy of Rousseau and Locke, common forefathers of the American and French Revolutions.

13. Faÿ, *op. cit.*, pp. 62-63. Brissot said that the reason "the celebrated pamphlet entitled *Common Sense* had such a widespread effect was that it was cited and reproduced hundreds of times in the gazettes, and devoured with avidity by artisans and farmers, as well as men of all other classes." (*J. P. Brissot: Mémoires* [ed. by Perroud, Cl.], II, 81.)

14. The complete French translation of *Common Sense* published in 1792 was the work of Lanthenas, who was to be a supernumerary of the first constitutional committee of 1793. This translation, appearing shortly after the overthrow of the monarchy in August — although excerpts from *Common Sense*, as already indicated, had appeared in French newspapers some years before — when republicanism was the dominant political ideology, would show that Paine's American Revolutionary pamphlet was regarded as a strong argument for republics. Brissot and Condorcet were both impressed by the sentiments of this early writing of Paine. (Gidney, Lucy M., *L'Influence des États-Unis d'Amérique sur Brissot, Condorcet, et Mme. Roland* [Paris, 1930], p. 18.)

Having great popularity in France,[15] it increased enthusiasm for the American cause still more.

Fervor for the independence of the rebellious British colonies increased with every year of Franklin's stay in France. The old American philosopher and statesman encouraged this passion amongst the many young nobles who flocked around him. Certain of the young nobles, either smitten by the philosophical doctrines of the time or burning for a war of revenge with England, beseeched Franklin for commissions in the American army.[16] They were anxious to serve the revolting colonials in some capacity. They were impatient with the apparent hesitancy of their government to take a more active course of action against Great Britain. Vergennes, Minister of Foreign Affairs, was especially criticized.[17] In reality, the government was doing much for Amer-

---

15. Aulard, *Histoire Politique*, p. 20. Doubtless, the fame derived from this pamphlet was later instrumental in causing Paine to be made a French citizen and to be elected to the Convention. Tom Paine's connection with the French monarchy was as unique as it was interesting. Through the French minister to America, Gerard, the monarchy offered to pay Paine for any further pamphlet he might write about America's struggle for liberty. (Fay, *op. cit.*, p. 87.) The French absolute government of 1776, in its hatred for England, was willing to pay one of the most violently anti-monarchical pamphleteers of the day to write doctrines which were later to be used, with unfortunate effects, against itself. Paine's writings were not only instrumental in advancing the cause of republicanism in America; they were also to be used to advance the same cause in France. Paine, however, was not against a king as an individual. Perhaps Paine recalled the king's proffered generosity in 1776 when, as a member of the Convention in 1793, he pleaded for clemency for the royal family and recommended its deportation to the United States.

16. Hale and Hale, *op. cit.*, I, 69.

17. Faÿ, *op. cit.*, p. 60.

ica through secret grants of money to the versatile merchant and speculator Beaumarchais,[18] who in turn supplied the colonials with war equipment. Vergennes personally put the American emissaries in touch with Beaumarchais. Active intervention by the government was not far in the offing.

The year 1778 can be regarded as an important year in Franco-American relations. Finally prodded by public opinion into openly upholding the cause of the American colonies, the French government, by a series of treaties exchanged in January and February with Franklin and the other American emissaries, recognized the independence of a republican United States. Soon French ships and French troops were fighting side by side with those of the Americans.[19] Perhaps the French monarchy thought it was only helping to bring grief to its adversary, Great Britain. However, the view of many Frenchmen was that they were fighting something quite different from a nationalistic war. A French writer by the name of Linguet, whose bold writings caused him to be imprisoned in the Bastille several times, wrote that in fight-

18. Beaumarchais, Augustin Pierre Caron de (1732–1799), the son of a Parisian watchmaker, could lay claim to a wide versatility of talents. During his lifetime he successfully engaged in such different occupations as statesman, playwright, and merchant. As a playwright, Beaumarchais is well known for *The Barber of Seville* and *The Marriage of Figaro*.

19. A discussion of French military and naval aid is not pertinent to our subject. Suffice it to say that such French leaders in the art of war as Admirals D'Estaing and De Grasse and Generals La Fayette and Rochambeau, with their well-trained European forces, were of considerable help to the revolting colonists. Moreover, France, because of her strategic position just opposite England, had a nuisance value and caused many good British regulars to remain at home to guard against any attempted invasion from France or from Ireland, a part of the British Isles that, because of the enforced inferior status of many of its inhabitants, was always open to the intrigues of England's enemies.

ing the crown of England they were attacking the abuses of all
monarchies. The reason there were so many friends of America
in France, wrote Linguet, was that they hoped to imitate the
example of the American colonials.[20] Linguet's claim seems to
have been proved by the increasing popularity of Franklin. Certainly this popularity could not be accounted for by a hatred of
England alone.[21] Undoubtedly, this popularity could be ascribed
as well to an ideal which Franklin represented. This ideal was a
faith in the reason of man and in his ability to govern himself.

In the same year that France and the United States became

20. Cited by Faÿ, *op. cit.*, p. 65.

21. Between 1713 and 1754, as Dr. Bonno pointed out in his
     work *La Constitution britannique devant l'Opinion française
     de Montesquieu à Bonaparte*, French and British relations were
     almost cordial. French writers, Montesquieu above all, praised
     British institutions. The outcome of the Seven Years War,
     however, resulting in the loss of French colonies, contemptu-
     ously referred to by Voltaire as a few *arpents* (an *arpent* is
     equal to one and a half acres) of snow, hurt French pride if
     not a sense of French values. During the American Revolution
     esteem for the British constitution considerably diminished.
     Several writers were even astonished by Montesquieu's
     admiration for the British government. (Bonno, G., *La Cons-
     titution britannique devant l'Opinion française de Montes-
     quieu à Bonaparte* [Paris, 1931], pp. 142-143.) The strongest
     criticism of the English constitution was found in the writings
     of Condorcet. (*Ibid.*, pp. 156-157.)
     There could be no better witness than Franklin himself
     to the fact that most Frenchmen were not fighting for revenge
     alone, even if the crown was. Writing to Dr. Cooper, a friend,
     in May 1778, Franklin said: "Here there is a common dictum
     that our cause is that of the human species and that we are
     fighting for European liberty while combatting for our own."
     (As quoted by Aulard, Francois V. Alphonse, "La Révolution
     américaine et la Révolution française: Franklin," in *La Révo-
     lution française* [September-October, 1918], LXXI, 399.)

allies, events of important historical symbolism occurred. There were a series of meetings between two of the greatest philosophers in the world, Franklin and Voltaire, men whose ideas and faith helped to shatter old systems and create new ones.

Voltaire, now an old man of eighty-four, was back in Paris after a long absence. He had endured twenty-seven years of exile, chiefly self-imposed, because of literary works regarded as treasonous by the French government.[22] Arriving in Paris on February 10, 1778, he threw this leading cultural center of the world into ecstasies of joy. Voltaire's plays were quickly revived at the Comédie Française, and he personally attended many. John Adams, one of the American emissaries to France, also attended some of the productions. He recounted in his diary how the appearance of the aged philosopher was greeted by theatre crowds with thunderous applause. Repeatedly, his name was called out between acts.[23]

Soon after his arrival, Voltaire expressed a desire to see Franklin. The desire was mutual. Franklin, with the other American commissioners, called on the old philosopher. Franklin took his grandson with him, and asked Voltaire if he would be kind enough to bestow upon the young man some form of blessing. Voltaire agreeably complied with the request. Placing his hand on the head of Franklin's grandson, he said, "God and Liberty is the only benediction fit for a grandson of Mr. Franklin."[24]

Voltaire and Franklin were both regular attendants at the Academy of Sciences. The former attended his first meeting, after returning to Paris, on March 30, 1778. By acclamation he was

22. *Ibid.*, LXXXI, 401.
23. As quoted by Hale and Hale, *op. cit.*, I, 167. Brissot attended some of Voltaire's plays in 1778. At the showing of *Irène*, Franklin's grandson, who accompanied the old philosopher to France, was pointed out to Brissot by a friend. (*J. P. Brissot: Mémoires* [ed. by Perroud, Cl., 2 vols., Paris, 1911], I, 142.)
24. Hale and Hale, *op. cit.*, I, 168-169.

chosen president of the Academy for the next three months.[25]
At the meeting of April 29, 1778, Franklin and Voltaire sat side
by side. Aulard refers to them as two deities sitting together in
the realm of world-moving philosophy.

One, says Aulard, was the liberal philosopher of a rising
democratic New World; the other, the liberal philosopher of a
decadent, despotic Old World. The Old World, however, was to
be regenerated through the liberal ideas of which these two men
were the outstanding exponents.[26] At this historical meeting in
April, to the accompanying applause of the enraptured Acade-
micians, these two white-haired old men first shook hands *à la
anglaise* and then embraced *à la française*.[27]

Besides having the honor of sharing plaudits with France's
greatest living philosopher at a famous public reception, Franklin
was further honored in 1778. The fifth edition of his complete
works, to date, was published. This edition made a singular impression on Paris and the provinces. All the journals recommended its reading.[28] In September he was dignified by his own
government by being made Minister Plenipotentiary to France
instead of mere commissioner.

The year 1778, so filled with honors for Franklin and Voltaire,
was perhaps not quite so happy for Rousseau. Voltaire, who,
like Rousseau, would die in this year,[29] had the gratification at
least of seeing himself almost deified by the French public before
his demise. Rousseau, on the other hand, died at his Ermenonville
retreat somewhat neglected by the public that he had for so long
endeavored to instruct. Still, after his death his political ideas —

25. *Ibid.*, I, 171.
26. Aulard, "La Révolution américaine et la Révolution fran-
    çaise: Franklin," *op. cit.*, LXXI, 9.
27. *Ibid.*, LXXI, 402. Condorcet was a witness of this episode
    and described the incident in his life of Voltaire.
28. Faÿ, *op. cit.*, p. 100.
29. Both Voltaire and Rousseau died in 1778.

being more precise than those of Voltaire, and more clearly stated — would have greater effect. That is, future French republicans, by their own admission, learned much more about republican institutions from Rousseau's works than from those of Voltaire.

Although the chief object of Franklin's mission was obtained by the series of treaties negotiated between the United States and France in 1778, he stayed in the latter country six more years. These were the years in which, through his writings and personal contacts, he spread a great deal of information regarding the idealistic form of government called "republican," a government which was actually working across the Atlantic.

It was due mainly to Franklin that three editions of American state constitutions were published in Paris between 1778 and 1783. These translations of the American state charters were soon circulating throughout France. Vergennes, the French Foreign Minister, without formally approving them, did not hinder their wide dissemination in any official way.[30] Franklin repaid this privilege by sending complimentary copies to Vergennes and the royal family.[31]

30. Faÿ, *op. cit.*, p. 97.
31. Chinard, Albert, *Les Amities Américaines de Madame D'Houdetot d'après sa Correspondance inédite avec Benjamin Franklin et Thomas Jefferson* (Paris, 1924), p. 20. The copy of American constitutions presented to the royal family was handsomely bound with fine engravings. At the taking of the Tuilleries by a Parisian mob in August, 1792, a roisterous member of the sovereign people, who probably could not read, threw the volume out of the window. It fell on the surprised head of an American, Robert Gilmor, who consoled himself over the unexpected shock by toting the unappreciated volume home to America. Today (1918) this historic volume, says Aulard, peacefully resides in the library of a Dr. Emmet of New York City. (Aulard, "La Révolution américaine et la Révolution française: William Penn et Locke," in *La Révo-*

A veritable cult was formed around the person of the distinguished American. Silas Deane, another American envoy sent by the Continental Congress, related how crowds went wild whenever Franklin appeared.[32] It was the mode of the day for everyone to have an engraving of Franklin over the mantelpiece.[33] Receptacles of all types had the benign face of the great philosopher engraved upon them.[34] Women especially worshiped the old

lution française [January-February, 1918], LXXI, 22, footnote 2.) Madame d'Houdetot (1730-1813), former mistress of Rousseau, and an acquaintance of Franklin, gloated over the fact that she received her copy before the royal family received its copy. (Chinard, *op. cit.*, p. 20.) Madame d'Houdetot, a liberally-minded Frenchwoman, was a strong exponent of the American cause and a great admirer of Franklin, its chief representative in France. With little respect for the memory of Rousseau, she called the American patriot the man of the century most worthy of being known. (*Ibid.*, p. 44.) She looked upon the American Revolution as the cause of humanity. Charitably inclined, she paid the debts of many American sailors held in French prisons for their indebtedness. Franklin was well acquainted with Madame d'Houdetot and visited her several times at her residence at Sannois. On one occasion she recited a series of poems in which she referred to him as the benefactor of the world. Through her, Franklin met Crèvecoeur, whose book on America was later to have such an appeal in France.

32. Aulard, "La Révolution américain et la Révolution française: Franklin," *op. cit.*, LXXI, 397.

33. Hale and Hale, *op. cit.*, I, 69-70. Franklin's grandson collected one hundred and fifty portraits of Franklin. (Aulard, "La Révolution américaine et la Révolution française: Franklin," *op. cit.*, LXXI, 398.)

34. Aulard, "La Révolution américaine et la Révolution française: Franklin," *op. cit.*, LXXI, 398. Aulard relates an amusing story about one receptacle that the king gave as a gift to one of his courtiers. In this incident King Louis XVI seems to have shown a rather Rabelaisian sense of humor. This state-

patriot. At one fête in his honor the most beautiful of three hundred women were designated to go and place on his white locks a crown of laurel. Then he was kissed by each one of the lovely ladies.[35]

Important for the future growth of a republican spirit in France was the fact that Franklin associated with the most liberally inclined men of Paris, publicists and philosophers who themselves scarcely concealed their sympathy toward republican principles. Cabanis, one of the coterie of the salon of Madame Helvetius, where he often encountered the great American, said that Benjamin Franklin passed his time with the men of Paris most distinguished for their knowledge and their love of liberty.[36] Condorcet, who wrote several articles about Franklin and American democratic institutions, was well acquainted with the American Min-

men may seem surprising to most people who have been fed with accounts of his dullness and his failure to show any signs of emotion, except when excited by a Gargantuan dinner or a particularly intricate piece of lockwork. The court of Louis XVI, during Franklin's stay in France, resounded with praises of the American patriot. One woman courtier was especially vociferous in her praise of Franklin to the king. Louis, perhaps bored with the constant mention of Poor Richard, sought to silence the lady by presenting her with a *pot de chambre* as a New Year's gift. Franklin's portrait was engraved upon the bottom of it. Aulard interprets the motive of this action somewhat differently. Adhering to the belief that Louis XVI was of a dull and crude nature, Aulard says that the king gave this gift, not as a sign of contempt for the American philosopher, but rather as a sign of homage. One is inclined to believe that Aulard, writing during the First World War, was being considerate of American patriotic sensibilities for the sake of Franco-American solidarity.

35. Hale and Hale, *op. cit.*, I, 363.
36. Aulard, "La Révolution américaine et la Révolution française: Franklin," *op. cit.*, LXXI, 395.

ister. They were both members of the Academy of Sciences.[37] Condorcet, a strong opponent of slavery, asked Franklin's advice about the aptitude of Negroes for liberty.[38] Abbé Mably, who in his old age was writing a series of articles on conditions in the United States, asked his opinion regarding laws in the new republic.[39] Mirabeau[40] and Benjamin Franklin collaborated on two works, *La Lettre aux Hessois (Letter to the Hessians)* and *Considerations sur l'Ordre des Cincinnatus (Reflections on the Order of Cincinnatus)*.[41] The latter work criticized the Cincinnatus Order as being aristocratic. This order was a fraternal society

37. Moreover, they were both Masons. The order had been introduced into France by Franklin with the aid of Madame Helvetius and her husband. It was concerned mainly with charitable and educational work. By its efforts a form of free university was established in France; this university became a foyer of liberalism.

38. Faÿ, *op. cit.*, p. 98.

39. *Loc. cit.*

40. Riqueti, Honoré Gabriel, Count de Mirabeau (1749-1791), although a member of the nobility, was elected to the States-General in 1789 as a representative of the Third State of Aix. He already had quite a reputation for his writings on political and economic questions. His dissolute life was also the source of some notoriety. He achieved lasting fame when, at the historic meeting of the States-General on June 23, 1789, he influenced the members of the Third State, by persuasive oratory, to disregard the king's order to disband. Ultimately, the king gave ground and ordered the two upper States to join the Commons.

41. Faÿ, *op. cit.*, p. 152. The Society of Cincinnatus was formed in 1782. Membership in this society was to be hereditary. It was this feature which made Franklin and Mirabeau view the order as aristocratic. Thomas Jefferson, Minister to France after Franklin, also was against the hereditary factor. It was largely through his efforts that it was removed. McKee, George H., *Thomas Jefferson: Ami de la Révolution française* (Paris, 1928), pp. 118-120.

made up of former American Revolutionary officers, both French and American. Saint-John de Crèvecoeur, who wrote one of the most popular and widely read books on America, was aided in his writing by the American statesman-philosopher.[42] Of all Franklin's wide list of acquaintances, the one on whom he had the greatest influence, however, was Condorcet.

In his *Éloge de Franklin* (*Praise of Franklin*), written shortly after the outbreak of the French Revolution, Condorcet told how much France owed to the American sage. Franklin, said Condorcet, waged a strong war against fanaticism. At the same time, in two different parts of the globe, philosophy waged war against this deadly sin.[43] Voltaire and Franklin were kindred spirits in the battle against intolerance.[44] The American Revolution proved that there existed in the forests of the New World men (such as Franklin) who had fathomed the principles of society. These men and their principles afforded lessons for Europe.[45] Franklin's celebrity in the sciences, moreover, won him friends amongst all those who loved or cultivated them. And every home he visited was won over to the American cause.[46]

Condorcet continued his praise by explaining precisely how enlightened France viewed the American Revolution as something in which she had a deep and personal interest. In as much as the American cause was favored by the Court, liberal Frenchmen, hiding behind the cloak of sympathy for the Americans, could openly express republican principles and applaud the maxims of liberty expressed in the theatres.[47] It was easy to foresee, prophesied Condorcet, that the French people, so worthy of liberty, would soon reconquer their own.[48]

42. Faÿ, *op. cit.*, p. 156.
43. Condorcet, *Éloge de Franklin*, in *Oeuvres complètes*, IV, 103.
44. *Ibid.*, IV, 103.
45. *Ibid.*, IV, 131.
46. *Ibid.*, IV, 141.
47. Condorcet, *Éloge de Franklin*, in *Oeuvres complètes*, IV, 146.
48. *Loc. cit.*

Brissot, a prominent French Revolutionary leader whose views were similar to those of Condorcet, was also impressed with Franklin. He never met the noted American while he was in France. However, a few years later Brissot made a trip to America. One of the highlights of the trip was his visit with the American sage. Of all the great men he met during the course of this tour, he found none who possessed to such a high degree the virtue of a real philosopher.[49] He called Franklin one of the fathers of modern philosophy.[50]

The last years of Franklin's stay in France were momentous ones. Great Britain finally, in 1783, made peace with her former colonies, recognizing their independence. A philosopher's dream was fulfilled with the creation of a republic in the New World. Those who vaunted the beauties of representative government now had an actual working example to which they could refer. Publicists need allude no longer to the virtues of the ancient republics of Greece and Rome, as described in the books of the ancient historians, or in those of the philosophers.

All the marvels of republicanism were to be found in the newly created United States. Liberals felt that it was their duty to inform France about America and its institutions. Between 1783 and the French Revolution, there were a number of books written describing life and institutions in republican America. Franklin had been the first important intermediary to spread amongst Frenchmen knowledge concerning America. Following him, there were to be others, such as Condorcet, Saint-John de Crèvecoeur, the Marquis de Chastellux and Brissot de Warville. These men would exert considerable influence over enlightened public opinion. When Franklin left France in 1785,[51] some publicists already

49. Brissot, *New Travels in the United States of America*, p. 215.
50. *Ibid.*, p. 219.
51. Franklin never returned again to France. Yet he kept up a heavy correspondence with his many French friends until his death. Franklin's name was not forgotten and was held

were openly discussing the advantages of republics in their descriptions of the United States.

In 1782 there was published in London a book by Saint-John
de Crèvecoeur[52] entitled *Letters from an American Farmer*. At

by the Revolutionaries in almost the same esteem as that
of Voltaire or Rousseau. When he died in 1790, Frenchmen
mourned his passing as much as did the Americans. Abbé
Sièyes was delegated by the Constituent Assembly, then
meeting, to write an address to the Congress of the United
States expressing the general sorrow which Franklin's death
had caused France. (Chinard, *op. cit.*, p. 52.) Both Condorcet
and Mirabeau spoke to the Constituents concerning the
greatness of Franklin. Condorcet compared him with Voltaire.
(Hale and Hale, *op. cit.*, II, 410-414.) Mirabeau called him
the genius who had liberated America and spread the lights
of his wisdom throughout Europe. Franklin, said Mirabeau,
more than any other man had spread the rights of man over
the face of the earth and was the greatest man that had ever
honored philosophy and liberty. (Brissot, *New Travels in
the United States of America*, pp. 230-231.)

52.   Saint-John de Crèvecoeur (1735-1813), born in Caën, France,
and educated at the Jesuit college there, left France when
only twenty years of age to go to Canada. He served as a
lieutenant in the French army of Montcalm during the Seven
Years War, fighting with distinction at Quebec. After the
fall of Quebec, Crèvecoeur left the army and made his way
to the British colonies. For the next ten years, while engaged
in various occupations, such as merchant and surveyor, he
did a great deal of traveling through all the colonies. Thus,
he became intimately acquainted with their economic and
social conditions. In 1769 he married and settled down in
Goshen, New York, as a gentleman farmer. The American
Revolution interrupted a quiet and idyllic life, which Crèvecoeur was later to describe in his famous book *Letters from
an American Farmer*. He was imprisoned by the British for
a few months in 1779; they suspected him of being a spy.
Finally released, Crèvecoeur decided to return to France,

the instigation of Madame d'Houdetot, [53] this book was soon

taking one of his three children with him. He arrived in France early in 1781. For two years Crèvecoeur lived largely off the charity of new-found friends, such as Turgot (brother of the former minister), Buffon, the famous naturalist, and, last but not least, Madame d'Houdetot. Making an impression on De Castries, Minister of Marine, through his writings on America, Crèvecoeur had the good fortune, in 1783, to be made French consul at New York. Returning to the former British colony of New York, now one of the thirteen original states of the republican United States, he learned to his sorrow that his wife had died while he was in France. The two children he had left behind were being cared for by a charitable American family. Saddened at the loss of his wife, but glad to find his children, Crèvecoeur conscientiously took up his duties as consul. He held this position intermittently between 1785 and 1790. He was an excellent consul and did much to make the United States and France acquainted with one another's economic status. Crèvecoeur also sent many items from American newspapers and books to France. Crèvecoeur's active career ended in 1790. After retiring as consul, he returned to France, where he was to remain for the rest of his life in relative seclusion. He died in 1813, the same year as his benefactor, Madame Houdetot. Crèvecoeur's chief claim to glory was his publication in 1782 of *Letters from an American Farmer*. One of the best accounts of the life of Crèvecoeur is Rice, Howard C., *Le Cultivateur Américain: Étude sur L'Oeuvre de Saint-John de Crèvecoeur* (Paris, 1933).

53.   See p. 75, footnote 31. After his first return to France in 1781, Crèvecoeur spent much of his time at the home of Madame d'Houdetot. She did everything she could to aid the repatriated Frenchman, including the writing of a letter to her friend Benjamin Franklin, asking him to introduce Crèvecoeur's book in America. (Chinard, *op. cit.*, p. 17.) Later Madame d'Houdetot adopted Crèvecoeur's children and raised them as her own.

made into a much longer French edition.[54] Although written in part before Britain's colonies revolted against her, it was not published until after the American Revolution. France was then eager to hear about America. Crèvecoeur's work was enthusiastically received. Through the medium of newspapers, its fame even reached the provinces most distant from Paris.[55] Brissot, who did much to publicize the book, said that all the women of quality were fascinated with this account of idyllic American life.[56]

According to Ludwig Lewissohn, who edited an edition of *Letters from an American Farmer*, Crèvecoeur's work should be regarded as a literary piece.[57] This is true, in so far as Crèvecoeur, a lover of nature like Rousseau, described in his work all the beauties of a simple life. However, even as Rousseau, he united revolutionary ideas with romantic tendencies in some of his most powerful passages. Under an inoffensive title were found startling ideas.[58]

Crèvecoeur dedicated his book to Abbé Raynal,[59] whose work *Philosophical and Political History of the Establishment of European Commerce in Both Indies* the "American Farmer" had read with "infinite pleasure."[60] Raynal, said Crèvecoeur, espoused the cause of humanity in espousing that of the Negro. Moreover, he saw the provinces of North America in their true light — as the asylum of freedom, the cradle of future nations, and the refuge

54. Rice, *op. cit.*, p. 76.
55. *Ibid.*, p. 90.
56. *J. P. Brissot: Mémoires* (ed. by Perroud, Cl.), II, 47-48.
57. Crèvecoeur, J. Hector Saint-John, *Letters from an American Farmer* (ed. by Lewissohn, Ludwig, New York, 1904), Introduction, pp. XV-XVI. This edition was used in the preparation of the monograph.
58. Rice, *op. cit.*, p. 204.
59. Refer to pp. 58-59.
60. Crèvecoeur, *op. cit.*, Dedication, p. XXXI.

of distressed Europeans.[61] Much that is revolutionary in *Letters from an American Farmer* can be attributed in part to the influence of Raynal.

The form adopted by Crèvecoeur in his writing was that of a series of letters written by an American cultivator to an imaginary English gentleman. Of course, the farmer in the case was Crèvecoeur. Mentioning that he, as a busy American cultivator, would find it difficult to keep up his correspondence, he poked fun at the British leisure class. Humorously he told of a remark that his wife had once made. "These Englishmen," she said, "are strange people. Because they can live upon what they call bank notes, without working, they think all the world can do the same."[62] However, in spite of his many duties, said the farmer, he would do his best to keep his English friend informed about American conditions. The series of letters that followed were a strong recommendation for republics and a criticism of all absolute governments. They were filled with praise for the democratic American way of life.

In one letter the American cultivator described the status of Americans. He introduced the topic of discussion by comparing the state of people in America with that of people in Europe. America was not over-supplied with great lords, who possessed everything, as in Europe. Here there were no aristocratic families, courts, kings, bishops; there were no ecclesiastical dominions, manufacturers employing thousands of slaves, and terrible extravagance. The rich and poor were not so far removed from one another as in Europe.[63] Laws were respected because they were equitable. If a European were to travel through the rural American districts, he would not see the hostile castle contrasted with the clay-built hut, or miserable cabin, where men and animals mingled

61. *Ibid.*, p. XXXII. Crèvecoeur's political and philosophical ideas were derived mainly from Raynal (Rice, *op. cit.*, p. 53).

62. Crèvecoeur, *op. cit.*, p. 18.

63. *Ibid.*, p. 49.

indiscriminately. He would find industry unfettered and the spirit of individualism encouraged.[64]

There were no foolish titles in this remarkable new land. "In his town," said the farmer, "lawyer and merchant were the fairest titles."[65] The American idiom was short in words of dignity and names of honor. "We have no princes for whom we toil, starve, and bleed," he continued. "We are the most perfect society now existing in the world. Here man is free, as he ought to be; here, equality is not so transitory as many other pleasures."[66]

America regenerated migrated Europeans, said the agriculturist. They found themselves under new laws and a new social system. They found that they had become men: "In Europe they were only so many useless plants, wanting vegetative mould and refreshing showers. They withered and were mowed down by want, hunger, and war. Now, by the power of transplantation, like all other plants, they had taken root and flourished."[67] Formerly, in Europe, they were not numbered in any civil list of their respective countries. In America they ranked as citizens and were governed by just laws that the people themselves ratified.[68]

The cultivator (Crèvecoeur) defined what he meant by an American in the following brilliant word picture:

> "What then is the American, this new man? He is either a European or the descendent of a European. Hence, that strange mixture of blood that you will find in no other country. I could point out to you a man, English by blood, whose wife is Dutch. Their four sons have wives, all of different nationalities. . . . Here individuals of all nations are melted into a new race of men, whose labours and posterity will one day cause great changes in the

64. *Ibid.*, p. 50.
65. *Loc. cit.*
66. *Loc. cit.*
67. *Ibid.*, p. 53.
68. *Loc. cit.*

world. . . . Here the rewards of an individual's industry follow with equal steps the progress of his labor, labor that is founded on that basis of nature — self-interest. . . . Wives and children, who before, in vain, demanded of him a morsel of bread,[69] now, fat and frolicsome, gladly help their husbands or fathers, as the case might be, to clear those fields whence exuberant crops arise. These crops will feed and clothe them all, without any part being claimed by a despotic prince, a rich abbot, or a mighty lord. Here religion demands but little of a person; a small voluntary salary to the minister and gratitude to God. Can one refuse these?"[70]

Emphasizing that in America there was equality and opportunity, the farmer said:

"This fair country alone is settled by freeholders, the possessors of the soil they cultivate, members of the government they obey, and framers of their own laws, by means of their representatives."[71]

There was every encouragement to become a citizen, and to acquire land. All European prejudices were laid aside and all were on equal terms.[72]

Besides the letters describing the political and social conditions of Americans, there were letters which depicted the many beauties of nature in the New World. Crèvecoeur's descriptions, given in simple but effective style, were much appreciated by Europeans for their literary merit. Still, it was the political philosophy, included within the letters, which had such an effect on future Revolutionary leaders.

69. In this sentence Crèvecoeur is referring to a transplanted European family.
70. Crèvecoeur, *op. cit.*, pp. 541-561.
71. *Ibid.*, p. 72.
72. *Ibid.*, p. 79.

Crèvecoeur had a real influence on the prominent French Revolutionaries, especially those who were to form the Girondin faction. Doubtless, they formed their idea of the United States in part from the images that *Letters from an American Farmer* had furnished.[73] In particular, Brissot was much impressed and, after reading the famous book, wished to meet Crèvecour. He felt that he must have "the strongest hate for tyranny and a profound contempt for kings and nobles."[74] Finally meeting Crèvecour, who, in 1786, happened to be in France at the time, Brissot became quite intimate with him. Incidentally, Saint-John de Crèvecoeur, French in extraction, served intermittently as French consul to the port of New York between 1785 and 1790. Largely through his acquaintanceship with the noted writer on America, Brissot himself developed the inclination to go to the New World. He told Crèvecoeur that he had decided to migrate to America, as he was tired of living under a despotism.[75] "To raise my children far from the sight of a tyrant was my fond hope and supreme desire," said the future leader of the Girondins. Although Brissot's trip to America, which finally eventuated, would change his ideas about Crèvecoeur,[76] the experience of knowing the renowned author undoubtedly had some influence on the man who, later, as one of the leading French publicists and politics, would have an important role in the creation of the first French Republic.

At the same time that *Letters from an American Farmer* was causing such a sensation in France, there was an influx of returning French officers[77] and men who had fought valiantly for

73. Rice, *op. cit.*, p. 204.
74. *J. P. Brissot: Mémoires* (ed. by Perroud, Cl.), II, 48.
75. *Ibid.*, II, 49.
76. *Loc. cit.*
77. The French officers, usually of the enlightened-nobility class, had fought for the American cause chiefly for idealistic reasons. As early as 1776, there were nineteen French gentlemen serving in the American army above the rank of colonel. By the end of the year 1777, the number had increased to 42.

American independence, and who could testify from first-hand experience as to the advantages of the American system. They brought back with them praise plus a feeling of pride for their part in the formation of the new nation.[78] An important factor in the spread of enthusiasm for America throughout the kingdom was that the officers and men making up the various French forces that had fought in the New World were representative of all sections of the country. Thus, when these forces were disbanded on their return from service abroad, the men composing them carried to their respective homes notions of democracy and freedom that were at variance with conditions in monarchical France.[79] And these notions would be easily communicated by the discharged veterans to their local compatriots.[80]

Memoirs of returning French officers were generally rather favorable in their opinions regarding the democratic transition that was taking place on the other side of the ocean. For instance, Alexander Lameth, a member of Rochambeau's army and later one of the important leaders in the early phase of the French Revolution, wrote in his *Histoire de l'Assemblée constituante (History of the Constituent Assembly)* that "the American war had the greatest influence on events which later took place in France." Significantly, he added that the young officers who had served under General Rochambeau "were all filled with ideas completely favorable to an order of things founded on the principles

The attitude of the majority of the French officers was that of the Marquis de la Fayette, who, in a letter to his wife, wrote that he was in the war as a defender of that liberty with which he was so "infatuated." "I carry to this task," he added, "only my frankness and good will, without ambition or personal interest." (Sagnac, Ph., "L'Influence américaine sur la Revolution française," in *Revue des Études Napoléoniennes* [January-February, 1924], pp. 28-29.)

78. Faÿ, *op. cit.*, p. 120.
79. Sagnac, *op. cit.*, pp. 29-30.
80. McKee, *op. cit.*, p. 153.

of liberty."[81] One French nobleman, the Marquis de Chastellux, who had attained the rank of general in the American army, wrote an interesting book about the new republic. His work won considerable notoriety. It carried the long title of *Voyages de M. le Marquis de Chastellux dans l'Amérique septentrionale dans les Années 1780, 1781, 1782*[82] *(Travels of the Marquis de Chastellux in North America During the Years 1780, 1781 and 1782)*.

Chastellux was an extremely cultured Frenchman[83] who had examined with care the people and institutions of America. During the American Revolution, with La Fayette and other French

81.   As quoted by McKee, *op. cit.*, p. 153. Faÿ differs with McKee as to the influence of the American Revolution on French officers. He says that the returning officers, with the exception of La Fayette, were not great admirers of American political institutions. (Faÿ, *op. cit.*, p. 122.) The most enthusiastic Frenchmen returning from America, says Faÿ, were the priests who had accompanied the army. "A whole part of the lower and middle clergy were filled with that American sentiment which led them to believe in the advent of a new world organized according to rational and universal religious principles." (*Ibid.*, pp. 121-122.) Memoirs of returning priests extolled republican virtues in America. Abbé Robin, almsman to the army of Rochambeau, wrote *Nouveau Voyage dans l'Amérique septentrionale (New Voyage into North America)*. In this work he interpreted the old American custom of bundling in a somewhat exaggerated sense. He said Americans were so virtuous that they even trusted their daughters to lie in the same beds with guests. (McKee, *op. cit.*, pp. 154-155, footnote I.)

82.   (2 vols., Paris, 1786.) The available edition consulted in the preparation of this work was a two-volume English translation appearing a year later in London with the title *Travels in North America in the Years 1780, 1781, and 1782*. This work will be the one cited.

83.   McKee calls him the most enlightened Frenchman who visited America. (McKee, *op. cit.*, p. 80.)

officers, he had attended frequently the deliberations of the Pennsylvania Assembly and gained an insight into republicanism in
action.[84] Moreover, he had attended the Philadelphia Academy, a
powerful foyer of republican thought and action.[85] His famous
republican acquaintances in America had included Thomas Jefferson, Samuel Adams and, of course, Benjamin Franklin. On one
occasion he had discussed with Adams the effect which the building of huge fortunes would have on American politics. He was of
the belief that political corruption and civil troubles might result
from the large number of fortunes accruing from increased trade.[86]
In 1782 Chastellux had had the privilege of being a guest of Jefferson at Monticello.[87] As a result of this visit with the great
American democrat, he would carry back to France some liberal
"Jeffersonian" principles.[88]

Even though Chastellux's *Voyages* was written in a light and
sometimes witty style, it was striking in its presentation and often
thought-provoking. Like Crèvecoeur, he compared the European
peasant with the American freeman. The latter enjoyed a holding
of his own and had the right to participate in the government.[89]
Showing the influence of Rousseau and Locke, he attributed the
type of government adopted by the Americans to their environ-
ment.[90] Although the constitutions of the thirteen states were not
similar, said Chastellux, there was in all of them a form of organization by which the people expressed their desires through delegates.[91]
One aspect of republicanism which appealed greatly to the visiting

84. Sagnac, *op. cit.*, p. 31.
85. *Loc. cit.*
86. *Ibid.*, p. 30.
87. McKee, *op. cit.*, p. 80.
88. Faÿ, *op. cit.* p. 80.
89. Chastellux, Marquis de, *Travels in North America in the
    Years 1780, 1781, and 1782* (translated by an English gentle-
    man, 2 vols., London, 1787), II, 56.
90. *Ibid.*, II, 338-339.
91. *Ibid.*, II, 340.

French officer, and which he found in all the state constitutions he examined, was the provision for annual assemblies. Furthermore, he admired the manner in which the executive branch of government was subject to control by the legislature. Finally, he approved of the easy opportunities for full citizenship.[92]

While admiring the political institutions of Pennsylvania, Chastellux had doubts about the virtues of the Quakers. He poked fun at their quaint customs and doubted that equality was really practiced amongst them. Apparently, like other American Revolutionary officers, he somewhat resented their pacifism during the war and their habit of business-as-usual.[93]

The most famous French nobleman who fought for the Americans was the Marquis de la Fayette (1737-1834), a gallant Frenchman who as a young man was a devotee of democratic ideas. The American cause, to him, was that of humanity and he was amongst the first French volunteers to go to America. When the war ended he returned to France, and his actions, before 1789, promised a continuance of the liberal career on which he had embarked. As one of the highest ranking as well as most progressive nobles in France, he was much respected and admired. Because of his great popularity and high station, the monarchy tolerated his seeming republican idiosyncrasies. On one of the

92. *Ibid.*, II, 342-343. He was critical, however, of the property requirement demanded by some of the state constitutions in order to vote. (*Ibid.*, II, 343-344.)

93. Brissot, an ardent admirer of the Quakers, wrote a book in refutation of Chastellux's charges against this sect, entitled *Examen critique du Voyage de Chastellux* (*Critical Examination of Chastellux's Voyage.*) Brissot described his own book as the best work that he had ever written. Moreover, said he, it marked the beginning of his liaison with the Quakers of America and his acquaintanceship with Crèvecoeur, who had written favorably about this religious group in his own famous book. (*J. P. Brissot: Mémoires* [ed. by Perroud, Cl.], II, 47.)

walls of his Parisian residence, he had the American Bill of Rights handsomely framed. Immediately contiguous was a space which he said was to be for the French Declaration of Rights. In his writing La Fayette often used the term "We republicans."[94] He was a close friend of Thomas Jefferson and frequently sought his advice on constitutional questions.[95] Jefferson, despite his reputation of being an ardent republican, recommended a gradual change in France, however. It would be best to begin with a limited monarchy.

La Fayette would follow Jefferson's advice, and during the Constituent Assembly phase of the French Revolution, while speaking for some republican principles, he still favored having a figurehead king. As he grew older, he grew more conservative and ended by working against the very spirit of republicanism that he had done so much to encourage when a young man. In the advancement of republicanism in France, La Fayette's importance was in his actions when he was young and full of idealism. He, a French

94. Aulard, *Histoire politique*, p. 22. Brissot summed up La Fayette's republicanism in the following caustic fashion: "The republic for him (La Fayette) was only a far-distant contemplation, liberty a form and not an essence. He only . . . loved her (liberty) as a eunuch loves woman." (*J. P. Brissot: Mémoires* [ed. by Perroud, Cl.], II, 164.) He added that La Fayette fooled the French people. They, believing him a disciple of Washington and Franklin, naturally thought him a republican. However, La Fayette was interested largely in a social position already brilliant, and wanted only to put a democratic polish on the old edifice of monarchy. He remained a monarchist, in spite of passing through the War of Independence and being exposed to the philosophy of Voltaire. (*Loc. cit.*)

95. McKee, *op. cit.*, pp. 161-162. Jefferson believed that the revolution in France would be carried out by the young and enlightened French nobles. He was ignorant of the power of the bourgeoisie, and he knew the people only from a distance. (Faÿ, *op. cit.*, p. 182.)

nobleman of high lineage, in fighting the cause of freedom and democracy in the American Revolution, seemed to herald the dawn of a new era in France. However, he was to offer the tragic example of a man who helped create an ideal that he himself feared to put into action.

While a few French nobles helped to arouse interest in American republicanism, it was men of lesser lineage but more facile pens who really informed France about the new political institutions of the United States. In this connection the names of Condorcet, born to the lesser nobility true, and Brissot would stand out. These two men were deeply affected by the political transition which took place across the Atlantic. Republican principles which had been eulogized in the writings of the philosophers were taking shape in the form of political organizations in America. Condorcet and Brissot were interested in seeing that these organizations were thoroughly understood by Frenchmen. These two future constitution-makers of 1793 not only derived many of their ideas on republican procedure from examples furnished by the United States, but also, through their writings, made many other Frenchmen acquainted with this procedure.

America's political influence on Condorcet was important in the light of his constitutional work in 1793. Many of the ideas in the plan which he presented to the Convention in that year could be traced back to their origin in certain American charters. Condorcet was an avid student of the workings of republican governments in the New World and enjoyed informing his fellow compatriots about them.

As already mentioned, between 1778 and the French Revolution there had been a number of editions of American constitutions published in France.[96] The study of these constitutions was

96. Refer to p. 75. Condorcet and his wife translated and published with commentaries the American Federal Constitution. This translation formed an appendix to his essay *De l'Influence de l'Amérique sur l'Europe* in *Oeuvres complètes*, XI, 332-365.

a powerful factor in the shaping of Condorcet's political theories. Besides studying these charters, the French philosopher was an interested reader of the American publication *The Federalist*, in which Hamilton, Adams, and Jay elaborated their views on representative government.[97] Acquaintanceship and discussions with great American republicans such as Benjamin Franklin, Thomas Jefferson,[98] and Tom Paine were also important in the confirmation of Condorcet's political beliefs. The writings of Condorcet before 1793, describing the politics of the United States, might, in part, be viewed as a prelude to his final work on republicanism — the constitutional plan submitted by the first constitutional committee in 1793.

Condorcet revered the Declarations of Rights (Bills of Rights) of the various American state constitutions. They clearly outlined to him certain natural rights of man, such as liberty, security, and property.[99] By reading Locke, Mably, and Rousseau he had become familiar already with many of these rights. Condorcet admired, above all, the Declaration of Rights of Virginia, which may have reflected some editorial influence by his friend, Jefferson. He thought that the French should have something like it.[100] "The author of this work has the right to the eternal gratitude of the human species," said Condorcet.[101] The Declaration of

97. Gidney, *op. cit.*, p. 17.
98. Jefferson had a great deal of respect for Condorcet's wisdom. In his library was a copy of *L'Esquisse des Progrés de l'Esprit humain* (*A Sketch of the Progress of the Human Mind*), written by the French philosopher. (McKee, *op. cit.*, p. 17.)
99. Sagnac, *op. cit.*, p. 35. Condorcet said that the Declaration of Rights guaranteed the people against arbitrary government. (Condorcet, *Éloge de Franklin* in *Oeuvres complètes*, IV, 146.)
100. Sagnac, *op. cit.*, p. 35.
101. As quoted by McKee, *op. cit.*, p. 208. The Virginia Declaration of Rights, which was anterior to the Declaration of American Independence, laid down the same principles for

Independence, largely written by Jefferson and resembling in some ways the Declaration of Rights of Virginia, also won Condorcet's hearty approval. In his essay *De l'Influence de l'Amérique sur l'Europe (Influence of America on Europe)*,[102] he referred to it as a "simple and sublime exposition of those rights so sacred, and for such a long time forgotten."[103] He thought that "the example of a great people among whom the rights of man are respected, is useful to all other peoples, despite differences of climate, customs, and constitutions."[104] (By the word "constitutions" Condorcet

its new governmental regime as were adopted by all the states of the United States. It was founded on natural law as defined by the French philosophers of the eighteenth century. (Herriot, Edouard, *The Wellsprings of Liberty* [tr. by Richard Duffy, New York, 1939], pp. 12-13.) Virginia was of interest to all the French philosophers because they believed that Locke had written the constitution. Aulard, "La Révolution américaine et la Révolution française: William Penn et Locke," *op. cit.*, LXXI, 33.

102. Condorcet, *De l'Influence de l'Amérique sur L'Europe*, in *Oeuvres complètes*, XI, 237. This work was dedicated to the Marquis de la Fayette, "who, at an age when ordinary men are scarcely known in society, had merited the title of benefactor of the Two Worlds" (*ibid.*, XI, 237). Condorcet wrote this essay because he was troubled by the indifference with which the French government viewed the independence of the United States, "a movement in which they had participated" (*ibid.*, XI, 233). He was also stimulated by a prize which the great Abbé Raynal had offered for the best book in answer to the question whether or not the discovery of America had been useful or harmful to the human species. (The philosopher-abbé had offered to the Academy of Lyons twelve hundred livres for the winner of the contest. McKee, *op. cit.*, p. 155.)

103. Condorcet, *De l'Influence de l'Amérique sur l'Europe*, in *Oeuvres complètes*, XI, 249.

104. *Ibid.*, XI, 251.

meant race). The American example could cure France of its lack of respect for natural law.[105]

As a summary of the most important rights of man found in America, Condorcet enumerated: 1. Security of one's person and assurance of not being troubled in the sanctity of one's home. 2. The right to use one's faculties in all ways that did not harm others. 3. Security and free enjoyment of property. 4. Man was submissive to laws that applied to all citizens equally; their interpretation could not be arbitrary, nor could their execution be entrusted to arbitrary hands. 5. Man was able to contribute either directly or indirectly to the law-making process. This was a necessary result, stemming from man's original equality before nature.[106] The last of these rights was nonexistent in most countries, including France, said Condorcet.[107]

There were other natural rights of man that Condorcet found in practically all the American state constitutions. In his writings he took great pains to enlarge upon these rights and to interpret them properly for Frenchmen. For example, here is how he interpreted some of the more important rights: The United States was most wise, said Condorcet, in guaranteeing freedom of press and conscience. Public discussion in the press would destroy prejudices and give wise legislation the support of public opinion.[108] The United States stood out as the one country in the world where people could freely express their opinions.[109] As for religion in America, that was a matter of the individual's own conscience, said the French philosopher, and no particular belief could be forced on anyone. He referred to the Virginian charter as one in which religion was separated from the civil rights and duties of citizens.[110] Condorcet admired the third article of Virginia's Declar-

105. *Ibid.*, XI, 260.
106. *Ibid.*, XI, 239-242.
107. *Ibid.*, XI, 243.
108. *Ibid.*, XI, 255-256.
109. Gidney, *op. cit.*, p. 48.
110. *Loc. cit.* Condorcet criticized those state constitutions which

ation of Rights especially. It stated that the people had the inalienable right to change their government if this step appeared necessary to the majority of them. Such action would prevent people from being tyrannized by their own government, commented Condorcet. It was not strange that he later put a similar article in to his own constitutional plan in 1793.[111]

In the mind of Condorcet, a declaration of man's rights, being of a permanent nature and not subject to change, was as important as a constitution itself. A declaration should be the base on which every constitution rested. These natural rights inherent in nature had been known to the philosophers but had never been drawn up in such a concise and convenient form as that found in the American constitutions. The Declarations that Condorcet presented to both the Constituent Assembly[112] and the

      authorized the establishment of taxes for the payment of religious expenses. (Sagnac, *op. cit.*, p. 38.)

111. McKee, *op. cit.*, p. 215, footnote 1.

112. Condorcet, early in his Revolutionary career, presented to the Constituent Assembly a Declaration. Several of its articles were taken from the Declarations of Rights found in the various state constitutions in the United States. (Gidney, *op. cit.*, p. 40.) In the discussions on other projects proposed to the Constituent Assembly, Brissot, like Condorcet a strong proponent of United States political institutions, extolled the American Declarations of Rights. (*Ibid.*, pp. 38-39.) Brissot and Condorcet were not the only ones affected by the American Declarations. The Archbishop of Bordeaux, reporter of the Constituent Constitutional Commitee, declared in July, 1789, that the French Declaration of Rights would be edited in imitation of those in America. "This noble idea" (that of having a Declaration), he said, "conceived in another hemisphere, ought preferably to be transplanted amongst us. We have taken part in the events that made America free. She has shown us on what principles we ought to support the conservation of our freedom. It is the New World, where formerly we had carried only irons, that teaches us today to

Convention were but a summary of the finest features of those of the state documents of the United States.

Condorcet would analyze the American Federal Constitution too. There were certain laudable features that he commended. On the other hand, there were parts of the Constitution that he thought were not democratic enough. He even wrote to Franklin that he mistrusted its "aristocratic spirit."[113]

What Condorcet meant by the "aristocratic spirit" of the Federal Constitution was the rather large powers granted the executive. He felt that it was dangerous to put too much power into the hands of one man, as this might be a threat to the republic. The president should not be commander-in-chief of the army and navy.[114] Neither should he have the right of veto over legislation.[115] Moreover, it

guarantee ourselves from the misfortune of wearing them ourselves." (*Moniteur universel,* July 27, 1789.) La Fayette, in the projected Declaration which he read to the Constituents on July 11, 1789, clearly showed that his source had been the Declaration of Independence, written mainly by Thomas Jefferson. (McKee, op. cit., p. 206.) Jellinek, eminent authority on French constitutional law, said that the French, in their sundry Declarations, adopted not only the ideas of Jefferson, but even the words by which they were expressed. (Jellinek, F., *La Déclaration des Droits de l'Homme* [*Declaration of Rights of Man*], [Paris, 1901], p. 46.)

113. As quoted by Bourne, H. E., "American Constitutional Precedents in the French National Assembly" in the *American Historical Review* (April, 1903), VIII, 471. Condorcet distinguished Franklin as being one of the most democratic American Conventionals. He mentioned that Franklin, as a member of the Constitutional Convention, did not always agree with the majority. The only reason he accepted an imperfect federal constitution was that he hoped it would be perfected later. (Condorcet, *Éloge de Franklin,* in *Oeuvres complètes,* IV, 151-152.)

114. Condorcet, *De l'Influence de l'Amérique sur l'Europe* in *Oeuvres complètes,* XI, 376.

115. Condorcet, *Éloge de Franklin,* in *Oeuvres complètes,* IV, 151.

was noted by Condorcet that the constitution of the United States did not provide an elective presidential council to check any impetuousity on his part.[116] Fearing that a long term of office might encourage foolish ambitions, Condorcet favored a shorter term.[117]

Another feature of the American Federal Constitution that Condorcet did not care for was the two-house legislature. In a federative state a simple one-house system would avoid complications, he thought.[118] Still, as long as the United States adopted a system of two houses, he remarked, it was wise that the republic had provided for one chamber to represent the states in proportion to their population.[119] Thus, the states that had the largest populations and paid the most taxes would be justly favored in the one house. There should be no taint of aristocracy in the Senate, however. Condorcet wondered why Senators might not be elected in the same manner as Representatives and their six-year term shortened.[120]

While favoring the American system of property qualifications in order to vote, Condorcet was of the opinion that voting qualifications might be more lenient in other respects. A strong champion of women's rights, he desired that they have the same voting rights as men.[121] Moreover, the age requirements seemed rather too

116. Condorcet, *De l'Influence de l'Amérique sur l'Europe*, in *Oeuvres complètes*, XI, 366. The French publicist was perhaps not familiar with the custom of having the President appoint a body of advisers, for various administrative details, called a "cabinet." Of course these appointees were subject to and appointed by the President with the advice and consent of the Senate. It was Condorcet's opinion that a presidential council should be elected by the people.

117. Condorcet, *Éloge de Franklin*, in *Oeuvres complètes*, IV, 151.

118. Condorcet, *De l'Influence de l'Amérique sur l'Europe*, in *Oeuvres complètes*, XI, 368.

119. *Ibid.*, XI, 371.

120. *Loc. cit.*

121. Gidney, *op. cit.*, pp. 56-57.

narrow to him. Saying, "Youth is not a sign of incapability," he cited, as an example of youth's achievements, that of Scipius Africanus, the brilliant Roman commander, who at twenty-two proved himself a master of strategy. He cited also the example of La Fayette, who was a general at nineteen.[122]

A distinctive feature of American government, thought the French publicist, was the judicial system. The selection and pay of judges by the republic was the only way to have an honest judiciary, thought the philosopher;[123] obviously, Condorcet was in no position to appreciate the intricacies and differences of the American judicial organization, on the national and state levels. Still a further guarantee against possible judicial oppression, remote as this might be, was the constitutional stipulation of jury trial in all criminal prosecutions.[124]

Of all the American constitutions, the one that Pennsylvania then had was viewed by Condorcet as the best and most democratic of all. It was this constitution which, in some respects, may have served as a pattern for the plan of the first republican constitutional committee in 1793. The former colony, now state, of Pennsylvania always had interested the French philosophers because of the humanity and believed liberalism of its government.[125] Its cons-

122. Condorcet, *De l'Influence de l'Amérique sur l'Europe*, in *Oeuvres complètes*, XI, 378, 380.

123. Gidney, *op. cit.*, p. 97.

124. *Ibid.*, p. 98.

125. The tolerance and wisdom of William Penn, the founder of Pennsylvania, was often praised. Abbé Raynal said that he made tolerance the foundation of his society. Every man who recognized a God could participate in the rights of the city. (Aulard, "La Révolution américaine et la Révolution française: William Penn et Locke," *op. cit.*, pp. 31-32.) Montesquieu wrote that Penn was a veritable Lycurgus. (*Ibid.*, p. 29.) Voltaire asserted that William Penn and his group carried out the original simplified religion of Christ without any intermediary priest group. (*Ibid.*, pp. 29-30.) Further-

titution, drawn up after the colonies declared their independence from England, was largely the work of Benjamin Franklin, said Condorcet.[126] It was distinguished from most of the others by its provisions for wider suffrage.[127] There were three characteristics of this constitution that Condorcet praised and was later to put into his own plan of government in 1793. These were: a single legislative assembly, a plural executive, and periodic conventions. The single-house idea was due to the sponsorship of Franklin alone, said the French publicist. The great American patriot realized that the establishment of two chambers would perpetuate existing errors.[128] A plural executive of twenty-four members was another interesting feature of the Pennsylvania charter of government. It was obliged to render an account of all its actions to the Assembly, in which it had no voice. Condorcet had a similar arrangement in the project of the first French republican constitutional committee in 1793; that is, in the so-called Girondin constitution of 1793, which was largely written by the philosopher himself. Provisions for periodic conventions, to keep the government from becoming reactionary, were found in both the Pennsylvania frame of government and the Girondin scheme of government.[129]

Thus, American political institutions had considerable sway

more, the maxim of Penn, that the people should participate in the making of laws, was according to the just principle that sovereignty should be exercised by the whole citizenry. (*Ibid.*, p. 26.)

126. Condorcet, *Éloge de Franklin*, in *Oeuvres complètes*, IV, 131-133.

127. *Ibid.*, IV, 133 Pennsylvania and Delaware, in their constitutions, had practically universal suffrage. There were no property qualifications in the constitutions.

128. *Ibid.*, IV, 133-135.

129. Condorcet might have been influenced by his friend, Tom Paine, who lauded this feature of the Pennsylvanian constitution. (Gidney, *op. cit.*, p. 108.)

over Condorcet. This influence was shown by his writings even before the French Revolution. After 1789, as an active politician and editor of several great newspapers, he was to mention, countless times, the worth of republican forms as proved by existing American institutions.

Another influential publicist and future proponent of republican institutions for France was Brissot de Warville. He too was impressed by the political developments in the United States. He realized the political significance of the American Revolution and was one of the first to affirm that the French Revolution was fathered by that of America.[130] His writings about America swayed a large group of French intellectuals. Faÿ refers to the group that followed Brissot as the most dynamic one in France.[131] His writings were a mine of information for Condorcet, Madame Roland, and other French intellectuals interested in the affairs of the new republic across the sea. He was considered by them an authority on American affairs.[132] Even as the fabulous Tom Paine,

130. Aulard, Francois V. Alphonse, ed., *La Société des Jacobins: Recueil de Documents pour l'Histoire du Club des Jacobins de Paris* (6 vols., Paris, 1891-1892), II, 262. In fact, he did all that he could after his return from America to promote a revolution in France by publicizing the success of the American Revolution. He said that he went to the United States in order to learn revolutionary procedure and to use this acquired knowledge to bring about a similar political upheaval in his own country. (*J. P. Brissot: Mémoires* [ed. by Perroud, Cl.], II, 275.)

131. Faÿ, *op. cit.*, p. 160.

132. Gidney, *op. cit.*, p. 33. Brissot de Warville was one of the first men in history to realize the importance of the newspaper as a means of creating or affirming public opinion. The American Revolution, in his eyes, was a splendid example of the dynamic influence of the written word. He saw how brochures such as Thomas Paine's *Common Sense* stirred millions when diffused amongst the people through the medium of journals. The only reason that the Canadians

who, like Brissot and Condorcet, would serve on the first republican constitutional committee in 1793, he too had had the opportunity actually to live in the United States for a period and to study republicanism in action. The American Revolution, to him, was a triumph of philosophy. An earnest student of the philosophers, he had absorbed many liberal ideas which were to find their justification, it seemed to him, when the thirteen British colonies threw off the monarchical yoke. It may be that his political views at this stage of his life were more clear-cut than they would be when France herself was in the throes of the Revolution.

Actually, before visiting the United States he had achieved his reputation as an authority on the newly founded republic by collaborating with the celebrated French physiocrat, Étienne Clavière, in the production of a volume which related the advantages for France in America's successful revolution. Published at London en 1787, this work bore the long title *De la France et des États-Unis ou de l'Importance de la Révolution de l'Amérique pour le Bonheur de la France, des Rapports de ce Royaume et des États-Unis, des Advantages réciproques qu'ils peuvent retirer de leurs Liaison de Commerce et enfin de la Situation actuelle des États-Unis (France and the United States or the Importance of the American Revolution for the Happiness of France, the Relationships of This Kingdom and the United States, the Reciprocal Advantages That They Can Gain from Their Commercial Liaison, and, Finally, the Present Situation of the United States).*

did not join the thirteen coastal colonies in the American Revolution, asserted Brissot, was that there were not enough newspapers in the former area to inspire people with revolutionary ideas. (*J. P. Brissot: Mémoires* [ed. by Perroud, Cl.], II, 81.) As editor of *Le Patriote français*, Brissot had a tremendous influence in spreading republican ideas in France between 1789 and 1792. It is significant that Brissot, Condorcet, and Thomas Paine, republicans and members of the first republican constitutional committee of 1793, were all prominent journalists.

A major purpose of the book, said the authors, was to encourage reciprocal trade between France and the United States. France would supply luxuries and the United States would supply raw materials.[133] Clavière, an expert on economic matters, wrote the section of the book relating to trade opportunities between the two countries. Brissot spoke of the scholarly Clavière, in the introduction, as being a republican whose ideas were the same as his.[134] The part of the book dealing with political and social conditions in America was written by the future Girondin leader himself. It is this part which appears more challenging and significant as far as the future history of France is concerned, because it contains many revolutionary statements.

Brissot said that America had avenged humanity by her revolution. Her democratic legislation was a revelation to the world. She was an eternal lesson to which all despotic governments should pay heed.[135] Some of the things to be learned from the American Revolution, said Brissot, were: America had done away with social prejudice, with a corresponding betterment of the general welfare. Furthermore, the social contract was proclaimed and civil liberty was recognized. Finally, there were formal declarations which legitimatized and sanctioned a people's insurrection — an insurrection which elevated the people to their proper position of sovereignty.[136]

France could learn much from the study of American government and manners, said Brissot. He thought the constitution of Pennsylvania a splendid frame of government, one worthy of being imitated.[137] He praised the simple republican habits of Americans and hoped that an increase in the number of large cities would not result in conditions that might corrup these simple manners. Cities

133. Clavière, Étienne and Brissot, J. P., *De la France et des États-Unis* (London, 1787), pp. 45-49.
134. *Ibid.*, Introduction, p. XXXVIII.
135. *Ibid.*, Introduction, p. XLII.
136. *Ibid.*, Introduction, p. XXXI.
137. *Loc. cit.*

would necessarily mean the beginning of factories, servitude, and concentration of wealth in the hands of a few. If America remained a simple agricultural state, she would have more chance of remaining republican, said this disciple of Rousseau.[138] We must not forget that one of the expressed purposes of the book was to encourage trade between France and the United States, the former state supplying luxury items to America, which in turn would supply raw materials to France.

The first book by Brissot in praise of America was the result of his thorough research about this land of liberty.[139] His research made him all the more desirous to see America. He was given this longed-for opportunity when Clavière, his collaborator, and a Monsieur Cazenove, who was a well-to-do financier, agreed to pay the costs of sending him to the New World. In return, he was to observe American affairs carefully and to find out if the new republic was capable of paying its debts. Brissot's backers were anxious to speculate in American stocks.[140]

After an uneventful voyage, Brissot arrived in America in July, 1788. His stay in the New World was to be of short duration, lasting only till December of the same year. Yet it was to be most fruitful in adding to the publicist's political experience. La Fayette, with whom Brissot had corresponded before leaving France, had given

138. *Ibid.*, pp. 61-63.
139. He said that he studied all the books possible which were able to inform him about America. (*J. P. Brissot: Mémoires* [ed. by Perroud, Cl.], II, 52.)
140. *J. P. Brissot: Correspondance et Papiers* (ed. by Perroud, Cl., Paris, 1912), pp. 179-181. The future Girondin leader had told Crèvecoeur that he was going to America to get away from despotism. Crèvecoeur, who was about to return to America as French consul at New York, advised against this. Doubtless he didn't want to embarrass his own position under the French monarchy by having relations with a man known to be strongly republican.

him several letters of introduction to important Americans.[141] One of these letters was to General Washington. La Fayette asked the celebrated American general to be useful to the visiting Frenchman and to let him run through whatever documents he might have, as Brissot was anxious to write a history of the United States.[142] Brissot carried similar letters to other famous American patriots.

While in America, Brissot interviewed the most prominent men of the republic. The substance of these conversations, plus his sharp observations of American life, were carefully recorded in notes. These notes were transcribed a few years later into a book entitled *New Travels in the United States of America*.[143] In this book he indicated precisely how American democratic ways and republican forms of government had impressed him.

His principal object in writing the book, said Brissot, was to examine the effects of liberty on the character of man, society,

141. La Fayette even had Montmorin, French Minister of Foreign Affairs, write a recommendation for Brissot to Count de Moustier, French Minister Plenipotentiary to the United States. Moustier, a strong monarchist, who knew of Brissot's republican leanings, would not do anything for him, however. *C. J. P. Brissot: Correspondance et Papiers* [ed. by Perroud, Cl.], pp. 176-177.)

142. *J. P. Brissot: Correspondance et Papiers* (ed. by Perroud, Cl.), p. 192.

143. The edition used in the writing of this monograph was: Brissot de Warville, J. P., *New Travels in the United States of America*, tr. from the French, Dublin, 1792. Brissot wrote his book early in 1791, when, as a political leader and newspaperman, he was extremely busy with many activities. In discussing his newspaper activities, he stressed that he alone was charged with compiling and publishing a daily newspaper (*Le Patriote français*) that had been established with the sole desire of shaping public opinion, "that powerful instrument of revolution."

and government.[144] Liberty, as the most perfect state of society, was most conspicuous under a republican form of government such as that of the United States. He hoped the portraits offered to view in his work might "justify that republicanism which knaves calumniate with design, and which ignorant men do not yet understand but will eventually learn to know and respect."[145] His purpose was to set forth truthfully "the advantages of the only form of government that merits any confidence."[146] Moreover, he wanted to remove any bad impressions about America that certain Frenchmen might have made by writing in a scurrilous way regarding this land of liberty.[147]

144. *Ibid.*, p. 75.
145. *Ibid.*, preface, p. XXXI.
146. *Ibid.*, preface, p. XXXIII.
147. He was especially angry over the French consular reports from the United States. Some of the consuls, between 1787 and 1792, were writing home that there was no stable government in America. "In the sight of these monarchists," said Brissot, "a republic is a monstrous sight, a monarch is an idol that they adore, and the people, in their mind, are a herd to be governed harshly." (Brissot, *New Travels in the United States of America*, preface, pp. XXXVI-XXXVII.) He was also angry with a few accounts written by certain dandified and cynical Frenchmen who, in their travels in America, had found that they were balked by republican morals. They were sour "because they could not strut idly along a vast boulevard, inanely sit in a coffee house, or seduce a pretty wench." (*Ibid.*, preface, p. XXXIX.) The Marquis de Chastellux, who, in the main, had written favorably about America, aroused Brissot's anger because of his unfavorable account of the Quakers. Brissot called Chastellux's book "a series of impertinences against the Quakers." (*J. P. Brissot: Mémoires* [ed. by Perroud, Cl.], II, 40.) Chastellux was irritated because the Quakers had not participated in the American Revolution. If he had studied this worthy group more thoroughly, however, he would never have written as

New Travels in the United States of America was an enthusiastic account of what Brissot referred to as an exemplary people living under the best type of government — one in which the individual was somebody and the state was his servant. The Frenchman was intrigued with the sight of a simple, moral,[148] democratic people enjoying all the blessings of liberty. He compared the condition of the inhabitants of an American city with that of the inhabitants of a French city. In the latter, Rouen, he had seen peasants living in misery — "a crowd of miserable beings who perish with hunger so as to enable others to swim in opulence."[149] In the former, Boston, he saw men on the street who had "the simple, dignified air of men who are conscious of liberty and who see in all men their brothers and equals."[150]

There was no foolish caste system[151] in the United States. All the

he did, said Brissot. (Brissot, *New Travels in the United States of America*, p. 390.)

148. The use of the word "moral" by Brissot shows the influence of Rousseau. Life in the new republic, to the future Girondin leader, was characterized by all the simple virtues of an individualistic people unspoiled by the hypocritical, despotic systems of Europe. The reason why the Americans possessed such pure morals was that nine-tenths of them lived dispersed in the country. Pure morals were encouraged, moreover, amongst Americans by the fact that they all had the chance to acquire property and gain personal independence. Private morals in a nation, said Brissot, led to public morals or to a wholly virtuous nation. (Brissot, *New Travels in the United States of America*, preface, pp. XIX-XXI.)

149. *Ibid.*, p. 87.

150. *Ibid.*, p. 94. He pointed out the efficiency and order in American municipal life. American cities might not have any great monuments or works of art but, in antithesis to conditions in European cities, the streets were well lighted at night. (*Ibid.*, p. 113.)

151. Brissot had a dislike for titles. He said that a man couldn't believe in equality if he allowed himself to be called "Your

inhabitants were simple citizens. Even her greatest patriots were not afraid to stoop to so-called menial occupations. Like the Roman republican, Cincinnatus, many of the American generals had gone back to their farms after the Revolution. Brissot, with some error as to military rank, mentions in this connection John Adams, General Heath, and the greatest of all, George Washington. The French traveler had visited the latter at Mount Vernon. He found Washington busy with the homely task of supervising the cultivation of his fields.[152] Other American patriots and leaders visited by Brissot were found to be modest, virtuous people who had no aristocratic ambitions.

The American spirit was characterized by individualism and confidence in one's own ability to make a place in the world. Brissot ascribed this to the limitless opportunities to acquire land,[153]

Lordship" and had numerous titles. (*Ibid.*, preface, p. XVII.) The brother-in-law of Brissot, Francois Dupont, was also an enthusiast for America. He migrated to the United States, arriving in the new country just as Brissot left. Buying several hundred acres of land, he settled down to a respectable career of farming. He too had a dislike for titles. In a letter written at Philadelphia, on March 15, 1789, to a Captain Jeaneret, governor of the Academy of Nobles at Berlin, he said: "In America they are not governed by sovereign or despotic idiots who plunder the people, hinder commerce, or put people in prison. Here merchants, artisans, and laborers are honored." (*J. P. Brissot: Correspondance et Papiers* [ed. by Perroud, Cl.], pp. 218-219.)

152. Brissot, *New Travels in the United States of America*, pp. 116-117, 127. Washington was also engaged in building a barn, according to plans sent him by Arthur Young, the famous English traveler.

153. The Western movement had just begun. People from Connecticut were migrating West to the Ohio River. According to the then-prevalent philosophy, if a man was nobody in Connecticut, he would go West, where he was somebody. (*Ibid.*, p. 136.)

and a government which represented the interests of all the people. Throughout his travels in America, Brissot noted the "happy condition" of the inhabitants. He attributed this largely to the freedom guaranteed by republican government. A government that made the people happy must be worthwhile. It should be studied and publicized so as to bring enlightenment to other parts of the world.[154] This was precisely what Brissot appeared to be doing. He carefully connected the condition of the people of the United States with the form of government under which they lived.

America wasn't subject to a tyrannical and arbitrary administration with all the burdens falling on the lower classes.[155] Government was not harsh because it was administered by the people, either directly or through their representatives. Liberty was of such a degree that it bordered on a state of nature. There was little need for strong government.[156] Brissot cited the Quakers of Pennsylvania as being so virtuous as almost to do without it.[157] The first constitution of the state of Pennsylvania was viewed by him, as by Condorcet, as the last word in democracy.[158] In the United States, power was certain to remain in the hands of the people for three reasons: 1. All important offices were elective (this was not completely accurate). 2. Legislative bodies were frequently changed.

154. "For valuable instruction, study the Americans. See to what degree of prosperity the blessings of freedom can elevate the industry of man. You will see how liberty is preserved. You will see independent Americans contemplating no other limits than those of the universe." (*Ibid.*, preface, p. XXVIII.)

155. *Ibid.*, p. 356.

156. Brissot, *New Travels in the United States of America*, preface, p. XXVIII. "Prosperity of a society is always in proportion to the extent of liberty; liberty is in an inverse proportion to the extent of the governing power," was the belief of Brissot.

157. *Ibid.*, preface, p. XXXI.

158. During the American Revolution he had written an ode on American liberty. As an appendix he had added a translation of the constitution of Pennsylvania. (Faÿ, *op. cit.*, p. 158.)

3. The executive had but little power[159] (obviously Brissot was mistaken on this last point). Government was not a burden as in Europe. By means of democratic institutions all administration was supervised by the people and was established only for their benefit. Government was something neither divine nor hereditary, and its officials had no honors other than that of being servants of the people. It was not permanent, and therefore was not exposed to the risk of becoming arbitrary. By the principle of conventions the American Federal Constitution or state constitutions could be altered or added to so as to conform to the changing conditions of time. It was realized that government was something that should progress, and not remain backward.

Thus Brissot, in his second book describing America, was able to recount the political development of the United States as he had beheld it with his own eyes. The book increased his prestige, already rather great, as an authority on the new republic.[160] After his return from the New World, he was to continue to publicize republican America through his writings as well as through a number of

159. Brissot, *New Travels in the United States of America*, preface, pp. XL-XLI. In regard to the last point, Brissot said there could be confidence in governments only where the executive power was elective and dependent on the will of the people. (*Ibid.*, preface, p. XLI.)

160. The Rolands, Madame and Monsieur, who were to play later such an important and tragic role in the French Revolution, wrote a letter to Brissot in March, 1789, in which they said that they envied his luck in having seen America. (*J. P. Brissot: Correspondance et Papiers* [ed. by Perroud, Cl.], p. 220.) Madame Roland said that all that pertained to the United States was of interest to those who had souls. (*Ibid.*, p. 223.) Monsieur Roland and Brissot had become acquainted through a mutual interest in one another's writings. They corresponded several years before actually meeting. Madame Roland referred to Brissot and herself as kindred spirits. (*Mémoires de Madame Roland* [ed. by Perroud, Cl., 2 vols. Paris, 1905], I, 61.)

speeches he would make before various Franco-American clubs, some of which were founded by him.[161] His purpose he admitted, was to tempt France to obtain her own liberties.[162] He joined with Condorcet in presenting, through the medium of the press, his judgments on the United States.

Condorcet and Brissot, possibly more than any other men, popularized the ideals of republicanism as they were seen in action on the other side of the Atlantic. These two were important in aiding in the creation of a republican state of mind amongst many middle-class intellectuals in France.[163] Between the American Revolution, and the French Revolution, Condorcet and Brissot kept alive the zeal with which all France had originally welcomed the courageous stand of the thirteen colonies against the British government. In the repeated references they made in their writings to the American frames of government, they endeavored to prove that the philosophers' theories about the virtues of representative institutions were not idle dreams. These two carried on the process of spreading publicity about the American republic, a process

161.   One club, of which he was a founder, was called the Gallo-American Society. Its object was to extend French commercial and intellectual relations with the United States and to keep France informed of all progress, including that of politics, in the new republic. As members, it boasted La Fayette, Condorcet and Crèvecoeur, besides other French liberals known to be sympathetic towards American progress. Discussions of political innovations were often the order of the day at the club's meetings. (*J. P. Brissot: Mémoires* [ed. by Perroud, Cl.], II, 54.) Brissot founded another club, the Friend of the Blacks, which was ostensibly for the purpose of attempting to alleviate the condition of the poor black slaves, but really was a society for discussing political questions. Condorcet was a prominent member of this club.

162.   As quoted by Gidney, *op. cit.*, p. 31.

163.   According to Sagnac, their theories and judgments about America spread amongst the enlightened classes of France. (Sagnac, *op. cit.*, p. 42.)

which had been inaugurated by Benjamin Franklin and continued by returning French volunteers and travelers. Moreover, through their study of constitutions, especially those of Pennsylvania and Virginia, they gained valuable ideas about representative government, ideas which later were to partly materialize in the Constitution of 1793.

So, when Louis XVI finally decided to call the States-General in May, 1789, a large part of the thinking public of France, through the increasingly important agency of the press, was already aware that there were certain glaring deficiencies in monarchical government. Publicists, quoting the philosophers, and making significant references to happy conditions in the United States, had caused thousands of Frenchmen to realize that they were more than mere subjects of an absolute sovereign. By 1789 there were enlightened, well-informed individuals capable of leading the French people along the path of representative government. And there were critics of absolutism whose constant activity seemed to be that of encouraging movements against any sort of monarchical rule.

Between the meeing of the States-General in 1789 and the deposition of Louis XVI in August, 1792, Brissot and Condorcet, with the aid of their famous Anglo-American friend Tom Paine, were possibly the most constant critics of the limited monarchy created by the Constituent Assembly (the States-General declared itself a constituent body in June, 1789). As newspaper editors, pamphleteers, and politicians, they and other dissatisfied individuals would take every opportunity they could to publicize the countless faults of even a limited French constitutional monarchy. It would have taken a far stronger individual than the easy-going, lock-tinkering King Louis XVI to maintain his throne against the rising tide of republican opposition.

Chapter III

Undermining of the Limited Monarchy by the Republicans

By 1789 there were quite a number of enlightened Frenchmen who had developed what appeared to be an almost passionate love for republican institutions. The liberal writings of eighteenth-century philosophers, and the practical fulfillment of many of these philosophers' theories in the creation of the United States of America, were largely the causes of this passion. It was certainly a possibility that if these enlightened ones ever had the opportunity to establish representative institutions in France, they would do so. When Louis XVI called the States-General in May, 1789, he was offering an undreamed-of opportunity to an ever-growing lot of discontented men.

Centuries of monarchical mismanagement had brought France to the brink of financial ruin. It was for the purpose of replenishing the royal treasury, only, that Louis and the leeching coterie around him finally decided to risk the calling of the States-General, an almost forgotten advisory body that absolute monarchy had dispensed with one hundred and seventy-five years before. They mistakenly believed that the States would meet but a short time and obediently grant the funds demanded. They had not counted on a recalcitrant Third State (composed chiefly of bourgeois members and allegedly representing the unprivileged classes) taking the stand that it did. This group forced the other two States (nobles and clergy) to join it,[1] abolished the unjust system of group voting,

1. According to tradition, the three groups met separately and voted separately. By that system of voting, all the members of each State voted as a group. Thus, the nobles and clergy always had two votes to the one of the bourgeoisie.

and assumed the title of "Constituent Assembly" (June 17-27, 1789).

France was not actually to become a republic until about three and one-half years later. Yet, between the creation of the Constituent Assembly in June, 1789, and the proclamation of the republic in September, 1792, agitation on the part of those already favoring completely representative government was to cease hardly for a moment.[2] Moreover, the trend of events during this period seemed to point ever more strongly towards republicanism.

The Constituent Assembly, coming under the control of the more conservative bourgeoisie, was not as democratic as it might have been. Still, in its two years of existence, it passed some forward legislation. Hereditary titles and feudal privileges were abolished, large landholdings of the clergy and nobles were broken up, and France was divided into efficient administrative units of *departments*,[3] *districts*,[4] and *municipalities*.[5] For the purpose of election,

2. Contemporary pamphlet literature is particularly enlightening on this. With the outbreak of the Revolution, pamphleteers found they had considerable license to write what they pleased. Taking advantage of the new freedom, republican-minded individuals published any number of tracts highly critical of the monarchy. The writer has read many of these contemporary French Revolutionary tracts.

3. The departments, named mainly after rivers and mountains, were created by breaking up the old royalist provinces. Governed by elective legislative councils and executive directories, they were important administrative units midway between the central government and the districts.

4. Chiefly units of coordination between the municipalities and the departmental administration, the district governments did have a few important functions. Two of their main duties were to assign tax quotas to the municipalities and to maintain law and order.

5. The municipality was the smallest unit of administration. The term "municipality" could be applied to the government of either a town (canton) or a city. Altogether, there were 44,000 of these units in France. A mayor and a council

primary assemblies and electoral assemblies[7] were established. Finally, the Constituents, after numerous distractions, created the monarchical Constitution of 1791.

France's first constitution was far from democratic. Still, it was a distinct step away from absolutism, containing some important features that were at least in the direction of liberalism. The Declaration of Rights, patterned after American declarations, guaranteed the citizens such rights as freedom of speech, assemblage, press, and religion. Moreover, the constitution proper provided for a single legislative body that was to make all laws. The executive, a king, could not arbitrarily proclaim laws and had only a suspensive veto over those passed by the assembly. Judges were elective, and in criminal matters citizens had the right of trial by jury.

The most undemocratic feature of the Constitution of 1791 was the restrictive suffrage requirements. Citizens were divided into two categories, *active* and *passive*. Only the first category, paying a certain tax rate, could vote. Besides, in order to be a member of the electoral assemblies, or to hold the position of deputy, one had to pay still higher tax rates. The effect of these requirements was that out of 24,000,000 French inhabitants, there were only 4,298,360 active citizens, and of the four-odd million active citizens,

> were the governing forces of the municipalities. Under their direction, public works were established, taxes were collected, men for the armed forces were requisitioned, and police officials were appointed.
>
> 6. The primary assemblies were originally founded for election purposes. Established in large numbers, they became important as foyers of democracy. No section of France, no matter how remote, lacked its assembly. By the Constitution of 1793, these small units were to figure prominently in the process of direct law-making by the people.
>
> 7. The electoral assemblies were only temporary bodies whose members were elected by the primary assemblies. As soon as their function of electing officers (local or national) was completed, they disbanded.

only about three-fourths were eligible to hold office. On an average, there were 500 to 600 members in each electoral assembly of a department. In eighty-three departments there were approximately 50,000 electors.[8]

Criticisms of the suffrage requirements were numerous. Liberals were quick to point out that suffrage based on a man's wealth was a contradiction of the Declaration of Rights, which stated all men were equal. Besides, it meant that the government would represent only the wealthier classes. Jean Paul Marat, the fiery editor of the journal *L'Ami du Peuple*, was not far wrong when he said, "What will we have gained if in destroying the aristocracy of nobles we have created an aristocracy of the rich? If we have to groan under the yoke of these newcomers, it would be better to preserve the privileged orders."[9] Condorcet said that France would no more be governed by the people than when it was ruled by an absolute monarch. Natural sovereignty would belong to the wealthy bourgeoisie.[10] Brissot's opinion was that of Condorcet. He added that the method of suffrage would violate the principle that man was subject only to laws he made himself.[11]

Differences among the members of the bourgeoisie, as to who should vote and who should not, caused a definite split in the French middle class. The wealthy members (who, incidentally, were profiting from confiscation of the nobles' lands) wanted to keep the suffrage in their own hands. They were afraid that any government

8. Sagnac, P., *La Révolution, 1789-1792*, in *Histoire de France contemporaine depuis la Révolution jusqu'à la Paix de 1919* (ed. by Lavisse, Ernest, 10 vols., Paris, 1920-1922), I, p. 165.

9. As quoted by Aulard, François V. Alphonse, *Histoire politique de la Révolution française: Origins et Développement de la Démocratie et de la République: 1789-1804* (Paris, 1901), pp. 78-79.

10. Cahen, L., *Condorcet et la Révolution française* (Paris, 1904), p. 189.

11. Ellery, Eloise, *Brissot de Warville: A Study in the History of the French Revolution* (Boston, 1915), p. 134.

by what they termed the "rabble" would threaten their own interests. On the other hand, the representatives of what might be termed the petty bourgeoisie — including small-town lawyers, publicists, poor scholars, and petty tradesmen — favored a suffrage system that would include all the people. It was this element that had been swayed greatly by the works of the philosophers and the institutions of the United States. As the revolution advanced, the petty bourgeoisie would further split. One group would continue to insist that a genuine republic based on universal suffrage would solve all France's political, economic, and social ills. The other ultimately favored a more centralized type of administration and strong executive leadership as the solution to France's ills, especially when France faced serious emergencies of an external and an internal nature. The apparatus of democracy could be set aside for a time, to be returned to the people later, at a more propitious time.

From the start of the Revolution the king and his advisers felt the increasing uncertainty of their position. The Constituents were passing legislation which destroyed all of the old aristocratic structure of society. The common people committed more and more acts of violence. The Paris prison fortress, the Bastille, was destroyed on July 14, 1789.[12] Many chateaux belonging to nobles were burned down by aroused French peasants. A hungry but good-natured mob forced the royal family to leave Versailles and come to Paris. The Constituents, who had also been meeting at Versailles, followed. So from early October, 1789, the king, his ministers, and the constitution-makers would be more directly under the watchful

12.   Brissot, in 1784, had been given the signal honor, for a republican, of serving a brief prison sentence in the old fortress. He was sentenced for writing scurrilous articles about the queen, Marie Antoinette, and the king's ministers. After being in jail for only two months, Brissot was released. He owed this release mainly to the efforts on his behalf of the Marquis de Condorcet and other liberals who petitioned the royal authorities to be lenient.

eyes of the sovereign people, who were concentrated in great numbers at Paris. Moreover, in this great city, political clubs were being formed. The most important of these that were early developing as molders of public opinion were the clubs that came to be known as the "Jacobins" and the "Cordeliers." Almost from the very beginning of their organization they had members who favored republican government. Finally, to harass royalty further, skillful publicists would write articles highly critical of monarchy.

In September, 1790, Hébert de Lavicomterie,[13] later to be a

13. Lavicomterie, Louis-Thomas Hébert (1746-1809), was chiefly famous as a persuasive republican pamphleteer. Before the Revolution he resided at Paris, trying to eke out a living by the then non-lucrative profession of law. His sparse legal income was supplemented by some money which he received as a writer. In 1782 he competed for a French Academy prize by writing *Éloge de Voltaire* (*Praise of Voltaire*). Although not even receiving an honorable mention for this writing, he had it published.

The Revolution, to Lavicomterie as to many other liberal, well-educated, and penurious lawyers, offered opportunities. Similar to Siéyès, who wrote the famous pamphlet *Qu'est-ce que le Tiers État* (*What the Third State Is*), he was sky rocketed to fame by one pamphlet bearing the title *Du Peuple et des Rois* (*Concerning People and Kings*). It was published in September, 1790. In August, 1792, appeared *La République sans Impôts* (*Republic without Taxes*). In this brochure Lavicomterie favored a federative republic in which even the name of "capital" would be forbidden. He argued for eighty-three autonomous republics, mistakenly believing that the United States had such a system. Two other works of this impecunious lawyer, *Crimes des Rois de France depuis Clovis jusqu'à Louis XVI* (*Crimes of the Kings of France from Clovis to Louis XVI*) and *Crimes des Papes* (*Crimes of the Popes*), added to his fame.

Lavicomterie's reputation as a writer and republican guaranteed his election to the Convention as a representative of

supernumerary of the first republican constitutional committee of 1793, published a pamphlet entitled *Du Peuple et des Rois (People and Kings)*. There was no such thing as a good king, said Lavicomterie. In time he hoped to see all such useless creatures extirpated from the earth.[14] Two months after Lavicomterie's publication, a Monsieur Pierre Robert published a brochure carrying the title *Le Républicanisme adapté à la France (Republicanism adapted to France)*. Robert made the bold assertion that a republican administration was the only one compatible with liberty and democracy.[15]

Early in 1791, Tom Paine, fabulous "citizen of the two worlds" and world revolutionary for republicanism, published a pamphlet that had much the same effect in France that his brochure *Common Sense* had had in America fifteen years before.[16] This writing, called

the Department of Paris in 1792. Because of his writings, like Siéyès, he was considered an authority on constitutional matters. He was appointed as one of the supernumeraries, in October, 1792, to the constitutional committee. He took no part in its proceedings, however. During the time of the ascendancy of Robespierre, he held important positions, such as member of the Committee of Public Security and Secretary (for a few days) of the Convention. Lavicomterie had such a dread of Robespierre that he tried to keep out of his way. During the Reign of Terror he developed a strong desire to continue living. Therefore he took no active part in the stormy issues of the Convention. He managed to keep a cool head, and one still attached to his torso, during the Terror, and lived to see Napoleon well established as emperor. Lavicomterie died in relative obscurity in 1809, holding the unimportant position of stamp administrator. (Kuscinski, A., *Dictionnaire des Conventionnels* [Paris, 1916], p. 380.)

14. Lavicometerie, M. de, *Du Peuple et des Rois* (Paris, 1791), p. 16.

15. As cited by Aulard, *Histoire politique*, p. 86.

16. Paine was already widely known in France as a leading American patriot and publicist who, by his pamphlet *Com-*

The Rights of Man,[17] was dedicated to the President of the United States, George Washington. Termed by some historians the earliest complete statement of republican principles,[18] it was given the widest publicity throughout France. Whole columns from it were printed

mon Sense, had done so much to inspire the thirteen original British colonies in their struggle for independence. His first trip to France had been in 1781; while in France he stayed with Benjamin Franklin at Passy. At the home of the American plenipotentiary he met Turgot, the deposed French minister, whose contemplated reforms might have prevented the French Revolution.

The second visit of Paine to France came in 1787. When he sailed from America in April of that year, he was perhaps as happy a man as any in the world. His intimate friend Thomas Jefferson had succeeded Franklin as United States Minister to France, and another friend, La Fayette, was the country's idol. Paine's fame had already preceded him. It was a guarantee that he would be heartily received by the same circle of savants and scholars that had surrounded Franklin ("The Editor's Introduction to the Rights of Man," in *The Writings of Thomas Paine* [ed. by Conway, Moncure Daniel, 4 vols., New York, 1894], II, 258.) He had been furnished by Benjamin Franklin with a letter of introduction to Madame Helvetius, widow of the philosopher Helvetius. It was at her home that the Anglo-American publicist first met Condorcet. He also met Danton, later to be one of the more brilliant orators at the Convention. (Alengry, Franck, *Condorcet: Guide de la Révolution française* [Paris, 1904], p. 198.) The main purpose of Paine's visit to Paris in 1787 was to present to the French Academy of Science plans for an iron bridge. The project was favorably received; no doubt the influence of Condorcet, one of the Academy's most honored members, had a great deal to do with its favorable reception. A common love of learning and a mutual interest in the political, social, and economic betterment of their fellowmen caused a strong friendship to develop between Condorcet and Paine. Whenever the latter was in Paris

in all the leading newspapers.[19] Probably, much of this publicity
was due to the philosopher Condorcet, who was a very close friend
of Tom Paine. He made sure that his friend's brilliant work was
circulated amongst all the influential liberals.[20]

Paine's treatise on the rights of man was written in answer to a
book by Edmund Burke, the British statesman. Burke, in his
Reflections on the French Revolution, had criticized all that had
taken place in France since the start of the Revolution. He took
the side of the king, nobles, and clergy against the people and

(between 1787 and 1791 Paine divided his time between
France and England), he spent most of his time with Condorcet. Madame Condorcet translated many of Paine's political treatises into French. (Alengry, *op. cit.,* p. 199.)

In the development of Condorcet's political philosophy
and, consequently, in the evolution of republicanism in
France, the friendship between the two men was important.
Paine, an expert on republican government, explained the
state and federal constitutions of the United States to Condorcet. On the other hand, Condorcet, through the medium
of newspapers and pamphlets, spread a great deal of Paine's
republican philosophy throughout the length and breadth
of France.

17. It was the first part of this work that was published in 1791.
The second part was published in 1792.

18. *The Writings of Thomas Paine, op. cit.,* II, 262.

19. According to Paul Desjardins, hundreds of thousands of
copies of *The Rights of Man* were printed in France. This
work was even appreciated by Napoleon Bonaparte. It was
so much appreciated by him that in 1797 he paid a visit to
Tom Paine, who was still residing in Paris. Napoleon told
Paine that *The Rights of Man* had been his favorite bedside
book. Its author deserved a statue of gold erected in his
honor, said the future dictator. (Desjardins, Paul, "Thomas
Paine républicain," in *Revue bleue* [April 20, 1901], XV, 483.)

20. It is possible that Condorcet helped Paine in the preparation
of the original manuscript. (Alengry, *op. cit.,* p. 92.)

claimed that the upheaval in France threatened not only Europe but the whole human race. Paine's answer to Burke was that the only place in the world where liberty was really manifest was in France and in the United States. Here the people had asserted their natural right of being able to change an unjust form of government. Monarchy, said Paine, was going out of fashion. In America, if one was asked whether he wanted to be king, he would retort, "Do you think I am an idiot?" In France the only thing maintaining the monarchy, such as it was, was some respect for the good personal character of Louis XVI. Monarchy, concluded Paine, was based on ignorance; republican government was the only administration based on reason. It was to be hoped that the principles of the latter would soon spread throughout the world).[21]

King Louis XVI's good personal character became very much a matter of doubt when (on June 20, 1791) he and his family tried to escape from the country and join the thousands of emigrant nobles who had fled France already. Stopped at the small town of Varennes, the royal family was quickly brought back to Paris. Royal authority was suspended for three months and France was governed solely by the Constituents. For a time it looked as though France was about to become a republic. Tom Paine, now a permanent resident of Paris, wrote to George Washington that it was only a matter of a short time before the country would have a republican administration.[22] Tom Paine should have been in a position to know. He and his friends, Condorcet and Brissot, were doing all in their power to have the monarchy ended then and there.[23]

21. *The Writings of Thomas Paine, op. cit.*, II, 265-288, *passim*.
22. Tom Paine to George Washington (July 21, 1791), in Conway, Moncure Daniel, *Thomas Paine (1737-1809) et la Révolution dans les deux Mondes* (tr. from the English by Felix Rabbe, Paris, 1900), p. 188.
23. Neither Condorcet nor Brissot were members of the Constituent Assembly. They contrasted with their future opponent, Robespierre, in this respect. However, they were both members of

On the morning of July 1, 1791, the citizenry of Paris found an important manifesto posted on practically all the walls of the capital. It was signed only by a Monsieur Du Chastellet, former aide-de-camp of La Fayette. Actually, the author of the inflammatory manifesto was Tom Paine. It is probable that he had been aided in its preparation by Brissot and Condorcet.[24] The essence of this republican declaration was that the king, by his own action in fleeing the country, had proved that he could not be trusted. Kings were a superfluity and an immense burden on the state anyway. Now was the opportunity for France to proclaim herself a republic.[25]

In the weeks following the king's flight to Varennes, Condorcet, Paine, and Brissot spoke and wrote against the monarchy. The speeches of Condorcet were especially effective in creating a strong public opinion for completely representative government. Condorcet, "the greatest thinker of the time, the disciple and heir of the Encyclopaedists," was listened to as an oracle. One speech of his, delivered at a Paris political club, was published and then distributed all over the country. In this he stated that an "unforeseen event" (the episode at Varennes) gave all Frenchmen the right to attack the monarchy and boast the excellencies of republican government. In fact, they ought to now call a republican convention.[27]

> the first elective municipal government of Paris. The chief occupation of these two republican leaders during the period of the Constituent Assembly was journalism. They were two of the most active republican propagandists in France. Brissot, as editor of *Le Patriote français,* and Condorcet, as editor of the *Chronique de Paris,* did much to make the position of Louis XVI, even as a limited monarch, untenable.

24. Alengry, *op. cit.,* p. 95.
25. *Ibid.,* pp. 95-96.
26. Aulard, *Histoire politique,* p. 138.
27. Condorcet, Marquis de, *De la République, ou un Roi est-il necessaire a la Conservation de la Liberté?* in *Oeuvres complètes* (21 vols., Paris, 1801-1804), XVII, 12.

Brissot praised Condorcet's address in *Le Patriote français.* Moreover, he announced that he was offering a prize of three hundred livres to anyone who could prove that a republican and a free citizen were not two inseparable things.[28]

Brissot, Condorcet, and Tom Paine all cooperated in founding the short-lived journal *Le Républicain ou le Défenseur du Gouvernement representatif par une Société de Républicains* (*The Republican or the Defender of Representative Government by a Republican Society*). There were only four numbers of this newspaper. In spreading republican propaganda it served a useful purpose, however. It reproduced well-written articles by Paine, Brissot, and Condorcet which described the various abuses of royalty and the beauties of republicanism.[29] Moreover, the famous reputations of the founders of the journal encouraged other newspapers to advocate the establishment of a republic. *Le Courrier de Provence,* widely read outside of Paris, predicted the coming acceptance of the principles found in the *Républicain.*[30] *Le Journal général de l'Europe* said that citizens from one end of the country to the other were now animated with republican zeal.[31]

Despite the endeavors of the leaders of the republican movement to have the monarchy abolished in 1791, this institution, growing ever more feeble, was granted a reprieve. Louis swore that he would support the constitution (September, 1791) and would never try to leave the country again. The wealthy bourgeoisie, rather numerous in the Constituent Assembly, were afraid that a re-

28. Ellery, *op. cit.,* p. 170.
29. *Ibid.,* p. 171.
30. *Le Courrier de Provence,* No. CCCXII, pp. 431-432, as cited by Pegg, Carl Hamilton, "Sentiments républicains dans la Presse parisienne à partir du Retour de Louis XVI jusqu'au Rapport des Sept Comités," in *Annales historiques de la Révolution française* (July-August, 1936), No. 76, pp. 344, 347.
31. *Le Journal général de l'Europe,* No. III, p. 69, as cited by Pegg, *op. cit.,* p. 353.

publican government might mean radical economic legislation. Hence, they were willing to accept the king's professions of good faith and place in operation the limited monarchical constitution that they thought guaranteed a government by the more affluent citizenry. The republicans would have to wait for another year before finally getting rid of the king. The Constituent Assembly disbanded on September 30, 1791, and France's first regular legislative body met on October 1, 1791.

As the elections for the Legislative Assembly had occurred during the months immediately following the Varennes incident, when republican agitation was strong, many of the new deputies were quite anti-monarchical. The restrictive suffrage qualifications apparently made little difference. Amongst the newly elected deputies were a large number of idealists who would give only lip service to the monarchy. It was to be expected that, given the least opportunity, they would overturn a form of rule obnoxious to themselves.

The newly elected deputies, with strong inclinations towards republicanism but sometimes to prove ineffective in the grim arena of practical politics, included such names as Condorcet, Brissot,[32] Gensonné,[33] Guadet,[34] and Vergniaud.[35] They were to be the more

32. Condorcet and Brissot were elected deputies to represent Paris.

33. Gensonné, Armand (1758-1793), was elected a deputy to both the Legislative Assembly and the Convention from the Department of Gironde. An ardent republican, after the flight of the king in June, 1791, he demanded (at the Assembly) that henceforth an oath of loyalty be taken only to the nation and never to a king. As a member of the Legislative Assembly's committee on diplomacy, he ceaselessly urged war, as did Brissot, the head of the committee, against Prussia and Austria. War to him was a war for the new way of life (representative government) against the old (despotism). At the Convention Gensonné was one of the leaders of the Girondin group. He was a close associate of Brissot, Guadet, Verg-

niaud, and Madame Roland, and his philosophy was their philosophy. He gloried in the establishment of the republic and anxiously awaited the completion of the first republican constitution. He himself was a member of the first constitutional committee and heartily favored the plan of the famous philosopher Condorcet. Like all the other Girondin chieftains, Gensonné was suspicious of the words and actions of Robespierre and Marat. He sarcastically, in speeches, referred to the former as one "who proclaimed himself the incorruptible defender of the people's rights," and to the latter as one "who said he was the people's friend." Gensonné, as a Girondin leader, was of course included in the June 2, 1793, list of those to be purged from the Convention. In a protest written against Robespierre's coup d'état, he said he would go to his death with the words "Long live the Republic" on his lips. The guillotine ended the career of another outstanding republican on October 31, 1793. (Kuscinski, *op. cit.*, pp. 289-291.)

34. Guadet, Marguerite Elie (1755-1794), was one of the most prominent Girondins of the Legislative Assembly and Convention. When the Revolution broke out, he was practicing law at Bordeaux. He immediately began to take his part in local Revolutionary affairs. His zealousness and capability won him many friends who were instrumental in having him elected, first, to the Legislative Assembly and then to the Convention. From the first days of the Legislative Assembly he felt that Robespierre, the Mountain chieftain, was developing unhealthy ambitions. He denounced him as a leader interested solely in his own glory, a leader who was building up an idolatrous following. For the good of his country, said Guadet, Robespierre should try to check the tendancy of some people to make him a public idol. Guadet continually harped on this refrain. At the Convention, on April 12, 1793, he made a parallel between Robespierre and Cicero: "But," said Guadet, "Cicero was an honest man. He did not accuse people without proof. He would not have built up a great reputation in order to subject the Republic. . . . I had best stop the comparison. . . . What could there be in common

between Cicero and Robespierre?" (Kuscinski, *op. cit.*, p. 313.) Guadet believed that Robespierre was using the Parisian masses as a tool to build up his own power. Instead of organizing means of checking this alleged tactic, Guadet made the mistake, a common one of the Girondins, of making brilliant but non-effective denunciatory speeches before the Convention. When the leading Girondins were indicted in May and June, 1793, Guadet escaped to the department of Gironde. With a few others he tried to arouse the departments against Paris. After a year of fruitless endeavor, during which he attempted to overcome the apathy of the departments, Guadet was arrested by Robespierre's followers. He was guillotined on June 20, 1794.

35. Vergniaud, Pierre Victurien (1753-1793), was one of the greatest orators of the Revolution and a leading Girondin. He was born in Limoges, in southern France. Like most of the other Girondins, he had had the advantage of an excellent education. Taking a degree in law, he was admitted to the bar at Bordeaux in 1781. From the beginning of his legal career he displayed an excellent legal mind and astounding oratorical ability. Unfortunately, he tended towards indolence and would take a case only when he was short of funds. One day a prospective client brought some voluminous case material to his office. Vergniaud stared at the material, estimated its bulk, and then walked over to his money drawer. Opening the drawer, he found that there were still a few livres left before he would be in want. The case was turned down. The Revolution was hailed as a marvelous regenerating force by Vergniaud. From the beginning he took an active interest in this political and social unpheaval. Elected an administrator of the department of Gironde, this able man was also a leader of the local Jacobin Club. Being a republican by political preference, Vergniaud, on learning of the king's flight in June, 1791, asked for his arraignment before the high court. If the king was found guilty, the people of France, through a plebiscite, should decide on his fate. At the Legislative

important leaders in the Legislative Assembly. They and the men who, through sympathy in aims and ideals, gathered around them have been distinguished by historians with the name "Girondins." This faction or party,[36] along with another small but eloquent

> Assembly, Vergniaud (chosen as a representative of Gironde) took his place on the left with his friends Ducos, Gensonné, Guadet, and Grangeneuve. As a staunch opponent of the Court, the brilliant orator from the South continually spoke against the king and condemned him for vetoing measures deemed necessary for the salvation of the country. He also supported his friend, Brissot, in demanding war with Austria, proposing this as early as January, 1792. In July, 1792, Vergniaud delivered a speech accusing the king of perfidy. This speech ranks as one of the "finest bits of modern eloquence." (Kuscinski, *op. cit.*, p. 599.) The king was blamed for arousing his brother monarchs against France. No doubt this speech helped to precipitate the event of August 10, 1792, in which the king was dethroned by a coup d'état. However, Vergniaud was an advocate of removing the king by constitutional means. No one fought harder than Vergniaud to make the Convention (to which he was elected as a deputy of Gironde) a success and to give France a republican constitution. He was a member of the first constitutional committee but left most of the editing work to Condorcet. On the Convention floor he spoke tirelessly in opposition to what he considered suspicious actions on the part of Robespierre and Marat. He was firmly against any tyrannical type of rule and would compromise for no diluted form of republicanism. Vergniaud, like so many other Girondin leaders who suffered from too much individualism, was to face extinction at the hands of the organized forces of Robespierre. He was guillotined on October 31, 1793.

> 36. Neither the Girondins nor the Mountain had any formal party organization. However, these factions acted as parties in that their policies were often formulated outside of the legislative halls (first of the Legislative Assembly and then of the Convention) by leaders who sometimes were not mem-

group termed "the Mountain," occupied the left side of the assembly hall. Their combined strength formed a majority against the monarchists of various degrees who occupied the right side of the hall. But in the center was the mass of uncommitted delegates, the "safe" bloc.

The Girondins, so-called because some of the leaders of this group came from the department of Gironde,[37] were largely young

> bers of the respective legislative bodies. For example, the policy of the Mountain was outlined chiefly by Robespierre at the Parisian Jacobin Club. On the other hand, the actions of the Girondins, to a lesser extent, were determined by the famous Madame Roland, at whose home important Girondin deputies were in the habit of gathering. Moreover, the two groups acted as parties in that they were quite consistent in their aims, having almost a party platform.
>
> Brissot first took the initiative in organizing a body of men sympathetic in views. From the opening of the Legislative Assembly he dominated a small political coterie composed of Condorcet, Clavière, Monsieur Roland and some of the deputies of the department of Gironde. They all agreed to meet three times a week, preferably some time before attending the Assembly sessions. These meetings finally grew into daily affairs. At first they met at the home of Madame Dudon, a friend of Brissot. Soon, however, Petion, Vergniaud, Clavière, and, of course, Madame Roland began to entertain their political co-workers. Many of the measures discussed at the Assembly had their origin at these politico-social gatherings. (Aulard, *Histoire politique*, pp. 388-389.)

37. Historians have designated the friends of Brissot, Vergniaud, Madame Roland and Buzot under the collective name of "Girondins." At the Legislative Assembly this group of men was variously called by its opponents (the Mountain) "Brissotines," "Bordelaisians" (because so many of its leaders were from the vicinity of Bordeaux), or "Guadet-Brissot faction." At the Convention it was still to be called the "Brissotine party." However, at times it was termed the "Rolandist" or "Buzotine" party after the Girondin guides, Roland

and inexperienced men; a number were lawyers by training. They seemed, in the main, to be filled with idealism and worthy sentiments. Through their classical education and their avid reading of the philosophers, they had come to view republican government as the only worthwhile form of administration. Since the start of the Revolution this idea had been still further impressed on their minds by the writings of Brissot and Condorcet,[38] men whom they

(both Madame and Monsieur) and Buzot (see p. 165, footnote 39.) Robespierre, the head of the Mountain, was one of the few contemporaries who sometimes referred to their political adversaries as "Girondins" (Kuscinski, *op. cit.*, p. 91). Usually, however, he spoke of them as "Brissotines" after their acknowledged chief, the famous republican, Brissot. In the course of the nineteenth century, for the sake of simplification and uniformity, historians universally, by tacit agreement, designated as "Girondins" those deputies of the Legislative Assembly and Convention who sympathized with the policies of Brissot, Condorcet, Vergniaud, Buzot, Barbaroux, Guadet, Pétion, and the Rolands.

38. The question of the philosopher's political affiliation is a mute one. Certainly, in political ideals, he sympathized with the Girondins. However, Condorcet always prided himself on being independent in politics. Near the end of the Legislative Assembly, and a few days before the opening of the Convention, Condorcet was to write: "Having belonged to no party as yet, I will not start by joining one now. During the Legislative Assembly I was affiliated with a small number of just, enlightened, and incorruptible men who were zealous defenders of the people and of the law [i.e., the Girondins]. Almost all these men are now members of the Convention. I will remain their friend. At the Convention [to which he had recently been elected] I will join a few former members of the Constituent Assembly [now elected to the Convention] and a few men newly called to represent the nation. However, we will not form a party, for none of us would wish to tolerate chiefs, or be chiefs ourselves. One speaks of the department of Gironde. It is true that her deputation

regarded as their chief leaders. It is little wonder that with two such men providing guidance, the Girondins looked to the future with over-optimism.

The feeling was prevalent amongst the Girondins that it was but a matter of time before their country would be rid of the onerous burden of a king. By the action of the Constituents, France had been bequeathed a limited monarchical constitution. But the election of many men to the Legislative Assembly who would have preferred a republic proved the growth of anti-monarchical feeling in France. The deputies composing the Girondin group, and even some in the Mountain, at the opening of the Assembly, ostensibly were limited monarchists, as were all the other deputies. In reality, they formed the first republican party in France. The happy evolution of real representative government was to depend on them. They had ideals and they had leaders. Time was to prove how strong were their ideals and how apt was their leader-

includes a rare group of pure men of distinguished merit. It is true that they were previously united by friendship and esteem. Brissot and myself were admitted to their society almost from the first days of the Legislative Assembly. (As quoted by Alengry, *op. cit.*, p. 314.) According to Alengry, Condorcet was even taken for a rabid Jacobin (he was at one time president of the Paris society) and a member of the Mountain. Chabot, a contemporary, declared at the Jacobin Club on October 12, 1792, that Condorcet had abandoned the party of Brissot. Two days later, at the same society, he announced that Condorcet with Danton and Barère were the only representatives of the Mountain on the constitutional committee (the first, the so-called Girondin committee). Moreover, the proscription list, directed against leading Girondins in June, 1793, did not contain Condorcet's name. A further proof that he was no Girondin, claims Alengry, is the fact that he would not be advised by Madame Roland. (*Ibid.*, p. 312.) The best conclusion would be that Condorcet was a Girondin sympathizer but independent in his actions and beliefs.

ship. There appeared few threats to Girondin ascendancy. Monarchism was being more discredited every day. Those deputies who honestly preferred a limited monarchy were not very well organized and offered no real leadership. The times, then, seemed propitious to France's first republicans. However, there was one element of doubt in French politics. The Mountain, so-called because the members of this faction occupied the most elevated part of the assembly, on the far left, did not appear to have any clear-cut platform at the moment. Individually the members were called "Montagnards." It was often customary, however, to call them "Robespierrists" after their capable but somewhat unfathomable leader, Maximilien Robespierre.[39] Ordinarily, they appeared to be

39. Maximilien Marie Robespierre (1758-1794) is too well known to call for much comment. Ranking second to Napoleon in importance as a Revolutionary figure, he has been the subject of numerous books. His character has been judged in so many ways that it is really hard to arrive at an objective conclusion as to what it really was. In his rise to power he took the role of a man fighting for the well-being of all the underprivileged. There can be little doubt that academically, at least, he sympathized with those that might be variously termed the "under-dogs," "common men" or "the masses." However, unlike Danton, he was too effete and "finicky" to feel really comfortable in their presence. Nor, like Marat, who was probably much better educated than Robespierre, could he divest himself of schoolmaster ways and take on the dress and demeanor of a Revolutionary Apache. Finally, obsessed with the notion of a perfect society, operating according to perfect rules, he regarded people as sociological statistics, rather than as flesh-and-blood realities.

During the early years of the Revolution (1789-1791) he was regarded as a mild and honest man by all groups, including many of the members of the later Girondin faction. The liberal leaders looked upon him as a champion of democratic rights. His speeches before the Jacobin Club were generally published and eagerly read before other societies. However, unlike Condorcet and Brissot, in the years

staunch defenders of the people's rights, and they were quick to denounce and accuse any individual or group who seemed to threaten these rights.[40] Taking their orders from Robespierre, who every day was becoming more and more powerful at the Paris Jacobin Club,[41] they were not afraid to criticize the king and the

> between the opening of the Revolution and the fall of the monarchy, he did not actively work for a republic. Although his principles might have had the appearance of being republican, he had a strange hesitancy in asking for the removal of the king, even after the episode of Varennes. And when a republic was finally established, he did not seem to strive too hard to maintain it. But then, perhaps, it should be observed that these were times of extreme emergency and Robespierre had such a messianic program preying on his mind that a personality already severely introverted became fanatical. In general, his plans for the underprivileged were quite good. But then again, whether because of the severe emergencies of the time or because of personality changes in himself (brought about by introversion and frustrations), he set aside democratic institutions, replacing them with a more highly centralized type of organization that he felt would more quickly and efficiently bring about the ideal state.

40. Truly, the Girondins themselves were not above reproach when it came to denouncements and accusations. However, as a general rule, their charges seemed to be better backed by evidence than the charges made by the Montagnards.

41. As a result of his own action, Robespierre was not a member of the Legislative Assembly. On his motion, the Constituent Assembly, before disbanding, had passed a self-denying ordinance excluding all its members from election to the succeeding assembly. Robespierre, being a Constituent, was thus included in this restriction. Possibly genuine disinterestedness had motivated him in making this motion. Perhaps he foresaw that he would be a far more important figure as a leader fully occupied at the Jacobins. At the Jacobin forum he could speak as an important tribune of all the people, and not solely as a representative of a single constituency.

Girondin leaders alike. Their speeches at the Assembly were to
contain by and large the same sentiments as those of Robespierre,
or those of his close follower Jean-Paul Marat, celebrated editor of
L'Ami du Peuple.[42]

42. Jean-Paul Marat (1743-1793) is a French Revolutionary
     character whose name — if not the details of his colorful
     life — is almost as well known as that of Robespierre. In
     fact, the names of the two can be coupled. It was due largely
     to the influence of Marat, through his newspaper L'Ami du
     Peuple, that public opinion was prepared for the eventual
     centralization of authority in the hands of Robespierre. It
     is unique that Marat, who appeared to be a rabid democrat,
     was never very strong for a republic. His democracy was
     not to be one sanctioned by the people themselves; rather,
     it was to be one dictated by a strong and virtuous man. Marat
     believed that Robespierre was the most suitable man.

        A common misconception is that Marat was only a mad,
     illiterate Revolutionary. On the contrary, amongst the well
     educated leaders of the Revolution, Marat was one of the
     best educated. He not only had a reputation for being an
     authority on social science; he was equally famous as a
     physical scientist. Moreover, prior to the Revolution, his fame
     as a doctor of medicine earned him the position of private
     physician to the Count of Artois, younger brother of Louis
     XVI, who later became King Charles X.

        As a youth, Marat studied medicine in France at Toulouse,
     Bordeaux, and Paris. He then went to Scotland to finish his
     studies, receiving his degree of Doctor of Medicine from
     the University of Saint Andrews, one of the best medical
     schools in Europe. While in the British Isles, Marat pub-
     lished a book entitled The Chains of Slavery, in which he un-
     masked the corruption of the British court and ministry.
     This work, by its vigorous style and objectivity, won him the
     reputation of being somewhat of a philosopher. Marat next
     wrote A Philosophical Essay on Man, in which he attacked
     the philosopher Helvetius. The greatest philosopher of the
     day, Voltaire, made Marat ridiculous by publishing a sharp

While the opinions of the Montagnard deputies certainly revealed that they were not monarchists, these opinions also cast some doubts on the nature of their political philosophy. They did, indeed, express great love for the people and said that they had only their interests at heart. At the same time, there were those who sometimes vaguely hinted that they did not thoroughly trust the capa-

criticism of this work. He reproached Marat for destructively criticizing one of the greatest French thinkers while offering no constructive criticism in return He hoped that Marat's medical prescriptions were not as bad as his philosophy. Marat never forgave Voltaire and, unlike most Revolutionary leaders, never praised the latter.

After returning from England (in 1776), he settled down in Paris where, until the Revolution, he engaged in many activities. He practiced medicine. He carried on electrical experiments. He did research on certain legal matters, publishing a few books. It was during this period that he became acquainted with Brissot and seems to have been quite friendly with the future Girondin leader. Later, at the Convention, they were to represent different factions and were to be strong enemies. In a letter written in 1783, Marat expressed his great esteem for Brissot. He wanted the latter to aid him in the sale of one of his books. (*J. P. Brissot: Correspondance et Papiers* [ed. by Perroud, Cl., Paris, 1912], p. 80.) For humanity's sake, said Brissot, he sometimes attempted to sell Marat's books and experiments. According to Brissot, the experiments were skillful and earned the praise of Franklin, then American minister to France. (*J. P. Brissot: Mémoires* [ed. by Perroud, Cl., 2 vols., Paris, 1911], I, 202.) In 1787 Brissot told Marat that they ought to join hands and campaign against despotism. Marat, to be one of the boldest as well as one of the bloodiest Revolutionaries, meekly replied that he would rather continue peacefully to perform his scientific experiments. Physics would never lead to the Bastille, said he. Moreover, the French people were not ripe for revolution, believed Dr. Marat. (*Ibid.*, I, 205-206.)

The Revolutionary career of Marat contrasted with that

bilities of the people to govern themselves at the time. They occasionally suggested that France needed an honest and virtuous man to guide her successfully down the path of complete revolution. The name of Robespierre came more and more frequently to their lips as the man possessing these qualities in abundance. Perhaps this was true; perhaps it was not. Historians are still arguing the matter. Undoubtedly, the Montagnards, even as the Girondins, promoted what they thought was best for France.

The story of the Legislative Assembly is chiefly the story of the

of his earlier years. From the start of the Revolution, he proclaimed himself a tribune of the people. Through the medium of his newspaper *L'Ami du Peuple*, established in 1789, he denounced privilege of any sort, that of wealth as well as that of title. Although appearing to be a strong democrat, he did not really favor republicanism. He desired a dictator and, believing that he had found one in Robespierre, was instrumental in pushing him into power. During the Convention, Marat was one of the leaders of the Mountain. Constantly attacked by members of the Girondin faction, including its leader and his former friend, Brissot, he was always on the verge of being expelled and imprisoned. However, supported by the Mountain and the Parisian populace, who worshiped him, he was able to turn the tide. The leading Girondins ended by being expelled themselves. In the downfall of the Girondins, Marat played a leading role. It was he who enabled the Mountain, under Robespierre, to proscribe the influential Girondins. Through his newspaper and pamphlets he had placed the populace of Paris almost unanimously behind the policies of Robespierre and the Mountain.

Marat, when at the height of his glory — just after the proscription of the Girondins — met death by an assassin's dagger. It was customary with him to receive petitions from the people. Sometimes he received petitioners while lolling sybaritically in a warm bath. We might compare him with Napoleon in this respect. However, bath treatments, with

continued struggle of republicans against monarchical rule. Brissot, who was recognized as the most powerful man in the Legislative Assembly, admittedly worked to end monarchy once and for all. Brissot seemed to realize that Louis XVI could not be completely trusted, and suspected that he was in correspondence with foreign rulers and emigrant nobles who were bent on re-establishing absolute monarchy in France.[43] He hoped that the king would not be long in revealing his guilty character by committing some act which would reveal a treasonous relationship with his brother rulers.[44] One sure way of getting Louis to commit treason, thought the Girondin leader, would be to have him declare war against his brother monarchs. In pursuit of this plan, Brissot, after some endeavor, had a Girondin ministry appointed on March 12, 1792. This ministry took the place of the stubborn Narbonne cabinet,

Marat, were not simply a means of calming nerves. Although a doctor of medicine from the famous Saint Andrews, he did not possess enough dermatological knowledge to cure his own scrofulous skin. However, he felt that baths would help. At any rate, one day, while at his bath, he received a young lady petitioner by the name of Charlotte Corday. It so happened that the young lady had a fanatical sympathy for the Girondin cause and attributed its recent downfall to the machinations of the "people's friend." So, instead of a petition, she presented a dagger to the unsuspecting Marat.

43.   The king of Austria, who was a brother of Queen Marie Antoinette, and the king of Prussia issued (on August 27, 1791) what was termed the "Declaration of Pillnitz." In this, the two sovereigns asked that other rulers join them in establishing order in France. Louis XVI of France secretly wrote (on December 3, 1791) a letter to the king of Prussia in which he stated that an armed congress (of sovereigns) was the best way of intimidating French factionalists and reestablishing a more durable order of things. (Aulard, *Histoire politique*, p. 177.)

44.   Brissot, J. P. *À Tous les Républicains de France; sur la Société des Jacobins de Paris* (Paris, 1792), p. 9.

which contained members suspected of being royalists. Most of the members of the new cabinet were picked by the Girondin leader. If he wanted war, they could be expected to force Louis XVI to declare war.

The newly appointed ministry was not to disappoint the Girondin chief. War was declared against Austria on April 20, 1792. For this war, which was to lead to the dethronement of the king and the founding of the republic, Brissot, more than any other man, was responsible.[45] As it was the war that carried the republicans to power, their reason for promoting it is not an unimportant digression.

For some months Brissot and Condorcet had been encouraging a warlike feeling among the French people. Condorcet's argument for the necessity of war was the threats against France by the monarchs of Austria and Prussia. This would be the obvious reason for fighting. The French people were aware of the threatening movements of Austrian, Prussian and émigré troops on the north-eastern border of their country. They knew that these troops menaced France with the possible restoration of the king to his absolute power, with the result that all the achievements of the Revolution would be lost.

Besides the manifest reason for war, Condorcet pointed out the glories which would redound to France if she could spread the emancipative doctrines of the Revolution to other parts of Europe.

Brissot proclaimed publically the same arguments as Condorcet. He, too, stressed what a great honor it would be for French troops to plant the standard of liberty upon the palaces of kings. He repeatedly cited the American example. The Americans had gone through a war of liberation safely. Why could not France? In his editorials in *Le Patriote francais*, and in his speeches to the Jacobins and at the Assembly, he referred to the need for war as the need for a political crusade. Without mentioning the world *republic* (France still had a king), he left no doubt but that he expected war to spread the principles of republicanism:

45. Ellery, *op. cit.*, p. 216.

"It will be an expiatory war which will renew the face
of the world and plant the standard of liberty upon the
palaces of kings, the seraglios of sultans, the chateaux
of petty feudal tyrants, and, finally, upon the temples of
muftis and popes."[46]

A political crusade was not the immediate object that Brissot
had in mind when he endeavored so hard to involve France in

46. *Le Patriote français*, December 17, 1791; as quoted by Ellery,
op. cit., p. 233. Brissot had grandiose schemes of not only
spreading republicanism throughout Europe, but of also
spreading its principles throughout the world. With the em-
barkation of France on the unpredictable seas of war, hopes
soared high. In a letter written to General Servan (sometime in November, 1792), commander of the army in the
Pyrenees, he said that war was now necessary with Spain. In
fact, France would only be tranquil when all Europe was on
fire. He thought that General Miranda, future South American
patriot who was then serving under General Dumouriez in
the North, should be sent back to South America, where he
could start a revolt of the Spanish colonies. In a letter to
General Dumouriez himself (on November 28, 1792), Brissot (who was head of the diplomatic committee of the Convention) asked that Miranda be excused so that he could
return to South America. The war against the hated Bourbons should be carried on everywhere. There should not be
one Bourbon left on any throne. He ended by congratulating
Dumouriez on his brilliant successes (the letter was written
shortly after the battle of Jemmapes, which led to the capture
of the Austrian Netherlands. This was some months before
Dumouriez began to suffer reverses and had to face the angry
criticism of the Convention), and, while urging that the
tree of liberty be planted everywhere, exaltedly proclaimed:
"Ah, my dear friend, who were Alberone and Richelieu, to
be so vaunted? What were their petty projects, compared
to these upheavals of the globe and grand revolutions that
we are called upon to make?" (*J. P. Brissot: Correspondance
et Papiers* [ed. by Perroud, Cl.], pp. 312-316.)

war. Never losing sight of his primary goal — to make France a republic — he resolved war was to be a means of ending the monarchy, and of establishing that type of government towards which he and other idealists had been steadily working since the start of the Revolution. As yet, the king had committed no great act of treason that would thoroughly discredit him. The incident of Varennes had been blamed on evil advisers. War with Austria appeared one sure way of involving the apparently naive and gullible Louis XVI in some disloyal deed. It took no imagination, thought Brissot, to see that the French king would naturally sympathize with the monarchical enemies of France who wished to restore him to his old power. He would, with the encouragement of the queen, the "Austrian woman," probably blunder willy-nilly into the final path of betrayal. It was a strong conviction of the Girondin chief that war would lead to great betrayals and the consequential end of the monarchy.[47] In a pamphlet published in October, 1792, after the war had been going on for some months and the king had been dethroned, Brissot was to affirm this:

"It was the abolition of royalty that I had in mind when I had war declared[48] . . . They accuse me of having provoked the war![49] Do they not realize that without war royalty would still exist[50] and France would be covered with ignominy? Without a war a thousand talents and a thousand virtues would be undeveloped! . . . They feared a war made by a king! But this was politics of a narrow view. It was precisely because a treasonous monarch

47. *J. P. Brissot: Mémoires* (ed. by Perroud, Cl.), II, 251.
48. *Brissot, À Tous les Républicains de France, sur la Société des Jacobins de Paris* (Paris, 1792), p. 8, footnote 1.
49. Brissot, in using the word "they," was making reference to Robespierre and his followers at the Jacobin Club who had voted to expel him on October, 1792. One of the main charges against the leader of the Girondins was that he had thrust France into war.

would direct the war, and because he would direct it
only as a traitor, that it was necessary to have war declared by the king. After all, it was this treason alone
which led him to his doom."[51]

Brissot was right. War ended the monarchy, for some years at
least. It also resulted in the establishment of a republic. But the
republic, so long dreamed of by Brissot, Condorcet, and other
exponents of government by and for the people, was to last but
a short time. War, with all its tendency to the unforeseen, was
to be mainly responsible for the destruction of the very thing it
had helped create — the republic.

France went light-heartedly into war. All groups seemed to
support it now, even the royalists. The king and his followers, who
had been against the war originally, had a change of heart for
cynical reasons. With nothing but contempt for the Revolutionary
armies, which had lost many royalist officers through emigration and
resignation, the royalists believed that within a short time France
would be defeated by the well-equipped and well-trained armies
of Austria and Prussia. Then royalty would be restored to its
former powers. Other classes likewise desired war for more legitimate reasons. The middle and lower classes faced hostilities with
France's foreign enemies with something of a religious fervor.

50.   The monarchy end in September, 1792. Refer to p. 165.
51.   Brissot, *À Tous les Républicains*, p. 8. The eagerness of
      Brissot for war was such that he was willing to stoop to
      almost anything to bring it about. As the Legislative Assem-
      bly, during the first months of its existence, did not appear
      quite ready to sanction war, he conceived a somewhat shady
      scheme. French soldiers disguised as Austrians would attack
      a French village. This, he rightly believed, would carry the
      Assembly unanimously for war. (Dumont, Étienne, *Souvenirs
      sur Mirabeau et sur les deux premières Assemblées*, p. 411.)
      With the course of time, however, there was no need for such
      a devious method of arousing public opinion for war.

Having won a large measure of liberty at home, they now wished to spread this cherished liberty to those people abroad who were still under the heel of absolute monarchs. Condorcet, Brissot, and other publicists had promoted the idea that animosity was to be against kings, and not against people. Thus, the opening of the Revolutionary Wars was characterized not by an excessive spirit of nationalism, but rather by a spirit of internationalism. There was an exaggerated feeling that people everywhere would be liberated from their hated monarchs.

There was one sceptic, however, who did not want war. This was Maximilien Robespierre, who, strangely enough, was to owe in part his own rise to great prominence through the fortunes of war.

Robespierre argued that any wild attempt to liberate foreign peoples would result in a loss of liberty at home. He believed, with some justification, that the then-dominant group on the left, the Girondins, would become more powerful than ever. Although not a member of the Assembly — as the former Constituents, of which Robespierre was one, had decreed themselves ineligible — he could exercise control over the Mountain through the powerful caucus of the Parisian Jacobin Club. Here his speeches set the keynote for the Mountain's action in the Legislative Assembly.[52]

52. Condorcet, one of the original members of the Jacobins, noting the increasing subserviency of the club to Robespierre and, suspecting the Montagnard leader's actions, ceased attending its meetings in March, 1792. He made a remark in references to Robespierre's air of sanctimoniousness that touched the latter to the quick. Robespierre, said Condorcet, "is a priest and will never be anything else," (As quoted by Alengry, op. cit., p. 144.) One of Robespierre's admirers, Chabot, denounced Condorcet in an insulting speech delivered the following April at the Jacobin Club. There had been talk about the morals of Madame Condorcet. Chabot foully said: "It doesn't matter whether his wife was seduced or not. But it does matter if he allows himself to be blinded by her." (As quoted by Alengry, op. cit., p. 145.) Brissot, who was to be expelled from the society in October, 1792, took up

Regarding the war, he pointed out that a crusade was dangerous.
People would not easily change their customs, especially when
confronted with armed missionaries. The best thing for France
to do was to set her own house in order and acquire her own

the defense of his friend in a reply to Chabot which sum-
marizes the immense prestige of the *philosophe:*

"The calumniators did not spare Phocion (402 [?]—
317 B. C.; an Athenian general and patriot, noted for
his honesty and extreme patriotism). He was the victim
of a flatterer of the people, even when he wished to save
them. Oh! That reminds me of the terrible calumny
raised against Condorcet. You calumniate this great
man at the very moment when he, struggling under the
handicap of an illness, is trying so hard to terminate
a plan for public education, and when he is endeavoring
to work out a suitable financial regime! Who are you to
presume this right! What have you done? Where are
your works, your writings? Can you cite, as he can,
along with Voltaire and D'Alembert, so many assaults
made for thirty years against the throne, superstition,
and parliamentary and ministerial fanaticism? If it
were not for the burning genius of these great men who,
by degrees, have fired other souls and made them dis-
cover the secret of their grandeur and strength, you,
today, would not speak so freely from the tribune about
liberty. . . . You dare to insult Condorcet, when his
Revolutionary life is only a sequence of sacrifices for the
people: philosopher, he made himself a politician; acad-
emician, he became a journalist; noble, he changed to
a Jacobin; placed by the court in an eminent place, he
left it in order to work for the people. He has ruined his
health for them. Now, who dares attack him in the midst
of his immortal works — those very men who pretend
to love the people and liberty. . . . They say that he is
unfeeling because he works in silence. They insinuate
that he is an enemy of the people because he is not
constantly appealing to the people's tribune." (The

liberty before trying to offer it to others.[53] One of his followers, Camille Desmoulins, an ardent republican who would be beheaded during the Terror, said that it was absurd to fight kings when they still had one themselves and were under royal officers.[54] Of course, Camille, not being of the inner circle of the Girondins, knew nothing of their plan to use the war as a means of getting rid of the king.

The king seems to have fallen rather readily into the snares of the Girondins. Although the king was never really caught committing any overt acts of treason, the anticipation of soon being rescued by the armies of the kings of Prussia and Austria made him a little careless in his dealings with the Legislative Assembly. He vetoed, as the constitution gave him a right to do, certain pet acts of the Girondin-controlled assembly. He dismissed the Girondin ministry. Louis' independent attitude towards an Assembly containing many hostile elements was not very wise. Moreover, the Duke of Brunswick, in command of the Prussian army, did not make Louis XVI any more popular when he issued a manifesto saying that he was going to restore the king to his former absolute powers (July 25, 1792). Brunswick also said that Paris would be completely destroyed if the royal family was in any way injured. The duke's manifesto practically sealed the fate of the French king.

In that many of the important leaders of the Legislative Assembly were republican in beliefs, it would seem to be almost a foregone conclusion that they would take the initiative in deposing

> tribune was the space, along the sides of the Assembly Hall and also along the sides of the Jacobin Club, where any of the citizenry might sit.) (Quotation from Alengry, *op. cit.*, pp. 145-146.)

53. Aulard, ed., *La Société des Jacobins*, III, 309.
54. Desmoulins, *Discours au Conseil général de la Commune*, p. 8. As was to be expected, many of the better officers had been trained in the pre-Revolutionary armies of the king. However, many of these, living on small salaries and with little chance of advancement in times of peace, welcomed the war as an opportunity to rise quickly in rank.

an unwanted monarch. They wanted the king removed, all right. However, it apears that they wished the deposition to come about through subtle methods. In other words, they wanted the king so to incriminate himself by some act of betrayal that his removal would take place according to regular processes of law.[55] The sovereign people could not wait on subtle methods, however. For some months the Legislative Assembly had been receiving petitions from various republican groups, representative of all France. The petitions constantly reiterated that the king should be removed at once. Finally, when the Assembly was just about to take action, there occured the people's movement of August 10, 1792.

This movement, apparently well planned, was directed by relatively unknown but capable republican leaders chosen from the forty-eight Paris sections[56] and the ranks of National Guardsmen who happened to be in the capital. These leaders brushed aside the regular Paris municipal government and set up what was known as the "Revolutionary Commune." Their actions were quick and effective. Acting under their orders, Guardsmen attacked the royal palace, the Tuileries, forcing the king and his family to seek refuge with the Legislative Assembly. The men of the Revolutionary Commune then demanded that the Assembly dethrone the king. However, the leaders of the Assembly, while acceding to the demands of the Revolutionary Commune, appear to have upheld the authority of the Legislative Assembly as the supreme authority.[57] The day following the coup d'état against the king, the

55. A contemporary of Condorcet, Étienne Dumont, said that "he wanted a republic formed by the Assembly so as not to have one created by the populace." (Dumont, *op. cit.*, p. 102.)
56. Paris in 1789 had been divided into forty-eight administrative sections.
57. The question as to who really governed France between August 10, 1792, and September 20, 1792, has never really been settled to the satisfaction of all historians. The best conclusion seems to be that the Legislative Assembly was the main authority. The Assembly did give the new com-

Assembly decreed the suspension of Louis XVI and arranged for the calling of another constituent body. The same day the undemocratic classification of active and passive citizenries was abolished. One no longer needed to pay a certain tax rate in order

munal authority tacit recognition, however, when it was charged with maintaining law and order in Paris. It also voted the insurrectional assembly a subsidy of 850 livres per month. The insurrectional assembly of the Hôtel de Ville (city hall), the governing body of the Revolutionary Commune, was composed of 288 members chosen by the sections. It gave itself the official title of "General Council of the Commune" (on August 11, 1792). (Aulard, *Histoire politique*, p. 220.)

It appears that Mathiez's claim that "the Legislative Assembly was subordinated to the revolutionary power issued from the direct choice of the people" may be too strong. (See Mathiez, A., "Le Gouvernement révolutionnaire," in *Annales historiques de la Révolution française* [March-April, 1937], No. 89, p. 100.) As Bord points out, the Assembly did feel obligated to the Revolutionary Commune for providing a solution to the embarrassing question of how to get rid of the king. (Bord, Gustave, "La Proclamation de la République," in *Revue de la Révolution* [January, 1883], I, 24.) Yet it retained its position as the legal and authoritative center of government in France in spite of a certain non-preventable division of power. A foremost authority on this period of French history says, "My years of research on the interregnum lead me to believe that the government of France during these forty days tended to the organization of national defense. Authority lay not in one, but in several hands. In Paris, to speak only of the capital, it proceeded from a collaboration between the new powers, issued from popular victories, and the National Assembly, the latter remaining the center and source of action." (Caron, P. "Conseil executif provisoire et Pouvoir ministeriel [1792-1794]," in *Annales historiques de la Révolution française* [January-February, 1937], No. 79, p. 5.)

to be eligible for membership in either the electoral assemblies or the Convention. The Girondin leaders felt confident that public opinion was such that the formation of a Convention would mean the definite end of a monarchy and the firm foundation of a republic. In the decree calling for a new constituent assembly (edited by Vergniaud), Louis was accused of having acted treasonously "against the Constitution when France was engaged in a war undertaken in his name."[58] This statement could be regarded as a recommendation for the end of monarchy and the establishment of a republic. Recommendations were really not necessary.

In the elections to the Convention (taking place from August 26 to September 23, 1792), the republicans were triumphant everywhere. The Girondins would carry many departments outside of Paris. The growing power of Robespierre in the capital was proved by the selection of twenty-four deputies all favorable to him.[59] Both

58. Cahen, Leon and Gujot, Raymond, L'Oeuvre législative de la Révolution (Paris, 1913), p. 54. The report sent by the Legislative Assembly to all the departments, stating why the king was suspended, was an excellent piece of republican propaganda. The fact that it was edited by Concorcet and signed by the president of the Assembly, Guadet, gave it an immense authoritative value. It not only accused the king of being a traitor in his conduct of the war, but it indicted the whole royal system—the king's ministers, disloyal priests, and the émigrés and foreign monarchs with whom the king allegedly conspired. The citizens were warned to suspect everything that smacked of royalty, even, in some cases, the directories of their departments. (Condorcet, Exposition des Motifs d'après lesquels l'Assemblée nationale a proclamé la Convocation d'une Convention nationale, et prononcé la Suspension du Pouvoir exécutif dans les Mains du Roi [Paris, 1792], pp. 1-16.)

59. Naturally, Robespierre was elected a deputy to represent Paris.

Brissot and Concorcet were disappointed in not being elected representatives for Paris. Proof of the popularity of these two prominent republicans in other departments, however, was shown by the fact that they both were elected deputies by several different constituencies. Brissot chose to represent the department of l'Eure-et-Loir, and Condorcet decided to represent the department of l'Aisne. Robespierre, of course, would be the chief of the Parisian delegation. Altogether, seven hundred and forty-nine delegates were elected. Of this number probably one hundred to one hundred and fifty were firm supporters of the Girondin faction. One might say they were hard-core party-line followers. A similar number would make up the hard-core Montagnard group. Between these two dynamic factions lay an amorphous body made up of some four hundred deputies. These deputies, collectively known as "the Plain" or "Belly," generally followed the rule of expediency in voting.

The elections were significant in that they revealed the strength of Robespierre in the capital. And doubtless, they proved to him that he must depend on the capital to maintain and consolidate his power. By all means Paris should remain the center of authority in France. On the other hand, the elections revealed to the Girondins that their power was waning in Paris and on the increase in the departments. Moreover, they regarded the city as containing too many unstable elements that were hard to control. They suspected that Robespierre had ways of controlling the mass of Parisians, however.

A few weeks before the opening of the Convention, apparent proof of growing instability in the capital was found in a bloody incident which has come to be known as the "September Massacres."

Using the pretext that Paris was full of traitors who sympathized with the Austrians and emigrant nobles, the Revolutionary Commune, now largely under the influence of Robespierre,[60] had filled

60. It is to be observed that the Montagnard chief joined the Commune only after the success of August 10. He was not one

Parisian prisons with some three thousand suspect citizens, including many priests who had refused to take an oath (which had been
required by the Constitution of 1791) agreeing to the secularization
of the religious establishment in France. On September 2 and 3,
hundreds of these were massacred with only the pretense of a trial.
Most of them were innocents who had not plotted against the
state. The excuse offered for the executions was that Paris volunteers, departing for the frontiers to meet the foreign foe, were
afraid to leave anyone behind who might harm their wives and
children.[61] The Legislative Assembly appears to have done what it
could. However, twelve deputies sent by the Assembly to the
prisons in order to stop the useless slaughter were insulted and
ignored. Mayor Pétion went alone to one of the prisons, La Force,
and strongly reproached any municipal officers who were condemning victims. Brissot pleaded with Danton, Minister of Justice, and
Santerre, recently appointed head of the Paris National Guard,[62]
to stop the massacres. Danton told Brissot that the massacres were

of the original members who planned the coup which ended
the monarchy. He did not really pretend to a belief in republicanism until after August 10, 1792.

61.   Tourneaux, Maurice, ed., *Procès-verbaux de la Commune, 10
Août 1792—1 Juin 1793* (Paris, 1894), p. 20.

62.   He took the place of Mandat, who had been suspended for his
attempts to reinforce the forces of the Tuileries on August 10.
Incidentally, La Fayette, the first commander of the National
Guard, was now a man without a country. He was impeached
and proscribed on August 20, 1792, by the Legislative Assembly for the desertion of his army while in line of duty.
He had been in charge of one the armies assigned to protect
the frontier. He was also charged with unlawfully interfering
with the country's legislators because of his attempts to free the
king from their control. The former champion of American
freedom avoided arrest by fleeing across the frontier. He was
captured by the Austrians and imprisoned at Olmütz, where he
remained until 1796.

necessary to appease the people.[63] However, as pointed out by the leader of the Girondins in a pamphlet published a little more than a month later, this was no spontaneous movement of the people or a logical outcome of August 10.[64] It was an organized campaign of terror carried out by the Revolutionary Commune[65] and some over-zealous citizens of the capital who looked to the Robespierrist faction as the only one really attuned to the people's interests.[66] Danton, if not directly implicated in the bloody actions of early September, was at least guilty of criminal neglect of duty in not taking proper steps to prevent them.[67]

The September massacres were perhaps a harbinger of things to come. They did show that some Parisians could be mobilized quickly and efficiently, with proper organization, to carry out "extra-legal" actions when such actions were deemed necessary by the

63. *J. P. Brissot: Mémoires* (ed. by Perroud, Cl.), II, 244-247.

64. Brissot, *À Tous les Républicains*, pp. 44-45.

65. An indication of the Commune's guilt appears to be found in the minutes of its proceedings for September 6. The Council allotted 1,463 livres to pay the salaries of the individuals who had carried out the executions. The minutes picturesquely described them as "those persons who, at the peril of their lives, worked to purify the atmosphere during the days of September 2, 3, and 5." (Tourneaux, ed., *Procès verbaux de la Commune*, p. 96.)

66. Robespierre once replied to a deputy from La Gironde who accused him of having ordered the assassinations: "Agreed. Neither you nor your friends would have had an aristocrat assassinated." (Brissot, *À Tous les Républicains*, p. 45, footnote 1.)

67. As though accusing Danton, Brissot said that the massacres had been meditated and prepared in the ministry itself. (Brissot, *À Tous les Républicains*, p. 44.) Danton was the only minister who was on anything like friendly terms with Robespierre.

controlling forces of the city.[68] However, the ordinary French mortal was incapable of seeing anything at all ominous in this.

Most Frenchmen in 1792 faced the future with confidence and good cheer. France no longer was burdened with a king. A Convention was about to meet which was certain to grant France her first republican constitution. Probably the majority of enlightened Frenchmen felt that the meeting of a new body of representatives, dedicated to the task of creating a republican organization for the country, would put an end to all factionable squabbles and bring unity and internal peace to the country.

68. These massacres were also significant in that they caused the first sharply defined disagreement between the Mountain and the Girondins. (*Débats de la Convention nationale ou Analyse complète des Séances avec les Noms de Tous les Membres, Pétitionnaires ou Pérsonnages qui ont figuré dans cette Assemblée, précédee d'une Introduction par Léon Thiessé* [4 vols, Paris 1889], Introduction, volume I, p. X.) A contemporary, Meillan, later pointed out in his memoirs that it was significant that some of the men who had plotted and encouraged the atrocities were the very leaders of the Mountain who were elected to the Convention. They now had the alternative either of going ahead with further illegalities and usurping power, or of being justly condemned and sent to the scaffold. (Meillan, Arnaud Jean, *Mémoires* [Paris, 1823], p. II.)

Chapter IV

Some Signs of Dictatorship

To all appearances, the results of the elections to the Convention were a guarantee that France would have that republican government so long passionately desired by a few and now equally desired by many. The task of the 749 elected deputies[1] seemed simple and clear-cut — to formally abolish the monarchy, decree France a republic, and grant the people a democratic charter. In fact, any divergence from this straightforward program could have but unfortunate results. Public opinion had been well prepared to view representative government without a king as the only worthwhile

1. Although a large number of deputies were elected, it was to be characteristic of the Convention sessions that rarely was the attendance above 350. The largest attendance was during the first months of the meetings of the constituent body, when the Girondins were still in control. For instance, at the session of October 4, 1792, the total number present was 460. This, if one excepts the few days in January, 1793, during which the fate of the monarch was voted, was a record. With the overthrow of the Girondins, the Convention would suffer a drastic drop in attendance. In fact, the members attending after June, 1793, made up such a small proportion of the total number of elected deputies that it would be proper to term the Convention a rump body. Between June, 1793, and October 26, 1795 (the end of the Convention), the average number of deputies at the meetings was somewhere between 220 and 260. (Gulffrey, Jules, ed., *Les Conventionnels: Listes par Départements et par Ordre alphabétique des Députés et des Suppléants à la Convention national* [Paris, 1889], Introduction, p. XXII.)

form of administration. As to the state of opinion at the time, deputy Barère[2] wrote, "To decree the form of republican govern-

2. Barère, Bertrand (1755-1841), the son of a lawyer, was following with considerable success in his father's footsteps when the Revolution broke out. He already had a reputation as a skillful man of the law when the epochal year 1789 dawned. He also had a reputation for being too well versed in the radical philosophy of that day — the philosophy of men such as Voltaire and Rousseau. One prominent judge of the period thought that this was a pity. Barère's career was certain to be a brilliant one, commented the judge to a friend. He then added the reservation: "But what a pity that he has been nourished with the impure milk of modern philosophy!"

    Barère's familiarity with "the impure milk of modern philosophy," as well as his abilities as a lawyer and talented writer (he was the author of many pamphlets on political philosophy as well as the editor of the *Point du Jour*, one of the best and most accurate chronicles of the Constituent Assembly), made him a figure of note throughout all phases of the Revolution. The perseverance with which he managed to hold important positions, despite the change in regime, causes some wonder. Although he had been saturated with the liberal readings of the philosophers, he was still able to support with equanimity such widely divergent systems as the republic and the authoritarian states of Robespierre and Napoleon. Adherence to the creed "When in Rome, do as the Romans do" enabled Barère to live and record for future historians many of the momentous events of the French Revolution.

    Among the numerous positions held by Barère were those of deputy to the Constituent Assembly, to the Convention, and to the Council of Five Hundred (during the period of the Directory). Under Napoleon he was elected a member of one of the rubber-stamp legislative bodies. He was also charged by Napoleon with writing a weekly report on public opinion.

ment from the first session of the Convention was to obey the national character and spirit of the epoch."[3] Another deputy said that if the republic had not been decreed, the fires of civil war would have been lighted.[4] With such a unity of feeling and purpose being evident at the time, the question is naturally asked: why, then, did the first republic have such a short and unfortunate existence?[5] The answer seems to be that although the country as a whole was fairly unified, there was not a proper feeling of harmony and unselfishness amongst some of the people's delegates to the Convention.

The delegates, as far as their political viewpoints were concerned, fell into three main groups. These have been termed by historians as the *Girondins* (interchangeable with *Brissotines*), the *Montagnards* (interchangeable with *the Mountain* or *Robespierrists*), and the *Plain* or *Belly*. The former two, having their origin during the period of the Legislative Assembly,[6] were dynamic bodies with

It was during the Conventional period that Barère was appointed to the Girondin constitutional committee (although he was not a Girondin himself). He often reported the committee's proceedings. When the Committee of Public Safety was created, he was the first member to be elected. Barère as an old man continued to show his political adaptability. In 1840, one year before his death, he was honored by being elected to the Chamber of Deputies, as well as to the General Council of King Louis Philippe. (Kuscinski, A., *Dictionnaire des Conventionnels* [Paris, 1916], pp. 23-29.)

3. Barère, Bertrand, *Mémoires*, II, 39; as quoted by Bord, Gustave, "La Proclamation de la République," *Revue de la Révolution* (January, 1883), I, 24-25.
4. *Loc. cit.*
5. Theoretically, France was a republic until Napoleon I, casting aside all sham and pretense, made himself emperor in 1804. Actually, France's first experiment in republicanism, beginning in August, 1792, ended in June, 1793, when the Convention fell under authoritarian control.
6. Refer to pp. 128-137.

almost the attributes of party organization. The latter, the Plain,[7] was a large, flaccid and irresolute group of representatives without leadership, organization, or plans. Its members were largely timorous individuals who were willing to follow the dictates of the strong.[8] No plan of action could be expected from them. They were followers, not leaders. Leadership, apparently, was a monopoly of the Girondins and Montagnards. At the opening of the Convention, the Girondin chiefs appear to have been recognized by the majority of the Conventionals as the heads of the republican movement. Moreover, the Girondins had shown some strength in the departments. The Mountain, on the other hand, had its greatest strength to begin with in the capital itself.[9] Still, within a few months this

7. It was so called because its members sat squarely in the center of the assembly hall, between the delegates of the Mountain and those of the Girondins, who sat at opposite ends of the hall and slightly above the center. The deputies of the Plain were to be almost as much to blame as the authoritarian-minded for the failure of France's first experiment in republicanism. They were fearful men whose crime was their supineness in the face of threats. Lacking any program of their own, they were willing to follow anyone who held the upper hand. At first they were supporters of the Girondins. However, when the Girondins began to lose ground before attacks of the Mountain, they were quick to switch their allegiance.

8. Illustrative of their attitude is the following anecdote: A spokesman for the Mountain once asked the members of the Plain whether he could depend on them. A member of the latter body gave the impudent answer, "Yes, if you are the stronger; no, if you are the weaker." (Durand-Maillane, P. T., *Mémoires* [Paris, 1825], Introduction, p. VI.) Durand-Maillane, a member of the undistinguished Plain, honestly admitted he howled with the wolves when this was the expedient thing to do. (*Ibid*, p. 33.)

9. Refer to p. 149. Both sides naturally had propagandized in order to have their own candidates elected. Perhaps a good

group, although a minority, would overcome the coalesced strength of the Girondins and the majority of the Plain who originally supported them.[10]

The Mountain had certain distinguishing attributes which were to figure prominently in the ultimate domination by its leaders of the whole Convention. Probably the Mountain's greatest characteristic was the genius and diversity of its leadership. Its guides were a strange and varied assortment of idealists, practical men, some dreamers, and a few individuals tinged with the brush of fanaticism. Perhaps the most important of them all, Robespierre, combined all of these qualities.[11] Doubtless, as with many leaders in different periods of history, they honestly believed that they were contriving to make a state in which the ever-suffering people would be more prosperous and content. Still, the fiery zeal of some, coupled with a certain impatience with democratic processes, especially when

proportion of the Parisian delegation met the standards established by Robespierre. Durand-Maillane asserts that the Montagnard leader, through his control of the Paris Commune, was able to direct the Paris electoral bodies in the choice of deputies. This was the only way in which Marat would have been elected, claims Durand-Maillane. (*Ibid.*, p. 30.) On the other hand, Barbaroux, a prominent Girondin, was influential in naming the deputies of the department of Bouches-du-Rhône. (*Ibid.*, p. 31.)

10. According to Brissot, the Mountain had only 150 members. The Girondin chief cited as his authority for this figure the records of his adversaries. (*J. P. Brissot: Mémoires* [ed. by Perroud, Cl., 2 vols, Paris, 1911], II, 344.) The 599 other members were divided between the Girondins and the Plain. The latter was a fluctuating group which, in voting, sided with either the right (Girondins) or the left (Montagnards). Expediency was more apt to direct the vote of the Plain than honest convictions.

11. Robespierre, Saint-Just, Marat, Camille Desmoulins, Hérault de Sechelles, Anacharsis Cloots, Chabot, Panis, and the Duc de Orléans (Égalité) all had one or several of these qualities.

these processes seemed to be to the advantage of the opposition, caused them sometimes to follow a rather dubious policy as far as democracy was concerned. But then, what is democratic and what is not may be hard to decide in times of revolution. And revolutionaries have been known to argue that the end justifies the means. Admittedly, however, the Montagnard involvement in the September massacres was rather hard to understand.[12]

The Montagnards were willing to take strong action when deemed necessary. There was an incisiveness about them that was largely lacking amongst the Girondins.[13] This trait helped

12. Refer to pp. 149-151. Meillan, a deputy affiliated with the Girondins, inferred that those members of the Mountain who were directly connected with the massacres might have paid for their crimes if the Girondins had more initiative and less fear of bloodshed. The leading Montagnards (Robespierre, Marat, and Danton) actually feared that their Girondin opponents might make them amenable to justice. They believed that the only alternative to going to the scaffold was to seize more power, alleged Meillan. (Meillan, Arnaud Jean, *Mémoires* [Paris, 1823], p. II.)

13. Leon Thiessé summarized the weakness of the leaders of the republican movement (Condorcet, Brissot, Vergniaud, etc.) in the following phrase: "Their hatred of crime, their aversion to the shedding of blood — these laudable traits that society wishes to find in man or state, became, because of the horrible and unfortunate situation of France, the very cause of their ruin." (*Débats de la Convention nationale ou Analyse complète des Séances avec les Noms de Tous les Membres, Pétitionnaires ou Pérsonnages qui ont figuré dans cette Assemblée, precédée d'une Introduction par Léon Thiessé* [ed. by Léon Thiessé, 4 vols., Paris, 1828], p. XV to the introduction of vol. I.) (Hereafter this work will be cited as *Débats de la Convention nationale.*) Thiessé seems to have overlooked the fact that Brissot, by his own admission, was willing to do anything — even using immoral means if necessary — to get France into war. War certainly involves bloodshed. See

them to make maximun use of their strength in the capital, where they had their greatest support.[14] Here were all the elements that could be used in preparing the way for a highly centralized administration.

First of all, there was the Parisian delegation of deputies to the Convention.[15] This delegation, including Robespierre himself, of course, was made up of some of the boldest and most enterprising minds in the country. For instance, Marat, Danton, and Collot d'Herbois[16] were representatives of the capital. Marat, whose newspaper, *L'Ami du Peuple,* had a great influence on the Parisian populace,[17] never tired of praising the virtues of Robespierre and suggesting that he was the one to lead France. Collot d'Herbois and Danton (the latter was to lose his head after Robespierre broke with him) promoted, even though perhaps unwittingly, his ascendancy to supreme power by using their influence with the Parisians to further his plans. Moreover, Robespierre himself, in speeches at

p. 142 and foonote 51 of this monograph. It is debatable whether Brissot's idealistic purpose — the establishment of the republic — would have compensated for a rather dubious means of involvement. I suppose that we can say that Brissot was an enthusiastic republican, ready to do almost anything for the cause.

14. Refer to p. 149.

15. Meillan's unflattering opinion of the Paris deputation was that the majority of its members were knaves, madmen, and plain dumbbells who had no interest in seeing the return of law and order. At its head were Robespierre, Danton, and Marat, said Meillan. (Meillan, *op. cit.,* pp. 8-9.) Reservations indeed should be applied to this strong view, given by one who had been affiliated with the Girondins.

16. Collot d'Herbois was one of the most prominent members of the Parisian Jacobin Club. He was also one of the Parisian deputies at the Convention.

17. "A word inserted in his paper was sufficient to agitate the populace and even cause an uprising," said Meillan. (Meillan, *op. cit.,* p. 3.)

the Convention and the Jacobin Club, promised, with undoubted sincerity, to look after the economic and social wants of the poor and underprivileged.[18] These categories were represented by large numbers in Paris. Finally, the Revolutionary Paris Commune[19] and the Jacobin and Cordeliers Clubs influenced capital opinion in favor of the Montagnard leader. The first two had come almost directly under Robespierre's control. At the Cordeliers Club,[20] Marat and Danton often spoke of the great qualities of their chief.

Thus, the Montagnard leaders found that despite minority status in the Convention,[21] there were other factors in their favor. Of

18. Meillan alleged that Robespierre, by dint of flattering the populace, had become its idol. This was not unusual, thought the conservative Girondin deputy. Any demi-god, he said, could become such an idol by similarly declaiming against the rich and causing to be born in the souls of the poor the desire for and hope of material gain. (*Ibid.*, p. 109.) While confessing that the Montagnard leader might have been a real patriot, Meillan criticized him for being a harsh and dictatorially inclined one. "Jealous, full of pride, stubborn, violent and sanguinary, he would have sacrificed three-fourths of the human species in order to make his system of government dominant over the remaining fourth," said Meillan. (*Ibid.*, p. 5.)

19. Refer to p. 146.

20. Condorcet was formerly an honored member.

21. It is probable that many of the deputies of the Mountain might have sided with the Girondins if the Girondin leaders had proved as efficient in their organizational ability as most of them were honest in their republicanism. Brissot was of the opinion, a bit over-enthusiastic perhaps, that two-thirds of the Montagnards were good republicans gone slightly astray. All the divisions and misfortunes which were to occur in the Convention during the next six months were blamed "on some twenty individuals who influenced the Mountain." (*J. P. Brissot: Mémoires* [ed. by Perroud, Cl.], II, 344-345.)

prime importance was their control of the capital. There they had maximum appeal. It was to be expected that Robespierre, in making what appeared to be audacious proposals, whether of a political, economic, or social nature, would appeal to the increasing number of "have-nots" in Paris.[22] The Girondins, ardently republican as most of them were, wanted to promote the general welfare of all the people. But they would prove to lack the organization and, perhaps, a certain degree of ruthlessness required in times of severe crisis.[23] The Montagnards took every advantage of their

22. *Débats de la Convention nationale*, p. VII to the introduction of vol. I.

23. The weaknesses of Girondin leadership can best be generalized by citing the opinion of two contemporaries who were closely associated with them. Allowing for a little exaggeration perhaps, the opinions seem to be fairly close to the truth. Madame Roland and Arnaud Meillan agreed that the men who guided the Girondins were, in general, persons of excellent character and ideals who had struggled constantly to make their country a successful republic. Their chief weakness was that they did not realize that man had weaknesses; he was not innately good, even in the exalted natural state idyllically described by their chief prophet, Rousseau. Humans sometimes had to be prodded and organized. The philosophical equanimity of the Girondin leaders was a source of constant vexation to the vigorous Roland woman: "Sometimes, my patience exhausted, I could have slapped those sages that I had learned to esteem more every day for the honesty of their souls and the purity of their intentions. Excellent reasoners, good philosophers, and political savants in discussions, they understood nothing about leading men and consequently influencing them in an assembly. Ordinarily, their science and minds were a pure loss." (*Mémoires de Madame Roland* [ed. by Perroud, Cl., 2 vols., Paris, 1905], I, 64.) Meillan agreed with Madame Roland that the Girondin chiefs failed in not properly organizing a strong following. If they, instead of tolerating too much independence amongst their

weaknesses and pressed the attack against their rivals almost from the opening of the Convention. However, the first few sessions of the new constituent body were reasonably peaceful; legislation vital to the well-being of France was passed.

At the first session, on September 20, 1792, held in one of the salons of the Tuileries, Girondin control of a majority of the Conventionals at that point was recognized in the election of Petion as president and Brissot, Condorcet, and Vergniaud as secretaries.[24] As certain Montagnard deputies complained that their present meeing place was too small,[25] it was agreed that meetings henceforth would be at the neighboring Riding Academy (Salle du Manège), an extremely large structure where formerly the Constituent and Legislative Assemblies had held their sessions. Several Girondin deputies, aware that a larger meeting place would only encourage more of the idle of Paris to gather in the galleries and perhaps disrupt the orderly business of legislating, grumbled that they had not been sent to capture popularity with the Parisian populace.[26]

There was never again to be so much unity amongst the Conventional deputies as at the memorable session of September 21, 1792. The representatives of all groups who spoke that day spoke only the purest of republican sentiments. All forms of

associates, had actually formed a party with bold policies, they might have easily overcome the Mountain, said Meillan. (Meillan, *op. cit.*, pp. 99-100.)

24. Other secretaries named at this session were Rabaut Saint-Étienne, La Source and Camus. These men were all Girondin sympathizers.

25. According to these deputies, a larger place of assembly was necessary so that some of the citizens of Paris could also attend the sessions of the Convention. (Hamel, Ernest, *Histoire de Robespierre d'après des Papiers de Famille: les Sources originals et des Documents entièrement inédits* [3 vols., Paris, 1866], II, 431.)

26. Hamel, *op. cit.*, II, 432.

absolutism were condemned. The honest principles of democracy were proclaimed. Danton, Couthon,[27] and other Montagnard deputies declaimed against absolutism as loudly as the Girondins. It was noted that Marat and Robespierre had nothing to say, however.

The contention of Chabot,[28] that the task of the assembled representatives was not to arbitrarily draw up a constitution and put it into operation without having the sanction of the people,[29] caused considerable discussion. Couthon remarked that, in so far as their duty was to edit a type of social contract, it should be taken for granted that any contract of this nature must of neces-

27. Couthon, Georges Auguste (1755-1794), originally republican, fell under the spell of Robespierre. Before the Revolution he had practiced law in the city of Clermont, where he had gained a reputation as a lawyer who handled cases for the poor. Elected as a deputy from Puy-de-Dome, first to the Legislative Assembly and then to the Convention, he became noted for his strong hatred of kings. Besides fulfilling his duties as a Conventional deputy and occasionally acting as a representative on mission to the armies, Couthon found time to become one of the most active members of the Jacobin Club. Furthermore, he became a member of the Committee of Public Safety on July 10, 1793. However, he was more assiduous in attending meetings at the Jacobin Club than he was in attending the Committee meetings. It was at the Jacobin Club that he fell completely under the spell of Robespierre. Although originally a strong exponent of republicanism, he became convinced that France needed a strong authoritarian rule. So he shared in the triumphs and he shared in the final defeat of Robespierre, being one of the casualties of the 9th Thermidor (July 27, 1794).

28. Chabot was one of the most violent Jacobins. He was also one of the most violent critics of the Girondins.

29. *Moniteur universel: Journal officiel de l'Empire français* [196 vols., Paris, 1789-1863], September 22, 1792).

sity be submitted to the people.[30] The state of public opinion
being such as it was, there need not be any fear that the people
would want a monarchical constitution. "France would be unworthy of the liberty she had conquered if she thought to conserve
a form of government marked by fourteen centuries of crimes,"
orated Couthon.[31] He added that the Conventionals must not only
draw up a constitution free of all vestiges of royalty; they should
make sure as well that it offered no encouragement for dictatorship
or any sort of individual power.[32] Danton agreed that a charter
of government ought to be submitted to the sanction of the
people. "No constitution could exist," said he, "which was not
accepted by the majority of the primary assemblies."[33] He further
prophesied that it would be practically impossible for a tyrant
to be voted into power by the people.[34]

After these expressions of trust in the French citizenry, two
declarations were accepted in a formal vote by the Convention.

30. *Loc. cit.*
31. *Loc. cit.*
32. *Loc. cit.*
33. *Loc. cit.* For the origins and functions of the primary assemblies, refer to p. 256, footnote 12. Doubtless Couthon
and Danton, in proposing a referendum, had been influenced
by recent petitions presented to the Jacobin Club. At the
August 17 session of the club, a deputation from the Marche
section of Paris had introduced a petition which asked for
a referendum on all decrees relating to a constitution. It went
further and demanded that all measures — those ruling
marriage, succession, the judiciary, etc. — have the sanction
of the primary assemblies before becoming valid laws. Boldly
the petition added that the Paris Commune, by dint of its
proximity to the Convention, could cause a second deliberation
on any measure passed by said Convention which was deemed
dangerous. (Aulard, François V. Alphonse, ed., *La Société
des Jacobins: Récueil de Documents pour l'Histoire du Club
des Jacobins de Paris* [6 vols., Paris, 1891-1892], IV, 213.)
34. *Moniteur universel*, September 22, 1792.

The first, made by Couthon, stated that there could be no constitution other than one accepted by the people. The second, made by Danton, guaranteed the security of persons and property.[35] Almost as an afterthought, it was decreed, by acclamation,[36] that monarchy was forever abolished. This decree was greeted by a thunderous applause which lasted for several minutes.[37] It was also decreed that in the future all time would be figured from September 21, 1792, a day which was to be known as the Day One of the French Republic.

Between September 21 and October 11, 1792, the latter date being the one on which the first constitutional committee — sometimes termed the "Girondin Constitutional Committee" — was appointed time, an inestimable and irretrievable treasure, which should have been properly utilized in quickly completing a constitution, was futilely wasted in charges and counter-charges. The Girondins, who actually controlled a majority in the Convention, while continually denouncing the tactics of those who seemed to be conspiring towards a highly centralized government[38] based on the support of the Paris masses, took no really effective action to check any threats to the republic. But then, they were restrained by their very passion for legality.

One of the more practical of the Girondins, however, Francois Buzot,[39] aware from the first of existing conditions that might

35. *Loc. cit.*
36. (Abbé) Gregoire, a former Jesuit priest, was the deputy who proposed (on September 21, 1792) that the end of the monarchy be decreed by acclamation. Kings, he said, were in the moral order what monsters were in the physical order. The history of kings was but the story of the martyrology of nations.
37. *Moniteur universel,* September 22, 1792.
38. Robespierre has sometimes been called the first modern dictator.
39. Buzot, François Nicolas Leonard (1760-1794), was one of the inner circle of Girondin leaders. He was a very close friend

threaten the Conventionals in their constitutional work, proposed measures to guarantee a relative degree of order in Paris. At the session of September 24, he remarked that, only recently returned to the capital after an absence of some months,[40] he was surprised by the growing turbulence in Paris. A stranger to the recent uprisings in the city,[41] he said he had arrived with the confidence that he would be able to preserve the independence of his soul.[42] He saw that it would require effort to maintain this independence, however. Whilst expressing faith that Monsieur Roland, the Minister of the Interior, was capable of preserving order, he still thought that legislation should be passed to safeguard the Conventionals. The recent political trends in Paris were alarming, thought Buzot. He, personally, did not choose to become the slave of those Parisian deputies who were beginning to assume too much authority. Moreover, like every other honest deputy, he would think of the interests of all France, and not of those of Paris alone.

Buzot proposed three measures which were eagerly adopted by the then-Girondin-dominated Convention. The most important, and the one which naturally alarmed the capital-centered Montagnard leaders, was that which provided for a committee of six to make a study of, and give a report on, the necessity of an armed force (representative of all eighty-three departments) to

of Madame Roland, and sometimes her adviser on matters of state. At the Convention (as a deputy of l'Eure) he almost rivaled Vergniaud in the number of speeches he delivered. He also rivaled him in the number of pointed references which he made to the suspicious actions of Robespierre.

40. Buzot had been a member of the Constituent Assembly, serving as a representative of the Third State for the constituency of Evreux. During the period of the Legislative Assembly he remained at Evreux, where he held the position of president of the criminal court. After August 10 he was given the opportunity to return to Paris again; he was elected a deputy from the department of Eure to the Convention.

41. Those of August 10 and September 2-3, 1792.

42. *Débats de la Convention nationale,* I, 29-30.

protect the meeting place of the people's representatives. This same committee was to report on the state of the whole republic, with especial reference to the position of the capital. It was to prepare a law aimed against any individual or individuals who organized or encouraged rebellion in opposition to the republic.[43]

Buzot's measures, which manifested an open suspicion of Paris, also revealed, without mentioning names, a suspicion of those who would seek to usurp authority through control of the unruly elements in the capital. The following day, September 25, in a session full of surprises, the names of suspect persons were actually given. Merlin (de Thionville), deputy from Moselle, bluntly stated that he would like to know the identities of those seeking dictatorship. He said that Marc David Lasource, representative from Tarn, had told him there were men in the Convention with such guilty ambitions. Lasource somewhat feebly denied Merlin's assertions. He did say, however, that he had heard two-thirds of the Convention denounced as wishing to crush the true friends of liberty. In Lasource's opinion, the people of Paris were essentially honest and trustworthy. He did not see the need of an armed guard for the deputies. The people were not to be feared. The ones to fear were those wretches who pretended to be the only true friends of the people.[44] The mention of the position of Paris in the political picture caused Buzot to take the floor.

Paris, said the irrepressible Buzot, should be reduced in political importance to the same proportion as each of the eighty-two other departments.[45] As to any potential dictators, said Buzot, he would denounce them as soon as he had enough definite proof. François Rebecqui, a Conventional from Boucher-du-Rhône, who followed Buzot as a speaker, caused a sensation when he bluntly asserted that it was Maximilien Robespierre who had desires of being a dictator.[46] After the tumult caused by Rebecqui's remarks had

43. *Ibid.,* I, 30-31.
44. *Débats de la Convention nationale,* I, 32-33.
45. *Ibid.,* I, 33-34.
46. *Ibid.,* I, 35.

died down, Danton quickly jumped to his feet and said that the whole Paris deputation should not be accused of unworthy ambition because of the actions of a few. With great sincerity, it appears, he stated that as a deputy he belonged to the entire nation, and not to Paris alone.[47] Moreover, he wanted it understood that there was no connection between himself and that political untouchable, Marat, who, as the editor of *L'Ami du Peuple*, hinted at times for the need of a strong man. Danton affirmed his republicanism by asking the death penalty for any attempted dictatorship. It was at this juncture that Robespierre, the number-one man of the Paris delegation, arose and said he would like to answer Rebecqui's charges.

Robespierre protested his innocence and public virtue. After considerable tangential asides (during which there were constant complaints for him to shorten his dialogue and get to the point), the Montagnard chief said he could not make a simple denial of Rebecqui's charges. Such an accusation was a crime against the public welfare.[48] His enemies were trying to calumniate him in the eyes of the people.[49] Moreover, they were seeking to lower the esteem of the citizens in the departments for Paris, the capital. It was only at Paris that one could gain an accurate political picture. Here, at least, the populace could attend assembly meetings and form their own opinions. In the departments they could only read newspapers, which distorted the truth. Robespierre displayed his fear of the recently appointed investigating committee.[50] And at the same time, he showed his distrust of any Girondin-dominated commissions, when he stated there was too much reference to committees. The whole Convention, charged with constructing an important constitutional edifice, ought to do as much of the work as possible. Government could not be a monopoly of a few individuals without compromising the interests of the people.

47. *Ibid.*, I, 36-37.
48. *Ibid.*, I, 39-42.
49. *Ibid.*, I, 43.
50. Refer to pp. 166-167.

He shrugged off charges of his own dictatorial ambitions by saying that the enlightened French citizenry would themselves take care of any would-be-dictator.[51] Robespierre had scarcely finished his protestations of honesty when he and, for that matter, the whole Convention were surprised by the sudden ascent to the speaker's platform of Barbaroux,[52] one of the more important Girondin deputies.

51. *Débats de la Convention national*, I, 44-45.
52. Barbaroux, Charles Jean Marie (1767-1794), was one of the younger and more versatile of the Girondins. He had been educated in law as well as in the sciences. As a devotee of science, he had once studied optometry, under Dr. Marat, the man whom he was later to denounce for his advocacy of a dictatorship.

Prior to his being elected a representative to the Convention from the department of Bouches-du-Rhône, he had held several local offices in the city of Marseilles. He was noted for his republican spirit and ambitions. He was one of the chief instigators responsible for the march of the Marseilles battalion to Paris (a battalion of National Guardsmen that played an important part in the events of August 10).

No deputy was more zealous than Barbaroux, as a member of the Convention, in defending the cause of the republic. He early suspected the designs of Robespierre and the men of the Paris Revolutionary Commune. He vigorously denounced them at the Convention and, with Buzot, proposed steps to definitely thwart all threats to representative government. Because of his attacks against those who wanted to make Paris dominant, and because of his close association with the Rolands (who were viewed by the Montagnard leaders as chiefs of the Federalist movement), he was accused of being a Federalist. Along with other leading Girondins, Barbaroux was to suffer in their gradual eclipse of power between September, 1792, and May, 1793. A marked man because of his attempted course of action against Robespierre, Marat, and other Montagnard chiefs, he was to undergo the fate of most of the important Girondins. His name was on the purge

Barbaroux sustained the charges of Rebecqui. He related to the constituent body that he had had knowledge of Robespierre's ambitions even before August 10. A few days before that significant date, at a gathering at the Montagnard leader's residence, Panis, later to be a Parisian delegate to the Convention,[53] had pointed out Robespierre to Barbaroux as "the virtuous man who ought to be dictator of France."[54] Barbarous said he was willing to sign an

lists of May 31 and June 2, 1793. He attempted to evade the clutches of his enemies by fleeing to the south of France. After leading the unhappy existence of a fugitive for over a year, he was finally captured by the Robespierrists at Bordeaux. He was tried and executed on June 25, 1794.

53. Panis (1757-1832) was one of the Parisian officials who helped prepare the way for Robespierre's authoritarian state. A municipal official, he was active in the events of August 10, 1792. Probably through personal ambition, he supported the rise of Robespierre. He knew of the latter's desire to make Paris the most important and powerful city in France. As a member of the Paris Committee of Surveillance, along with Robespierre and Marat (the latter of whom he personally appointed to the Committee on September 2, 1792), he seems to have been rather high-handed in his actions during the bloody days of the September Massacres. Municipal archives were illegally broken into and confiscated. Panis authorized illegal arrests. He permitted false witnesses to testify in the local courts. His name was found on a circular which Marat sent to all the departments, asking them to take the same bloody actions as the capital in suppressing alleged traitors. The extent of Panis' connection with Robespierre is hard to ascertain to an exact degree. However, he was one of the first to mention his name as being the man to lead France. Moreover, through the aid of Robespierre he was one of the twenty-four Parisian delegates elected to the Convention. Finally, as indicated, Panis as a municipal official certainly promoted the interests of the powerful leader of the Mountain.

54. *Débats de la Convention national*, I, 46.

affidavit as to the truth of his testimony. Panis denied ever having made such a statement and asked the Girondin to produce witnesses. He was considerably nonplussed when Rebecqui dramatically took the stand and, striking his chest with both hands, loudly shouted, "I am his witness."[55]

Besides denouncing Robespierre, Barbaroux pointed out the suspicious actions of the Parisian extra-legal bodies that had sprung up since August 10. By inference he connected the actions of these bodies with the plot of the Montagnard chief to seize the reins of government. A dictatorship already existed, said Barbaroux, when a disorganizing commune could send commissioners into all parts of the republic and dare to command that other communes join the extra-legal one of Paris. Moreover, the Paris Revolutionary Commune[56] had had the boldness to issue warrants of arrest against deputies of the Legislative Assembly immediately after the events of August 10.[57] Such a state of affairs should not be allowed to

55. *Ibid.*, I, 50. Two Conventionals, Durand-Maillane and Meillan, in their memoirs corroborated the accusations of Barbaroux and Rebecqui. They both agreed that it was certain that from August 10, 1792, on, Robespierre aspired to personal power. According to Durand-Maillane, the Montagnard chief's henchmen worked from this date at the Jacobin Club and other Paris societies to gain converts to the idea of dictatorship. (Durand-Maillane, *op. cit.*, pp. 129-130.) Meillan said that he had ample proof of Robespierre's aims from Barbaroux, an acquaintance of his. He supported this hearsay evidence with the following little anecdote. He happened to be at a reception one day where Barbaroux and Robespierre were also in attendance. Barbaroux brashly accused Robespierre point-blank of seeking absolute power. Robespierre appeared to deny the charge with too much passion to make his denial genuine, thought Meillan. (Meillan, *op. cit.*, pp. 9-10.)

56. Refer to p. 146.

57. *Débats de la Convention national*, I, 46-47. A warrant of arrest had been issued against Brissot, The Revolutionary

continue, asserted Barbaroux. The Conventionals should hasten to pass laws which would protect the sanctuary of the people's representatives by providing an armed guard composed of soldiers chosen from all the departments.[58] In conclusion, the Girondin deputy pleaded for Robespierre to recognize his faults and become again the honest citizen they had all once loved and esteemed.

The statements of Buzot, Rebecqui, and Barbaroux encouraged other Girondin deputies to mention what they believed to be suspicious actions on the part of Robespierre since August 10. Jacques Boilleau, representative of Yonne, said that while serving as a member of the electoral assembly of Auxerre, he had witnessed the arrival of commissioners in that city from the Paris Commune. They came in pursuance of a plan to unify all French communes with that of the capital, Boilleau alleged.[59] Cambon,[60] deputy from

Communal authorities later said that this had been a mistake and apologized.

58. *Loc. cit.*
59. *Ibid.*, I, 48.
60. Cambon, Pierre Joseph (1756-1820), because of his keen knowledge of finance, served on various financial committees of the Legislative Assembly and the Convention. Although he was not affiliated with either the Girondins or the Montagnards, his ideals were similar, it appears, to those championed by the former group. During the days immediately following the king's flight to Varennes, Cambon, then president of the Jacobin Club of Montpelier, had written a plea for a republic which was so dynamic and timely that many copies of it were printed and sent to all the popular societies in France. During the early period of the Convention, Cambon joined the Girondins in denouncing the tyrannical actions of the Paris Commune and in condemning it for its open promotion of dictatorship. In the struggle between the Girondins and the Montagnards he remained neutral, trying to iron out differences between them. After the downfall of the Girondins, although cool in his relations with Robespierre, he nevertheless maintained an important position because of

Hérault, an independent in politics and known for his honesty, said that he had seen municipal commissioners in Paris take possession of public funds and records without even leaving receipts. The Girondin leader, Brissot, asked Panis, who had been Paris police commissioner during the exciting days following August 10, what right he had to issue warrants of arrest against deputies of the Legislative Assembly.[61] Panis said that he was compelled to do this in order to save his own neck. In regard to the attempted arrest of Brissot, Panis excused himself by saying he had sent police officials to the Girondin chief's home in order to protect him.[62]

Vergniaud, the greatest of the Girondin orators, spoke eloquently about the suspicious actions of the Robespierrists since August 10. In addition, he produced a circular letter, dated September 3, 1792, that was signed by Marat. This letter, which had been sent to all the departments, was but a tissue of lies directed against real republicans, accused Vergniaud. It was part of a plot to join all the communes of France with the Revolutionary one of Paris. In it, the claim was made that the new Paris Commune had prevented plots against the government. Moreover, it had been given extraordinary power by the Legislative Assembly to govern France during the emergency. Paris was to be a concentric authority around which the departments were to rally. An accusation of

his great reputation as a financial expert. He was a member of the Committee of Public Safety. He was also a member of the Committee of Finance. Cambon was unique in that he was able to live and enjoy a certain amount of power during the dark days of the Terror. In the years following the Ninth Thermidor, Cambon never again approached the power he had had prior to, and even during, the days of Robespierre's sway. He was one of the lost generation of republicans who actually lived through a return to authoritarianism and, finally, even witnessed a return of the hated Bourbons.

61. *Débats de la Convention nationale*, I, 53.
62. *Loc. cit.*

Robespierre, to the effect that Brissot, Condorcet, Guadet, and Vergniaud had wanted to turn France over to the Duke of Brunswick, the man who was leading the forces of the enemy against France, was also inserted in the letter.[63] This seems to have been a very strange accusation to make against men who had written and spoken for republicanism for a number of years now. Perhaps we should remember that the French Revolution was a period of innovation in modern European history. At the same time that it introduced certain advanced principles along political, economic, and social lines, it introduced political tactics that might subvert these very principles. Rumor, innuendo, character assassination, whispering campaigns, and the like, were tactics applied by some members of all Revolutionary factions.

The last testimony by deputy Boilleau on September 25 was one which aroused the whole Convention. Deputies jumped to their feet and shouted for indictments against Marat and Robespierre. Boilleau read an article written by Marat which had appeared some days before in Marat's newspaper, L'Ami du Peuple. In the article Marat had bemoaned the fact that all his recent efforts to "save the people" had not led to a new insurrection. He had prophesied that France would face fifty years of anarchy if the bases of a constitution were not laid in the first eight sessions of the Convention. At this point, Boilleau interrupted his reading to claim that this was impossible and that Marat knew it. Continuing his reading, Boilleau soon came to the part where the editor of L'Ami du Peuple deliberately asked for a dictator to save France from

63.　Ibid., I, 60. Brissot had answered the slander in a notice which had been inserted on page one of the Moniteur (universel) for September 7, 1792. He viewed this defamation of character as one so contemptible as hardly to warrant an answer. It was well known, said Brissot, that he had always been the enemy of kings and not waited until 1789 to manifest his hate. "He the partisan of a duke! He had rather die a thousand deaths than ever to recognize a despot!" (Moniteur universel, September 7, 1792.)

pending anarchy. This was a bit more than the Girondin-dominated Convention could take. Cries of "To the Abbaye!" (prison) or "To the guillotine!" were heard from all sides. Marat, sardonic and cool, as he usually was, boldly took the stand. Far from disavowing the writing, he said he was proud to admit its authorship. It has been written ten days ago in a moment of passion, said Marat, when he had been indignant at the way unfaithful deputies were elected to the Convention. The ones he viewed as particularly unfaithful were those connected with that faction called Girondin, he concluded.[64] This remark was received with a roar by the deputies of opposite views. Boilleau asked for the arrest of Marat. The "people's friend" intensified the drama by suddenly pulling a pistol from his pocket and pointing it at his pock-marked temple. He threatened to kill himself on the spot if the Convention dared to arrest him. The day was saved for Marat and perhaps, Robespierre, when a representative from the department of Seineet-Oise, Tallien,[65] pleaded opportunely and sucessfully for the Convention to cease occupying itself with individuals and turn its attentions to matters of state.[66]

Marat apparently did not frighten very easily. With his encouragement and that of fellow deputy Panis, a deputation from the Paris Committee of Surveillance[67] appeared before the Convention

64. *Débats de la Convention nationale,* I, 61-63; *Moniteur universel,* September 27, 1792.

65. Jean Lambert Tallien (1767-1820) had been the chief secretary of the Paris Revolutionary Commune between August 10 and the opening of the Convention. Important during the Terror as a rather unsavory Montagnard proconsul, he was one of the plotters against his own chief on the Ninth Thermidor. Finally, like Fouché, who masterminded the coup, he was clever enough to survive the various reactions following the overthrow of Robespierre.

66. *Débats de la Convention nationale,* I, 63.

67. This committee had figured prominently in the events of the capital since August 10. Its main function seemed to be that

on October 1. Marat and Panis had been members of this committee. The deputation claimed to have papers taken from the municipal archives[68] which showed who the real traitors of the country were. The inference was that the names of some Girondins were to be found in these papers guiltily linked with those of former royalist officials. A commission was named immediately by the Convention to examine all these papers and prepare an analysis of them.[69] A few days later the chairman of the commission made a report to the Convention. It was the finding of the commission, said the chairman, that the evidence presented had been submitted only with the purpose of defaming honest citizens. It would show that those offering this material, supposed to be damaging to the character of important Girondins, were more at fault than the ones they sought to accuse.[70] The president of the Convention at the time, Jean Michel Lacroix, said that it was his opinion that certain individuals had presented the material only for the purpose of obstructionism.[71] A deputy, Lecoint-Puyraveau, said this was but part of Marat's plan to excite Paris against the people's representatives. He added that Marat's newsboys were already crying about the streets that a great plot of the Brissotin (Girondin) faction has been discovered.[72]

Not discouraged by the commission's report, Marat arose to defend his opinions. After the usual difficulties encountered when-

of aiding the police department. Any information of a nature deemed to be useful to the new authorities of Paris was obtained, legally or illegally, and analyzed by this body. Like other extra-legal Parisian bodies of the time, it had become a tool of Robespierre.

68. The Revolutionary Commune which superseded the regular municipal government after August 10 appropriated all the archives of the former communal government.

69. *Débats de la Convention nationale*, I, 101.

70. *Ibid.*, I, 110.

71. *Ibid.*, I, 113.

72. *Ibid.*, I, 115-116.

ever he tried to speak,[73] he finally was able to say a few words. A dangerous faction did exist, said Marat. He named as its leaders the deputies from Gironde. Specifically the names of Brissot, Guadet, Vergniaud, and Lasource were mentioned. It was this faction which had proposed a disastrous war and was now demanding the suppression of the Paris Revolutionary Commune, the agency which had saved France on August 10.[74]

Charges and counter-charges continued to be hurled by members of the two dynamic Conventional factions. Girondins kept asking for a Conventional guard[75] to prevent a coup d'état by the Robespierrists. The Robespierrist countered with charges that the Girondins were "Federalists." This title had been effectively used already

73. Marat was never a very popular man in the Convention. Whenever he spoke he was constantly interrupted by hoots and howls and sarcastic remarks. On this occasion (October 4) he was greeted with the following comment pertaining to his popularity: "Marat is not worth the money he costs France. Since Paris has inflicted the torture of Marat upon us, I guess that we will have to listen to him." At one point in his speech Marat, in a spirit of benevolence, said that he regarded the majority in the Convention as being pure. Several deputies qualified this statement for him by adding, "With the exception of yourself." (*Ibid.*, I, 118-120.)

74. *Ibid.*, I, 121.

75. Buzot renewed his plea for a guard at the October 8 meeting of the Convention. Such a guard, he said, chosen from all the departments and changed with each successive legislative assembly, would prevent tyranny and dictatorship. He observed that the only ones who did not want a guard were "those men born of political upsets who, like reptiles, came out of the ground in times of storm." These individuals "needed anarchy in order to dominate." (*Ibid.*, I, 129-131.) Brissot gave great publicity to this speech of Buzot in the *Patriote français* for October 9, 1792. (Ellery, *Brissot de Warville: A Study in the History of the French Revolution* [Boston, 1915], p. 307.)

against Girondin leaders at the time of the Paris elections for deputies to the Convention.[76] The word, which then had been interpreted in such a way as to mean something aristocratic, was so interpreted again.[77] By dint of its constant repetition, and its association with the idea of a diminution of power for the capital, the Montagnards were ultimately to create amongst the multitudes of Paris suspicion and hate against the Girondins.[78] When Girondin leaders became too vociferous in their complaints about Robespierrists' ambitions, their opponents threw back at them the accusation of being Federalists.

76. It was due largely to this charge that Brissot and Condorcet were not elected deputies to represent Paris, a city which formerly had been the scene of all their triumphs.

77. The comments of one contemporary and one near-contemporary of the Revolution *à propos* the name "Federalist" reveal the importance which they attached to its use by the Montagnards. Leon Thiessé, in his introduction to the *Débats de la Convention nationale* (vol. I, p. XIII), said that it was so used by the Montagnards that the Parisian multitudes not only began to fear federated republics but actually believed that they were something akin to monarchy. Durand-Maillane, himself a member of the Convention, said that it was by accusing the Girondins of being Federalists that Robespierre finally was able to overcome them. (Durand-Maillane, *op. cit.*, p. 7.)

78. "By the calling of names such as 'Federalist' or 'calumniator of Paris,' they sought to build up public opinion against honest people." (*Mémoires de Madame Roland* [ed. by Perroud, Cl., Paris, 1905], I, 99-100.) Madame Roland believed that it was one Jean Baptiste Cloots (a German nobleman who gave up title and fortune to became a citizen of the French Republic. Having an international viewpoint, he dreamed and wrote about a universal republic with "all men belonging to one nation, with free and unrestricted commerce between them." Elected a deputy from Oise to the Convention, he was kept by his extremist views from being grouped with either the Girondins or Montagnards) who first

At the stormy session of September 25, when Robespierre had been openly accused of wanting to be a dictator, he had apparently sought to direct attention from himself by asserting that his opponents were Federalists. When the revolutionary government (Commune) of Paris was censured, said the Montagnard leader, he and his followers immediately suspected that certain persons wished to make France a mass of federated republics. This would cause disunity and, possibly, civil war.[79] Robespierre was using arguments which he had already presented at the Jacobin Club of Paris, which was now one of his main strongholds of power.[80] Chabot, speaking there a few days before, had argued that a federal government might suit America with its small population, but not France with a population of millions. In a federation there

charged the Girondins with being Federalists. Naïvely she attributed Cloots' action to the fact that his pride was wounded by her studied disrespect of him. Whenever he happened to be present at any of her little dinner parties, she always served him last. (*Ibid.*, I, 107.) More practically, however, Madame Roland claimed that the Montagnards made use of the charge to besmirch the character of the Girondins. They feared the unity that republicans were trying to bring about, she alleged. After the events of August 10, Monsieur Roland, Minister of the Interior, sent thousands of circulars to the departments which justified the end of monarchy, advocated the forming of schools to teach republicanism and encouraged the formation of correspondence societies. "Suspicious and jealous men saw in the triumph of liberty and the affirmation of the republic an end to their intrigues," said the Minister's wife. (*Ibid.*, I, 122-125.)

79. *Débats de la Convention*, I, 44.
80. By now the Jacobin Club of Paris was a well disciplined body under Robespierre's will. Speaking of its importance at this period, Durand-Maillane said that nothing was proposed at the Convention by the Montagnards which had not first been discussed at the Jacobin Club. (Durand-Maillane, *op. cit.*, p. 59.)

was always danger that the separate parts might not cooperate in time of need. As an example of this, he cited the lack of cooperation among the colonies during the American Revolution. With strange distortion of truth, he said that federalism was tending towards monarchy in America. Congress, said Chabot, had originally conferred the presidency on Washington for two years. Now (after his re-election) they were making him ruler for life. The reason for these arguments was revealed when Chabot said that with a federal government one could not be sure that Paris would be the capital. "Paris must be the center of the government," said this Jacobin, who, like Robespierre, knew where the Montagnards could depend on their strongest support.[81]

Brissot, being the recognized leader of the Girondins, was naturally subject to many attacks. His denunciations in the *Patriote français* against the Paris Commune, for its undue interference with legal authorities, were becoming more bothersome every day. Perhaps as one means of checking him, the Robespierrists said that his pleas for equality amongst all the departments, which he frequently made, were simply another way of promoting feder-

81. Aulard, François V. Alphonse, ed., *La Société des Jacobins: Récueil de Documents pour l'Histoire du Club des Jacobins de Paris* (6 vols., Paris, 1891-1892), IV, 275-277. The probable reason why Chabot used the example of the United States as an argument against federalism was that the Girondin leaders were constantly lauding the American form of government in their speeches and writings. In fact, on one occasion, Buzot defended federalism by referring to the Greek republics in ancient times and the Republic of the United States in his own time as being practical samples of federal government. (*Mémoires de Madame Roland* [ed. by Perroud, Cl.], I, 108.) Brissot's great admiration for the system of government of the United States was well known through the medium of his writings. He always upheld the United States as having the ideal type of administration. (Ellery, *op. cit.*, p. 348.)

alism.[82] Actually, at the opening of the Convention, Brissot had informed Robespierre that he had always been opposed to a system of federated republics.[83] As he made clear in a pamphlet appearing a bit later, his idea of a republican system of government was one whereby each of the eighty-three departments would be coordinated with all the others. All would have their central point of control in a national assembly.[84]

On October 10, 1792, Brissot suffered the humiliation of being voted out of the Jacobin Club. In justification of this step, the Paris society sent to all affiliated societies a circular listing charges against the head of the Girondins. One was that he was a half-hearted republican. The other accusations were that he had calumniated Paris, had been a close friend of La Fayette, had temporized with the king, and had injured the country by bringing on a foreign war.[85] Brissot's answers to these allegations were given in a pamphlet which was published in the latter part of October, 1792.

In answer to the charges made against him, Brissot was short and to the point. His republicanism, he said, was too well known to require much comment. Kings and other members of royalty had been his supreme hate since he first began to reason.[86] If he had ever been friendly to La Fayette, it was only because he believed that the man who fought for republicanism in the New World would also support it in the Old. (La Fayette had recently deserted his army command and fled across the border.) As to his bringing on a foreign war, Brissot was proud to be accused of this. If it had not been for the war, they would still have a king.[87]

82. At the time of his trial, some months later, he was accused of being the leader of the mythical "Federalists." (Ellery, *op. cit.*, p. 347.)

83. Brissot, J. P., *À Tous les Républicains de France; sur la Société des Jacobins de Paris* (Paris, 1792), p. 26.

84. *Ibid.*, p. 25.

85. Aulard, ed., *La Société des Jacobins*, IV, 377-378.

86. Brissot, *À Tous les Republicains*, p. 14.

87. *Ibid.*, p. 8.

Brissot had quite a bit to say about the men whom he called "disorganizers" and "intriguers." It was these men who tried to invest a municipality with all the national power. It was they who made use of the phrase "sovereignty of the people" only in order to carry on with impunity against it.[88] Moreover, they dared to preach political equality of departments, when, in fact, they raised Paris above all the others. Then they raised themselves above Paris! A constitution was not desired by these disorganizers. They wanted more bloodshed and revolution.[89] It was almost superfluous to mention the names of the intriguers. They were to be found on any of Marat's placards, stuck on practically any wall of the capital. To be specific, their names were Robespierre, Marat, Chabot, and Collot d'Herbois.[90] These "anarchists" often used the phrase "Brissotine" or "Girondin faction" to frighten the people and to detract attention from their own faction. Yes, said Brissot, he was willing to admit that he was congenially associated with a group of men.[91] It was these men whose principles had proved to be the right ones when France had proclaimed a republic on September 21. They had prepared the way for August 10.

Where were the Robespierrists on the memorable day in which the king was removed, asked Brissot? He then gave the answer. Robespierre and Marat were in mortal fear on August 10. They were conspicuous by their absence from any site of action. The victories of that day were attributed by the Girondin leader to the action of the National Guardsmen and the decrees of the Legislative Assembly.[92] Now Robespierre and his followers were seeking to derive profit from the achievement of others.

88. *Ibid.*, pp. 5-6.
89. *Ibid.*, pp. 6-7.
90. *Ibid.*, p. 7.
91. The Girondin chief said that he was proud of his acquaintanceship with men like Guadet, Vergniaud, Ducos, and Gensonné. He thanked heaven for the honor of being united to them. (*Ibid.*, p. 11.)
92. Refer to pp. 146-147.

Brissot concluded his brochure by saying that he was glad that his name had been removed from the rolls of the Jacobins. It had lost its identity as a fraternal society and a foyer of instruction. It was now but a tool for conspirators and a place where false charges were made against honest citizens. As to a recent accusation that the Girondins wanted to make a constitution only in order to monopolize the governmental positions, his answer was that the constitution would be based on a system of frequent rotations of office and popular elections. With these two principles, there could be no factions or intriguers. He prayed that the constitution would be finished before next spring.[93]

In asking for quick completion of the constitution, Brissot was voicing the sentiments of most of the Conventionals. They were eager to finish the work which had been assigned them, a task to which they looked forward with some anticipation. Since the opening of the Convention, there had been deputies who expressed the hope that France would soon have its republican constitution. Indeed, the day after the formal proclamation of the end of monarchy and the beginning of the French Republic, deputy Tallien had stated his desire of seeing the constitution completed within six months.[94] About a week later (on September 29, 1792), after a few expressions of differences of opinion, it was finally decreed that the constitutional committee would be made up of nine members.[95] When the committee had finished preparing

93. Brissot, *À Tous les Républicains*, pp. 42-43.
94. Frayssinet, Marc, *La République des Girondins* (Toulouse, 1904), p. 31.
95. The consensus of opinion amongst the Conventionals was that the committee should be small. If there were too many members, the Convention might be presented with a bulky, ill-planned charter, believed Cambon. Kersaint said that if they had men of the caliber of J. J Rousseau, Solon, or Lycurgus, they would need only three members. (*Archives parlementaires, 1787-1860: Recueil complèt des Débats des Chambres françaises* [ed. by Mavidal, Jérôme, Laurent, Émile, and

a constitution, it was to be presented *en masse* to the whole Convention for discussion. The committee would see that each deputy of the constituent body was given a printed copy of the charter as an aid to discussion.[96]

Despite the need for hurry, a motion was made and carried that there would be no debates over the constitution for at least two months after presentation by the committee. This, it was believed, would permit its examination and criticism by all the enlightened minds of Europe.[97] The desire to make a real people's charter, in which the people themselves had some part, was nicely expressed a few days latter by Bertrand Barère when he said, "The constitution of a great republic cannot be the work of a few minds; it must be the work of many."[98] Barère was then speaking in the name of the recently appointed Constitutional Committee (October 11, 1792) of which he was a member. This group, containing a galaxy of noted French republican names, is entitled to a chapter apart.

others, series I, 1787-1799, 82 vols., Paris, 1879-1913; series II, 1800-1860, 137 vols., Paris, 1862-1913], LII, 232.)

96. *Procès-verbal de la Convention national* (72 vols., Paris, 1792-1796), I, 117.

97. *Archives parlementaires*, LII, 232.

98. *Ibid.*, LII, 577. A like feeling had been manifested at the Jacobin Club over a month before. A proposal by a Monsieur Gerbet, to the effect that all citizens be invited to appear before the club and state their views on a constitution, had been decreed. (Aulard, ed., *La Société des Jacobins*, IV, 204.)

Chapter V

The First French Republican
Constitutional Committee

In the appointment of its first constitutional committee, the Convention appears to have made a selection of distinguished men. The names of some of the men selected (on October 11, 1792) were names not only famous in French republican circles; they were also well known amongst the enlightened elements of both the New and the Old Worlds. The members were chosen in the following order: First, the regulars — Emmanuel Joseph Siéyès, Thomas Paine, Jacques Pierre Brissot, Jerome Pétion, Pierre Victurnien Vergniaud, Armand Gensonné, Bertrand Barère, Georges Jacques Danton, and, last but certainly not least, Marie Jean Antoine Nicolas Caritat (better known as the Marquis de Condorcet). The supernumeraries were: Charles Jean Marie Barbaroux, Marie Jean Hérault de Séchelles, Francois Xavier Lanthenas, Jean Antoine Joseph de Bry, Claude Fauchet, and Louis Thomas Hebert de Lavicomterie.[1] Of the nine regulars, six were considered as belonging to the Girondins (or Brissotines). These were Paine, Brissot, Petion, Vergniaud, Gensonné and Condorcet.[2] Danton and Barère

1. *Archives parlementaires 1787-1880: Recueil Complèt des Débats des Chambres françaises* (ed. by Mavidal, Jérôme; Laurent, Émile, and others, series I, 1787-1799, 82 vols., Paris, 1879-1913; series II, 1800-1860, 137 vols., Paris, 1862-1913), series I, vol. LII, 455. Hereafter to be cited as *Archives parlementaires* (volume and page).

2. The question of Condorcet's political affiliations has already been discussed. Refer to p. 131, note 38. The eminent philosopher often expressed the desire of being considered a member of no political group. Through his friendships and ideals, how-

were classed with the Montagnards (or Robespierrists). Siéyès
was not classified with any group. Of the six supernumeraries,
Barbaroux, Lanthenas, and Fauchet were regarded as Girondins.
De Bry, Hérault de Séchelles, and Lavicomterie were independents
in politics, being affiliated with no faction.

Out of the fifteen committee members, then, nine were Girondins.[3]
In so far as the majority of the Conventionals belonged to or
supported this party[4] at the time, the composition was probably
neither unjust nor illogical. The Robespierrists were not satisfied
with the make-up of the committee, however. Objections were
voiced at the Jacobin Club. There were sarcastic remarks as to the
"nice arrangement" of the committee. One individual asserted that
now "everyone's eyes were opened."[5] At the suggestion of Danton,
who personally had no ill-will against the Brissotines,[6] the Paris

> ever, he was inevitably drawn to those men who appeared to be
> working most diligently for the cause of representative
> government — the Girondins. Yet both major political factions
> liked to believe him one of them; in the words of Alengry,
> they wanted "to shelter themselves behind his illustrious
> name." (Alengry, Franck, *Condorcet: Guide de la Révolution
> française: Théoricien du Droit constitutionnel et Précurseur
> de la Science sociale* [Paris, 1904], p. 191.) At the Jacobin
> Club (on October 12, 1792), Chabot took exception to a
> comment made by a member that the philosopher was rightly
> included in the Girondin-controlled constitutional committee.
> Condorcet was no longer associated with the Brissotines, said
> Chabot. (Aulard, ed., *La Société des Jacobins de Paris:
> Récueil de Documents pour l'Histoire du Club des Jacobins de
> Paris* [6 vols., Paris, 1891-1892], IV, 383.) Hereafter to be
> cited as Aulard, ed., *La Société des Jacobins* (volume and
> page).

3. Alengry, *op. cit.*, p. 190.
4. In regard to the use of the word "party," refer to p. 129,
   note 36.
5. Aulard, *op. cit.*, IV, 382.
6. From the end of the Legislative Assembly until as late as
   March, 1793, Danton tried to bring about a reconciliation

Jacobin Club decreed (on October 14, 1792) that it would form a constitutional committee of its own.[7] The exact purpose of this auxiliary committee was not stated. Presumably it was to act as a guide and advisory body to the Montagnard deputies in any ensuing constitutional debates at the Convention.[8]

between the Montagnards and the Girondins. At the time of the Paris elections for Conventionals, he proposed that both factions name an equal number of deputies to comprise the Paris delegation. At one time or another Brissot and Condorcet had shown that they trusted Danton above all the other Montagnards. After the proscription of the Girondins (in May and June, 1793), he was genuinely concerned over the fate of the ostracized. Tears even came into his eyes when he thought of their fate. He complained to a friend about the fact that he had not been able to affect some sort of a reconciliation. (*"Memoires de Garat," Histoire parlementaire de la Révolution française ou Journal des Assemblées nationales depuis 1789 jusqu'en 1815* [ed. by Buchez, P. B., and Roux, P. C., 40 vols., Paris, 1834-1838], XVIII.) One historian, perhaps with oversimplification, attributed the failure of Danton to bring about a truce to the terrible enmity felt against him by Madame Roland. The female confidante of the Girondins could never forgive the man who, unlike her husband, figured so prominently in the events of August 10, 1792. (Frayssinet, Març., *La République des Girondins* [Toulouse, 1904], p. 62.)

7. Aulard, ed., *La Société des Jacobins*, IV, 386.
8. The names of those appointed to the Jacobin committee (on October 17, 1792) were: Jean Maris Collot d'Herbois, Jacques Nicolas Billaud-Varenne, François Chabot, Georges Auguste Couthon, Georges Jacques Danton, and Maximilien Robespierre. These men, especially Robespierre, not only led the Paris Jacobins; they were also the most important of the Montagnards. At a later date, on February 18, 1793, there was a fresh election in which two of the six original members were temporarily eliminated, two were permanently eliminated, and six new members were added. The composition of the reshuffled committee was: Jeanbon Saint-André, Pierre

Constitutional debates were not to be on the calendar of the Convention for some months to come. As has already been mentioned, it had been decreed that there were to be no formal discussions on the charter for at least two months after its presentation by the committee.[9] Although it was to France's interest to have a constitution as soon as possible, no date was fixed upon which the committee should finish its work. Little was heard from the fifteen experts on government during the interval between their appointment on October 11, 1792, and the day on which the Convention was notified that a constitution was completed at last.

On February 15, 1793, Condorcet, the Committee's editor, presented a remarkable frame of government which has been dubbed the "Girondin Constitution of 1793." The presumption is that during the four-month period the committee had followed a regular plan of work in fulfilling its assigned task. Yet its place of meeting,[10] the discussions of members, and their degree of respon-

> François Joseph Robert, Jacques Alexis Thuriot, Pierre Louis Bentabole, Maximilien Robespierre, Jacques Nicolas Billaud-Varenne, François Paul Nicolas Anthoine, and Louis Antoine Saint-Just. This committee was finally completed (on February 18, 1793) by the re-election of Collot d'Herbois and Couthon and the election of Edmond Louis Alexis Dubois-Crancé and Jean Baptiste du Val de Grace Cloots.

9. Refer to p. 184.

10. It appears that Madame Roland, close friend and adviser of some of the Girondin committee members (Petion, Gensonné, and Barbaroux), did not have the privilege of opening her home to those entrusted with the creation of a republican charter. Condorcet, mainstay of the fifteen, much preferred that they meet either at the home of Julie Talma (wife of the great actor) or at his own home, presided over by his charming and intelligent wife, the former Sophie de Grouchy. The mild and unassuming philosopher, recognized as one of the greatest minds of the day, was not one to be dominated by the inquisitive and somewhat shrewish Roland woman. (Frayssinet, *op. cit.*, pp. 65-67.) The Revolutionary Aspasia

sibility for certain parts of the constitution must be partly con-
jectured. It is surprising that of all the Revolutionary committees
this particularly important one should not have left a clearer
record as its activities. However, by a study of memoirs and other
materials of the time, many of the more bothersome gaps can
be filled in.

Fifteen men were appointed to prepare France's first republican
frame of government — all capable men who seem to have been
selected because of their believed expert understanding of governmental principles. However, as far as can be learned, out of the
fifteen only three, possibly four, actually participated in the creation
of the charter which emanated from the committee on February 15,
1793. Of these four the work of one stood out far above that of
the others. This was the work of Condorcet, last of the *philosophes*,
whose writings for democracy and republicanism, before and after
1789, entitled him to the great distinction of being one of the
founding fathers of the First French Republic. Taking the premise
that the Girondin constitution was principally the creation of
Condorcet, and in a way a *résumé* of his political ideas expressed
in earlier works, it is proper that some space be devoted to the
life and ideals of the great Frenchman. The other members of
the committee, one of whom (Brissot) perhaps played just as
important a part as the philosopher in the founding of the republic,
will be discussed in a somewhat briefer fashion. However, Tom

doubtless was offended at what she considered his contempt
for her capabilities. Her description of him in her memoirs
was not flattering. Condorcet, she said, was as weak of heart
as he was weak in health (his health was never very good).
She had never seen one so timid. Before a noisy assembly he
would, through fear, deny things which he had written. Such
men, said Madame Roland, should only write. They should
never be imployed in vigorous activities. (*Mémoires de
Madame Roland* [ed. by Perroud, Cl., 2 vols., Paris, 1905],
I, 273.)

Paine, because of his direct influence on Condorcet, will be treated in a little more detail.[11]

In tracing the beginnings, indeed the very foundation, of republicanism in both the United States and France, it is dicovered that the name of a humble English corset-maker's son[12] must

11.   Condorcet and Paine, because of their ages as well as their international renown, could well be considered the doyens of the committee. With the exception of one, they were older than all the others. The ages of the committee members in 1793 were: Condorcet — 50; Paine — 56; Siéyès — 45; Brissot — 39; Petion — 38; Vergniaud — 40; Gensonné — 35; Barère 38; Danton—33; Barbaroux—25; Hérault de Sechelles—34; Lanthenas — 38; Fauchet — 49; and De Bry — 33. Lavicomterie, a supernumerary, was 61. (Alengry, *op. cit.*, pp. 192-193.)

12.   Paine, Thomas (1737-1809), was born in Thetford, England, where he spent the first thirty-seven years of his life. These years, although filled with troubles, were formative ones in the development of Paine's character. Not favored with much formal learning, he nevertheless, by dint of his own perseverance and eagerness to learn, gained a good practical education. When quite young, he had to earn his own living. This he did by working, first in his father's corset shop and then as a customs official and tobacco merchant. None of these professions were very lucrative and young Paine found that he was steadily going deeper into debt. To add to his worries, he had taken unto himself a wife. Finding that creditors were becoming more and more troublesome, he decided to chuck it all, including his wife, and come to America. This he did in 1774. Paine's thirty-seven years of life in England may not have advanced his social or economic position very much. They had, however, through his own experiences and the observations of the conditions of others, shown him the terrible injustices which existed under the absolute British monarchy of the late eightteenth century. He developed a strong hatred for aristocracy and all that it stood for: political, social, and economic in-

stand with those of history's truly great characters.[13] Tom Paine, fired by his own love for truth, justice, and freedom, took up his pen to fight despotism wherever he found it. His impassioned

equality and the misgovernment of a people by a few better-born or wealthier individuals.

In coming to America, originally to Pennsylvania, he came to a land where the flag of freedom was about to be raised. The American Revolution appealed to the republican soul of Paine and he entered wholeheartedly into the movement. Already a publicist by the time the Revolution broke out (a friend and collaborator of Benjamin Franklin, he edited the *Pennsylvania Magazine*), he eagerly took up his pen for the cause of liberty. The pamphlets *The American Crisis* and *Common Sense* kindled the fighting spirits of American patriots. Not satisfied with being a propagandist alone, Paine became a soldier. He served for a period as aide-de-camp to General Green. For a time, during the Revolution, he was secretary to the Department of Foreign Affairs. Because of personal difficulties, however, he renounced this post and became secretary-general of the Pennsylvania Assembly. The years immediately following the American War for Independence were not especially prosperous for Tom Paine. He made several trips to France, where his fame had already preceded him. (Refer to p. 120, note 16 of this monograph.) He stayed in England for a while, but, because of the incendiary pamphlet *The Rights of Man,* had to flee across the Channel. (Refer to pp. 120-123.)

The eleven years between 1791 and 1802 were spent by Paine in France. Part of this period (1791-1793) has already been discussed (refer to pp. 120-125). Shortly after the overthrow of the Girondins, Paine, possibly because of his known sympathies with them, was imprisoned. However, because of appreciation for the great services which he had rendered France, he was soon set free again and was reinstated in the Convention. Following the dissolution of the Convention, Paine was elected a deputy of the Council of Five Hundred (during the period of the Directory). He was holding this position

words propagated through his writings, and appealing to the head as well as the heart, were a major factor in inducing freedom-loving Americans and Frenchmen to throw off the shackles of tyranny engendered by centuries of ignorance and lethargy. He was one of the chief prophets of the period 1776–1793, years during which the United States and France, generally sympathetic and sometimes helpful to one another, underwent rather similar transitions, passing through the trials and tribulations of becoming, and being, infant republics.

When Tom Paine, in his flight from the vengeful wrath of aroused British aristocrats early in 1791, was compelled to cross

> when Bonaparte came into power. Tiring of French politics, perhaps discouraged, the man who had done so much for republicanism in the two worlds returned to the United States in 1802. His last years were spent in relative poverty and neglect. He died in 1809 and was buried at New Rochelle, New York.

13. After an exhaustive study of Tom Paine and his works, a French historian, Paul Desjardins, expressed surprise that the astounding importance of the Anglo-American-French publicist had not been properly emphasized, placed, or synthesized in the story of man and his progress. Of course Desjardins was writing in 1901. Even so, it was unusual that not much had been done on the really fabulous career of one of modern history's first great republicans. Of course, since 1901 studies have been made of this great figure in the republican movement of both the New and the Old Worlds.

Desjardins said that when he finished reading about Tom Paine, the name Paine seemed to him to be of more consequence to history than that of Franklin, Condorcet, or Robespierre. (Desjardins, Paul, "Thomas Paine, Républicain," *Revue Bleue* [April 20, 1901], series IV, vol. XV, no. p. 484.) He also said that his study of the evolution of the word "republican" in France led him to believe that Paine was the first to popularize it there, as he likewise was the first to popularize it in America. (*Ibid.*, p. 482.)

the Channel and take refuge in France, he took asylum in a country where he was greatly loved and respected. Proof that his fame had preceded him was the magnificent reception awaiting him when he disembarked at Calais; the Anglo-American publicist was honored by artillery salvos, flag-waving, bouquet-throwing and patriotic speeches.[14] Indeed Paine was no stranger to France! How could the man who wrote *Common Sense* be a stranger? The book, which had called Americans to freedom in 1776, had also aroused the freedom-loving instincts of many Frenchmen.[15] Besides, Paine was already known among the enlightened classes through the several visits he had made to the country since 1781.[16] He was a close friend of Condorcet;[17] the philosopher probably owed many of his ideas about republicanism to the author of *Common Sense*.

It was logical that the republican Tom Paine should seek refuge in a country which so heartily welcomed his ideas. Moreover, his flight from England was the result of a book he had written in defense of the momentous changes taking place in French politics. This book, *The Rights of Man*, written in answer to Edmund Burke's *Reflexions on the French Revolution*, may have wounded the sensibilities of British aristocrats and earned Paine the charge of committing treason. Yet in France it caused the name of Paine to be all the more respected.[18] For the next year and a half, in the closest cooperation with Condorcet, Brissot, and other republicans, he worked towards a government for the people and by the people.[19] His part in the events leading up to August 10, 1792, was no small one. Appreciation for Paine's effort was shown by the Legislative Assembly when it conferred (on August 26, 1792) the title of French citizen upon him and

14. Desjardins, *op. cit.*, p. 482.
15. For the effect of *Common Sense* on France, refer to p. 69.
16. Refer to p. 120, note 16.
17. Refer to pp. 120-123.
18. Refer to pp. 120-123.
19. For his activities during these months, refer to pp. 120-125.

eighteen other prominent foreigners for "having prepared the freedom of the French people."[20]

Elected to the Convention by the departments of Aisne, Oise, Puy-de-Dôme, and Pas-de-Calais, Paine chose to be the representative of the last named. He must have been proud when he was given the signal honor of being selected to France's first republican constitutional committee. Now, with his close friend Condorcet, he would be able to work openly on a project embodying ideas which, until now, they had had to discuss in a guarded fashion.

It is generally agreed that the work of framing the Girondin Constitution of 1793 was entrusted mainly to Condorcet and Paine.[21] There is a possibility that the newly adopted French citizen may have suggested to Condorcet the project that finally emerged from the committee on February 15, 1793.[22] Through the memoirs of an eye-witness, Dr. John Moore, we know that the two prominent committee members were in almost daily contact with one another from October, 1792, to February, 1793. Moore described the two at their work.[23] Madame Condorcet translated for her husband, from English into French, the notes of Paine.[24] Perhaps she translated the complete constitution which the Anglo-American-French publicist had prepared for the committee.[25] Seemingly strong evidence of Paine's participations in the constitution-making was a letter published on April 17, 1793, in the British newspaper *Morning Herald*. In this letter, purported to be one from

20. Desjardins, *op. cit.*, p. 483.
21. Conway, Moncure Daniel, ed., *The Writings of Thomas Paine* (4 vols., New York, 1894-1909), III, 128, note 1.
22. Desjardins, *op. cit.*, p. 483.
23. Conway, ed., *The Writings of Thomas Paine*, III, 128.
24. Alengry, *op. cit.*, p. 201.
25. Although this document has never been found, it is known that such a document really existed. Paine, in his appeal from prison in 1794, said that he had prepared a constitution and turned it over to Barère, another committee member. (Conway, ed., *The Writings of Thomas Paine*, III, 128.)

a Britisher by the name of King to Tom Paine, the statement was made ". . . that you (Paine) are the chief editor of the new constitution" (Girondin).[26] As pointed out by one historian of the Revolution, this statement is probably only an exaggeration.[27]

No definite conclusion, then, can be arrived at in regard to the role which Tom Paine had in drawing up the Girondin Constitution of 1793. There can be but little doubt that he had an immense influence on Condorcet both through his writings and through personal contact. Yet one is not far from right in regarding the French philosopher as the most important editor of the constitution. Even though some of Paine's ideas did find their way into the charter,[28] it was only after they had been analyzed and synthesized by one of the greatest minds in Europe.[29]

26. Alengry, *op. cit.*, p. 213.
27. *Loc. cit.*
28. Alengry has shown (*op. cit.*, pp. 204-212) that it is possible to reconstruct the constitution of Condorcet (Girondin) by taking parts from these works of which Paine was either the sole or a joint author: 1. *Common Sense*; 2. *The Rights of Man*; 3. *Reply to the Four Questions of May, 1791*; 4. The proclamation of July 1, 1791; 5. Articles by Paine in the *Républicain (ou le Defenseur du Gouvernement représentatif)*; 6. The constitution of Pennsylvania; 7. *Sur les premiers Principes de Gouvernement*. Since items 1, 2, 4, 5, and 6 have already been discussed respectively on the following pages: 69, 120-123, 124, 100-102, there is no need for further comment in regard to them. Item 3, *Reply to the Four Questions of May 1791*, was written in response to four theoretical questions asked by an unknown citizen about the Constitution of 1791. The questions appertained to the legislative power, the executive power, a unicameral assembly, and the organization of the administrative system. Paine's answers to these questions were translated by Condorcet and his wife. In them, statements were made to the effect that all law proceeded from the nation (through the legislative assembly); the executive should be limited in his functions; and there should not be a second chamber, as a simple major-

Another member of the committee, whose fame was almost equal to that of Paine, was Abbé Siéyès. He was one of the first to be named. The man who, in 1789, had expressed the feelings of all enlightened Frenchmen in his pamphlet *What Is the Third State?*[30] had not been forgotten when deputies were elected to the Convenion in 1792. Chosen in three departments, Gironde, Orme, and Sarthe, he had decided to represent the last. In keeping with his timid nature, he took his seat amongst members of the Plain. Owing to his celebrated reputation as a writer of pamphlets on government, and his consistent advocacy of a constitution which represented the will of the whole nation, it was practically a foregone conclusion that he would be selected to the constitutional committee. However, once on the committee, he had to take a back seat in relation to Condorcet, whose star was then at its zenith.[31] Yet evidence would indicate that Siéyès managed to impress a number of his ideas upon his colleague.[32]

ity of the second house might defeat a unanimous first house. Division of a single house into two sections for purposes of discussion was recommended, however, and periodic revision of a constitution was necessary. Item 7, *Sur les premiers Principes de Gouvernement,* was not published until 1795. Nevertheless it is an excellent *résumé* of Paine's early works.

29. In the words of Alengry, "One can call the Girondin Constitution of 1793 the work of Condorcet without overlooking the merit of Paine." (*Op. cit.,* p. 228.)

30. In this pamphlet, written before the meeting of the States-General in 1789, Siéyès said that the Third State was more important than the two privileged States. The Third State, in that it represented the people, was the true sovereign, said Siéyès.

31. Neton, A., *Siéyès (1748-1836), d'apres des Documents inédits* (Paris, 1900), p. 176.

32. A brochure, by an unknown author, appeared within Siéyès' own lifetime, entitled *Des Opinions politiques du Citoyen Siéyès et sa Vie comme Homme public (The Political Beliefs of Sieyes and His Life as a Public Official)* (Paris,

The former abbé presented to the committee a few general observations about division of power in government and the

1800). Perhaps the accuracy of its comments can be attested by the fact that they were not, as far as can be learned, denied by Siéyès himself. In this work it was stated that the author of *What Is the Third State?* undoubtedly worked at the construction of the new social edifice, and that the principles which he had previously developed might have served, in part at least, as its foundation. (*Des Opinions politiques,* p. 234.)

By studying the pamphlet one appreciates the farsighted and liberal nature of Siéyès. In answer to any doubts as to his belief in government by and for the people, the assertion is made that some writers opined that Siéyès, even before the Revolution, had conceived the design of delivering the French nation from royal tyranny. (*Ibid.,* p. 108.) The former abbé's principles, as found in the brochure, constitute the basis of a true republicanism and can be listed as follows: The national will, resulting from all the individual will, is the origin of all equality. (*Ibid.,* p. 39.) Equality of political rights is a fundamental principle of government. (*Ibid.,* p. 138.) The object of the social union (government) is to promote the happiness of all and to assure that all are protected from the natural but nevertheless harmful inequality of means. (*Ibid.,* p. 133.) A large country must of necessity have a representative government. Yet the people's representatives should be closely watched. It should never be forgotten that the point of departure in a free nation is in the primary assemblies (small governmental units in which the people directly participate in public affairs). (*Ibid.,* p. 236.) A true legislator should never forget that he is charged with preventing the bad effects of certain natural inequalities. His task is to assure that every individual has the right of freely disposing of his person and property. (*Ibid.,* p. 99.) All functions of the executive power should be limited. It is the duty of the legislative power to see that they are limited. (*Ibid.,* p. 101.) By the lessons of history one learns to dread any actions by the executive power. (*Ibid.,*

advantage of a representative system.[33] Some of his advice in regard to representative government was doubtless acceptable,[34] as evidenced by the legislative arrangement found in Condorcet's project. However, the editor, or, more correctly, author, of the Girondin Constitution of 1793, to Siéyès' disgust,[35] was to make certain that his preference for direct rule by the people predominated.

We have the word of Madame Roland that one more amongst the fifteen constitutional authorities was active in the affairs of the committee.[36] This was Gensonné.[37] As he was a laborious worker and a stickler for phraseology, it is quite conceivable that he participated in many of the discussions.[38] However, bound

p. 155.) The length of time a government has endured is no criterion of its worth. After all, history shows that despotism sometimes lasted a long time. (*Ibid.*, pp. 51-55.) Trial by jury is the veritable guarantee of individual liberty in all the countries of the world where one aspires to be free. (*Ibid.*, p. 52.)

33. *Des Opinions politiques du Citoyen Siéyès*, p. 235.
34. By no means, said Siéyès, should the ignorant workingman be deprived of his right to vote. However, as the majority of people did not have the time or education to participate in public affairs, it was but logical to believe that they should be represented. (Alengry, *op. cit.*, p. 193.)
35. Undoubtedly there was a sharp discussion between Siéyès and Condorcet. A few years later Siéyès made allusion to the committee debates of 1793. He said that he had argued for a completely representative arrangement but because of the influence of unnamed individuals his arguments were fruitless: "In their gross ignorance they believed the representative system incompatible with democracy. Then, as at present, a very harmful impression held sway — the people should delegate only those powers that they could not handle themselves." (Alengry, *op. cit.*, p. 194.)
36. *Mémoires de Madame Roland* (ed. by Perroud, Cl.), I, 155.
37. Refer to p. 126, note 33.
38. Alengry, *op. cit.*, p. 197.

by the available records, which are largely silent in regard to Gensonné's constitutional work, we cannot say to what extent he did participate.

Of the remaining twelve committee members, it appears that all except Condorcet were too busy with other political matters between October, 1792, and February, 1793, to occupy themselves with the framing of the charter. The vexatious issues between the Girondons and Montagnards, the trial of the king, and the declaration of war on England were problems which immediately concerned Brissot,[39] Vergniaud, Pétion, Danton, and Barère, more

39. Brissot, Jacques Pierre (1754-1793), ranks with Condorcet as one of the important founders of the French republican movement. Since his activities have of necessity entered integrally into the story of the whole monograph, some of the facts of this interesting Frenchman's life have already been mentioned. Still, to round out the discussion, a few more details will not be superfluous.

The outline of Brissot's life anterior to 1789, briefly sketched, is as follows: He was born in Chartres, the thirteenth child of the owner of a small restaurant. Despite the handicap of poverty, he received a good education; graduation from the *collège* of Chartres was followed by apprenticeship, in the same city, to a lawyer. Soon tiring of Chartres, however, the young apprentice eagerly accepted an offer to go to Paris and work in a law office there. Brissot, incidentally, would finally receive his law degree from the University of Rheims, which he colloquially described as a "diploma factory." Roland, Danton, and Lanthenas all received their degrees at this institution, Roland after the supreme effort of four days' work. (*J. P. Brissot: Mémoires* [ed. by Perroud, Cl., 2 vols., Paris, 1911], I, 193.)

Crowded with activities were the years between Brissot's first arrival in Paris and the outbreak of the French Revolution. He divided his time between England and France, plus a very few significant months spent in the United States. (Refer to pp. 102-111 of this monograph.) His chief and most loved occupation was writing; many articles about political, legal,

than the making of the constitution. Hérault de Séchelles, who was later to be the reporter of the Montagnard Constitution of 1793, was absent as a deputy on mission from November 29, 1792, to May, 1793. Lanthenas gave himself entirely to the work of the

and economic matters appeared under the name of Brissot; the enterprising Frenchman was also a reporter for the important pre-Revolutionary paper *Courrier de l'Europe*. Besides writing, Brissot was quite a founder of cultural clubs for the purpose of propagating liberal ideas. At various times he formed, or tried to form, an Anglo-French philosophical club (he conferred with the three French philosophers Condorcet, d'Alembert and Bossuet over the scheme [*J. P. Brissot: Correspondence et Papiers* (ed. By Perroud, Cl., Paris, 1911), pp. 74-77]), a Gallo-American club (for the purpose of informing Europe of the marvels of the United States [*J. P. Brissot: Correspondance*, p. 117]), and a society for alleviating the unfortunate condition of the blacks. Through his writings and organizing activities, the future leader of the Girondins had by 1789 a wide circle of acquaintances, including such names as Condorcet, La Fayette, Roland, Mirabeau, Jefferson, Franklin, Gibbons, Madame de Genlis, Bentham, and Washington.

As to many others, the Revolution gave Brissot a chance to pass from the state of being a theorist for democratic causes to one in which he could be an active man of affairs in politics. From 1789 to 1793 he was one of the foremost men in France. However, in so far as his work relating to the evolution of French republicanism during the Revolution has formed, and will continue to form, an important part of the monograph, there is no need for repetition of it here.

Practically the whole of Brissot's life was dedicated to the eradication of despotism and the advancement of free goverment by free peoples. When only a youth, through his reading of Plutarch, Rousseau, and books dealing with the story of Cromwell and Charles I, he learned to detest kings and dreamed of overthrowing them one day. The idea of an emancipative revolution for his own country was always

Committee of Public Instruction, another Conventional division to which he had been chosen. De Bry was busy writing a report on national education, and La Vicomterie was dividing his time between political activities and the composition of a didactic poem relating to the crimes of French kings from Clovis to Louis XVI.[40]

dominant in his mind. (*J. P. Brissot: Mémoires* [ed. by Perroud, Cl.], I, 1-38.) He would have liked to lead a quiet philosopher's life similar to that of his hero, Rousseau, to whom he often compared himself, but felt that his mission was to enter the stormy arena of politics and free philosophy from the yoke of despotism. (*J. P. Brissot: Mémoires* [ed. by Perroud, Cl.], I, 15.) Before 1789 Brissot's fight against despotism was in the form of a number of writings that had the avowed purpose of extending information and educating public opinion. (Ellery, Eloise, *Brissot de Warville: A Study in the History of the French Revolution* [Boston, 1915], p. 52.) For example, he wrote *The Theory of Criminal Law* with the desire of "attacking political tyranny and breaking that idol of government which, under the name of monarchy, practiced despotism (*J. P. Brissot: Mémoires* [ed. by Perroud, Cl.], II, 22.) This was part of his project against absolutism. As Voltaire used his writing to attack the church, so would Brissot use his to attack the absolute state. The American Revolution was of exceeding interest to the future Girondin leader. He even went to America in 1788 so as to learn how he might bring about a similar revolution in his own country. (*J. P. Brissot: Mémoires* [ed. by Perroud, Cl.], II, 275.) The outbreak of the French Revolution in 1789 was to Brissot the fulfillment of a long cherished dream. He was now able, as an active politician, to work not only for the end of tyrannical government, but also for the foundation of a republic. As has already been told in this work, this is exactly what he did.

40. Another person who might have had some influence on the committee was David Williams, the British political-economist. He was summoned from England early in 1793 by Brissot. The Girondin leader had to write several urgent letters before Williams consented to come. With some self-flattery, the

If the eleven above-mentioned men did not enter into the task of preparing France's first republican articles of government, it was not from lack of interest. Far from this! The majority of them, republicans by sentiment for years, knew only too well the necessity of giving their country a charter as soon as possible. Yet they probably felt that Condorcet, Paine, and Siéyès, all renowned for their deep study of governments, were sufficient unto themselves to frame a project at least suitable to open discussions at the Convention. Then, if they wanted to offer any amendments, this could be done on the days when constitutional questions were open to debate by the whole constituent body. It was not surprising that the work of editing a charter was entrusted almost entirely to one man, especially when he had the reputation of being one of the greatest philosophers of the day.

Condorcet was perhaps the most noted living Frenchman. The Conventionals, at first even the more rabid Montagnards, were

> Englishman claimed that the constitutional committee was so beset with difficulties that outside aid was deemed necessary. However, once in France, he had no access to the meetings of the committee. He was told that all they wanted from him was his objections in writing to the Constitution of 1791. These objections were to be compared with comments on the same subject by Condorcet, Brissot, and Gensonné. ("Un Document inedit sur la Gironde: David Williams," *Annales historiques de la Revolution française* [September-October, 1938], fifth year, no. 89, pp. 411-431.)
>
> Madame Roland was not a woman to waste ink in writing flattering remarks about men other than her husband. Notwithstanding, she did leave in her memoirs a complimentary description of David Williams. It was her opinion that he was an excellent man for legislative work. He was calm and collected. In a comparison with Tom Paine, Paine suffered. The author of *The Rights of Man* was better at lighting a revolution than making a constitution, said the sharp-tongued confidante of the Girondins. (*Mémoires de Madame Roland* [ed. by Perroud, Cl.], I, 270-271.)

honored to have such a famous personage sitting with them. They were glad that he had been selected to help work out their republican destiny. Certainly it was fitting and proper that the last of an imposing line of eighteenth-century philosophers — one which included the names of Montesquieu, Rousseau, Voltaire, Franklin, D'Alembert, and Mably — should be given the major share in a work which was, so to speak, to represent the culmination of that century's liberal philosophic ideals. Seemingly, it would not be a mistake to trust the calm and objective mind[41] of a highly trained and much informed scholar, a mind long admired for its humanity, progressiveness and extreme reasonableness.

Although Condorcet's career as a celebrated scientist and philosopher is interesting, it can, within the limitations of this monograph, only be touched upon.[42] It is well, however, after indicating something of the scope of this career, to discuss certain of Condorcet's writings.[43] In them we find many advanced political

41. Objectivity was a cardinal principle of Condorcet. Although he might be deeply impassioned over some subject, he never allowed his emotions to effect his reason — or so he believed. Despite his appreciation and use of Rousseau's principles (popular censure, the referendum, the social pact, and others), he criticized his extreme emotionalism. Rousseau, believed Condorcet, had too much false sensibility and tended to exaggerate all his opinions. (Condorcet, Marquis de, *Éloge de M. de Comte de Buffon*, in *Oeuvres complètes* [21 vols., Paris, 1801-1804], IV, 67.)

42. To understand the philosophy behind the French Revolution and to appreciate the full significance of the eighteenth-century intellectual upheaval and its effects on Revolutionary leaders, there is no better method than a study of the life and works of Condorcet. He was prominent both in the intellectual movement preceding the Revolution and in the Revolution itself.

43. Since a few of the philosopher's works have been relevant to earlier chapters of this work, they have already been analyzed.

principles similar to those found in the Girondin constitution. Of course, one might argue as to the practicability of some of these principles.

Marie Jean Antoine Nicolas Caritat, the Marquis de Condorcet, was born at Bourg-la-Reine on September 17, 1743, to parents of rather considerable means. Destined for a military career, he received an excellent education in mathematics and other exact sciences. While showing a remarkable proficiency in those subjects which were tools of war, he gave no indications of wishing to follow the profession of a soldier. His proficiency was such that he achieved fame when still a young man.[44] At the age of twenty-six Condorcet was elected to the Academy of Sciences. In 1777 he became its permanent secretary. In 1782 he received the coveted honor of an appointment to the French Academy. Condorcet's first paper before this noted body carried the tittle *Avantages que l'Union des Sciences morales aux Sciences physiques pourrait procurer a la Société* (*Advantages That Society Would Gain from the Union of the Social and Physical Sciences*). The subject of the report was in keeping with the French scholar's whole philosophy of life. It was one about which he was never to grow tired of writing or speaking. It was Condorcet's opinion that all sciences, whether social or physical, should be studied with only one purpose in mind, namely, to better the condition of all mankind. The physical scientists should also be aware of the principles of social science. If they were not, their subjects were liable to be misused for the detriment, rather than the advancement, of society.

Condorcet's convictions were not mere idle musings; they were firmly believed and, when feasible, were practiced by this Father of French Republicanism. He, himself, had an encyclopaedic knowledge of both physical and social sciences, knowledge firmly based on long and hard study. After winning laurels for his

44. Condorcet, while yet in his twenties, had written several distingushed treatises on scientific subjects, one of which, *La Théorie des Comètes*, earned him a prize from the Berlin Academy of Science.

outstanding achievements in such exacting subjects as mathematics and astronomy, he was not satisfied to rest on these accomplishments and bask in the declining sun of a fainéant monarchy. Yet, in the light of his shy and retiring nature,[45] this might have been the easiest thing to do. The illogical absolute system of the Old Regime, however, oppressed the great scientist too much in order for him to remain quiet and unprotesting. When still a relatively young man, Condorcet began to spend less and less time writing about the generally unnoticed abstractions of mathematics and more and more time writing about the sensitive, often antagonistic subjects of government and human relations.[46] The democratic and republican principles for which, as we have seen, Condorcet as a political leader fought so hard between 1789 and 1792 had been proclaimed by him in numerous essays appearing since 1778. A brief survey of a few of the tenets found in these will further help one to understand the far-sighted and humanitarian political, economic, and social views of this great man.

Although Condorcet believed in man's progress in general, he had a rather critical outlook as to the ability of any form of government to guarantee the individual complete liberty, equality, and fraternity. As long as governments were made by humans, for the control of humans, there would be a certain amount of error in them, regardless of their form. There would always be the necessary, but nevertheless disquieting, inequality between those who ruled (the governors) and those who were ruled (the governed). Inequality due to education and intellectual ability, however, was far more equitable than that due to hereditary rights or wealth.[47] Still, there was the constant

45. Madame Roland said that she never met such a shy and timorous individual.
46. In 1792 he wrote that for thirty years he had rarely missed a day without studying political science. (Condorcet, *Réponse à l'Adresse aux Provinces ou Réflexions sur les Écrits publiés contre l'Assemblée nationale* in *Oeuvres complètes*, XVI, 33.)
47. *De la Nature des Pouvoirs politiques dans une Nation libre* in

danger that even necessary inequalities might sometimes tend to political embarrassments. This was encouraged by the carelessness and ignorance of most people in regard to their governors, even those elected by themselves. With a vein of cynicism, Condorcet once wrote that men had become so accustomed to the habit of obeying other men that liberty, for most of them, meant only the right of being submitted to masters chosen by themselves.[48] Moreover, the steps taken by government chiefs and their agents would continue to be, despite publicity, a secret for the generality of citizens, who were not capable of understanding these steps.[49] Yet, regardless of seeming governmental inevitabilities because of human frailties, man must never cease to strive for perfection of rule. The more the people could limit the powers and actions of their governors, the closer they would be to supreme excellence in government.[50] Of all types of government, Condorcet believed that a republic was as close to perfection as practicable. His writings along political lines were filled with the principles of this preferable type of administration.

It was during the early months of 1789 that Condorcet, in several articles, made clear that he believed the rule of despotism was ended and the rule of the people just beginning.[51] While not

Oeuvres complètes, XVI, 133. In a work written several years earlier (1789), the French philosopher wrote that inequalities of personality, fortune, and opinion were legitimate because inherent in the nature of man and things. (Condorcet, *Lettres d' un Gentilhomme. Messieurs du Tiers État* in *Oeuvres complètes*, XII, 313-314.)

48. Condorcet, *De la Nature des Pouvoirs politiques* . . . in *Oeuvres complètes*, XVI, III.

49. *Ibid.*, XVI, 137.

50. Condorcet, *De la Nature des Pouvoirs politiques* . . . in *Oeuvres complètes*, XVI, 137.

51. In one article with the significant title of *Sentiments d'un Républicain sur les Assemblées provinciales et les États-Generaux*, in *Oeuvres complètes*, XII, 177-202, he over-opti-

asking, at first, for the end of monarchy, he wished nevertheless to so limit its powers and those of the aristocratic classes dependent on it that it would be a monarchy in name only. The rights of the nation were to come before those of the monarch or any favored class. In the coming States-General the people's representatives (the Third State) should outnumber those of the other two classes, as they really represented the nation. It would be a crime if their numbers were so small that they represented only one-third of the French people.[52] Although the deputies of the Third State might collectively have greater powers than the king, they must never forget that they were but servants to the real sovereign — the citizenry.[53] They were elected to carry out the general will, the source of all law and authority.[54] If the general will was always consulted and followed, despotism would have a difficult time taking root again. To make sure the rule of absolutism was over, however, precautions should be taken. In an article Condorcet indicated what, in his mind, were necessary precautions.

The despotism of a small number of men over a larger number was a common thing, said the philosopher. Perhaps this could be attributed to the fact that sometimes a smaller number had either

mistically stated (p. 194) that despotism could not last long in Europe.

52. Condorcet, *Lettres d'un Gentilhomme à Messieurs du Tiers-État* in *Oeuvres complètes*, XII, 298-299.

53. "Veritable right is with those who elect, and not with those who represent. The right of the first is preserved if the form of representation permits them to elect men on whom they can depend." (Condorcet, *Sentiments d'un Républicain . . .* in *Oeuvres complètes*, XII, 192.)

54. "The general will being the law, all legislative power, whether in matters of borrowing, taxes, or other matters, belongs to the nation. (Condorcet, *Réflexions sur les Pouvoirs et Instructions à donner par les Provinces à leurs Députés aux États-Generaux* in *Oeuvres complètes*, XII, 375.)

better organizing ability or greater sources of wealth.[55] Still, there
was a way by which the tyranny of a few could be prevented.
The way was to make complete use of the democratic machinery
found in republican government.[56] Condorcet then listed some
of the things necessary to make such a government function
adequately: No tax measures, or any other measures, should be
considered legal until approved by the people's deputies. There
should be no distinction among individuals regarding admission
to office, payment of taxes, or trial by civil or criminal courts.[57]
Freedom of religion[58] and press were necessities in a free government. The election of judges would prevent any despotism
due to arbitrary appointment. To thwart any absolute tendencies
of the executive, the legislative body should be quite free from
executive control; the time of reunion and the duration of each
assembly should be matters for the deputies to decide themselves.
The legislative body itself could be kept from becoming too
absolute by frequent and democratic elections.[59]

55. Condorcet, *Idées sur le Despotisme* in *Oeuvres complètes*,
XII, 205.

56. The reason that despotism did not exist in the United States,
said Condorcet, was that there the people had a legislative
body composed of their own delegates. (*Ibid.*, XII, 211.) In
England, despite the appearance of representation, the people
were still absolutely ruled. The king and Chamber of Peers
could veto any measure of the Commons. Besides, the Commons, which should have worked for the good of all, was
really an aristocratic body dominated by forty or fifty members
(whether ministers, peers, or ordinary individuals). (*Ibid.*,
XII, 207-208.)

57. "Every nation which legally recognizes class distinctions
cannot be a free nation." (Condorcet, *Idées sur le Despotisme*
in *Oeuvres complètes*, XII, 214.)

58. "In countries where there is freedom of religion, a priest
class does not become dominant. Neither in one where there
is freedom of the press." (*Ibid.*, XII, 214-215.)

59. *Ibid.*, XII, 212, 214-217.

Condorcet not only opposed possible tyrannical deeds by government officials; he also feared the extreme brutality of mobs when dominated by rabble-rousers. In his essay about despotism, he, with the usual political foresight and sagacity that he displayed when writing on political matters, stated that despotism of the populace was to be regarded as a possibility in all states where great capitals and large commercial cities existed.[60] However, this could be checked if the condition of the people was bettered to such an extent that they would not listen to the wheedling words of false prophets.[61]

Tyranny of any sort, said Concorcet, would have difficulty in establishing itself if the rights of the people, stated with clarity and detail, were published and distributed amongst all the French inhabitants.[62] As Concorcet was to believe in 1793, so thought he

60. *Ibid.*, XII, 224. From the start of the Revolution, Condorcet never felt quite sure of Parisian politics. The constant influx of vagabonds to the capital, eager for material gain, and following any person who might promise it to them, worried the philosopher. He was especially anxious when, during the Legislative Assembly, Robespierre gained control over Paris politics. It was a bitter disappointment to him when he was not elected to represent the capital at the Convention. However, disregarding personal disappointment, he pleaded for unity between Paris and the departments. Discord would be fatal to liberty, he prophesied. (Condorcet, *Sur le Préjugé qui suppose une Contrariété d'Interêt entre la Capitale et les Départements* in *Oeuvres complètes*, XV, 159.) He suggested that the preponderance of the capital be lessened by making it part of a larger department, and not a complete department by itself. This would perhaps make other parts of France less suspicious of their capital, opined Condorcet. (Condorcet, *Sur l'Étendue des Pouvoirs de l'Assemblée nationale* in *Oeuvres complètes*, XV, 181-182.)

61. Condorcet, *Idées sur le Despotisme* in *Oeuvres complètes*, XII, 226-227.

62. *Ibid.*, XII, 228-229.

in 1789. A declaration of rights was the most important part of a constitutional edifice.[63] Those rights which Rousseau had done so much to reveal[64] should be the basic philosophy behind the constitution. They were the people's guarantee that their servant, the government, would not forget that it was a servant and seek arbitrary powers. During the meeting of the States-General, Condorcet drew up a declaration which specifically stated that its purpose was to protect the citizenry against the government.[65] The whole tenor of the various articles was directed towards this end:

Besides prerogatives such as freedom of speech, religion,[66]

63. Condorcet, *Lettres d'un Gentilhomme à Messieurs du Tiers-État* in *Oeuvres complètes*, XII, 308.

64. The idea of a Declaration of Rights introducing a constitution was, of course, gleaned by Condorcet from his study of American institutions. (Refer to pp. 93-102.) However, the philosophy which he would place within the various articles of a Declaration would contain many principles taken from Rousseau and Voltaire: "Rousseau revealed the veritable rights of man to those that Voltaire had re-established in their rights of reason." (Condorcet, *Réponse à l'Adresse aux Provinces, ou Réflexions sur les Écrits publiés contre l'Assemblée nationale* in *Oeuvres complètes*, XVI, 93.)

65. Condorcet, *Déclaration des Droits* in *Oeuvres complètes*, XII, 251-252.

66. With cynicism Condorcet in 1779 had written quite disparagingly of organized religions. "National religions," said he, "make men stupid and cruel towards foreigners; universal religion leads to proselytism and intolerance. Religions full of dogma make men cruel and senseless." (*Condorcet, Dissertation philosophique et politique* in *Bibliothèque de l'Homme public* [ed. by L. S. Balestrier de Canilhac, 128 vols., *in 14*, Paris, 1790-1792], IV, 35.) Patriotism, like religion, was often diverted to devious ends, said the philosopher. Similarly, it sometimes smacked of unreasoning fanaticism. Unscrupulous leaders would render their people emotionally intoxicated by preaching superiority, invinc-

press,[67] association, etc. (common to federal and state declarations in the constitutions of the United States), there were other rights which, even today, would be considered most advanced. Many of these were phrased as prohibitions applying to the various administrative branches. For instance, the legislative body could not forbid any action which was not contrary to the rights of others; levy hidden taxes or demand exactions which would embarrass the personal liberty of citizens;[68] penalize except by express law; appoint judges; employ the armed forces against citizens or use them to hinder the citizens' freedom of action in civil and religious life; declare war unless so petitioned by a majority of the people; or create exceptional qualifications in order to hold office, such as having a certain degree of wealth. The judiciary could not name other judges, perform executive and legislative functions, or make harsh and excessive sentences.[69] Rather strangely, Condorcet in his declaration, scarcely mentioned an executive power. In the light of his other political works, in which the executive power is always negligible, it can be surmised

ibility, and belief of a better life to come for those who died for their country. A fanatical soldier, with one exception, was the same as a drunken person. The exception was that a drunken person was soon over his drunkenness. Not so with the soldier. However, love of country, momentary and blind with most men, could be enlightened and durable in great souls. (*Ibid.*, VI, 38-41.)

67. Regarding the press, Condorcet once said that opposition, more or less strong, to the right to print was a true thermometer by which one could judge the intentions of public men or political bodies. (Condorcet, *Lettres d'un Citoyen des États-Unis à un Francais sur les Affaires présentes* in *Oeuvres complètes*, XII, 149-150.)

68. A citizen should contribute to the state only in direct proportion to his benefits from the state. (Condorcet, *Déclaration des Droits* in Oeuvres complètes, XII, 275.)

69. *Ibid.*, XII, *passim*, 247-293.

that he believed that political evolution was tending away from too much executive control.

There were some unusual rights to be found in the declaration. For example, no man, under any pretext whatsoever, could be made subject against his will to military or any other public service.[70] Neither could he be deprived of his freedom, except by reason of criminal or insane actions.[71] If a person was imprisoned, he had the right of enjoying the physical comfort of healthful surroundings and the mental comfort of knowing that the state would take care of his wife and children.[72]

Although not found in his Declaration of 1789, there was one other right[73] which Condorcet never tired of emphasizing. This was the people's prerogative of being able to resist the oppression of their own government when it became too arbitrary.[74] However, this right need not necessarily tend to insurrection. A

70. *Ibid.*, XII, 264.
71. *Ibid.*, XII, 265.
72. *Ibid.*, XII, 270-271.
73. Of course, there were other rights about which the philosopher liked to write. For example, he wrote that women should have the same rights as men. Republican government was not truly republican if women were deprived of political freedom. (Condorcet, *Lettres d'un Citoyen des États-Unis à un Francais sur les Affaires présentes*, in *Oeuvres complètes*, XII, 20, 27.) Moreover, the slave trade should be abolished. The blacks, endowed with the same reason and virtues as whites, should be freed. (Condorcet, *Réflexions sur l'Esclavage des Nègres* in *Oeuvres complètes*, XI, 85.) Finally, a free system of public education, teaching the wisdom of the eighteenth-century philosophers, should be instigated by the government. (Condorcet, *Discours sur l'Office de l'Empereur* in *Oeuvres complètes*, XVII, 226.)
74. When people were betrayed by their representatives, they had the inalienable and natural right to seek salvation in any way they chose. (Condorcet, *Instruction sur l'Exercice du Droit de Souveraineté* in *Oeuvres complètes*, XVII, 393.)

government, if it carried out the people's will reasonably and wisely, would find them willing to remain submissive and obedient. Moreover, the way to avoid insurrection was to give the citizenry a legal means of resistance. If the people could freely manifest their opinions, they would not be tempted to take up arms.[75] They would gladly obey laws which they themselves had the power to change.

Although firmly believing in the sacred right of insurrection, Condorcet thought that this right need not be utilized as long as the citizenry had a legal way to resist any tyranny. The legal means of resistance should be some method of changing the constitution to meet the desires of the people. In fact, this was a necessity. Any charter dictated by reason should be subject to change.[76] In conformity with his belief in the progressive evolution of man and his institutions, Condorcet recommended that constitutional laws should be reviewed and, if necessary, revised every generation.[77] However, to prevent constant and fickle changes, there should be a logical, well organized manner of either amending or completely altering a frame of government. Admirer that he was of American institutions, it was only natural that he

75. Condorcet, *De la Nature des Pouvoirs politiques dans une Nation libre* in *Oeuvres complètes*, XVI, 144.

76. Condorcet, *Discours sur les Conventions nationales prononcé a l'Assemblée des Amis de la Constitution séante aux Jacobins le 7 Août, 1791* in *Oeuvres complètes*, XVI, 213. Brissot was of a like opinion. Every constitution, being man-made, necessarily had faults. Such being the case, it was not right that future generations should be saddled with a hereditary charter. (Brissot, J.P., *Discours sur les Conventions nationales prononcé a la Société des Amis de la Constitution séante aux Jacobins le 8 Août, 1791* [Paris, 1791], p. 10.)

77. Condorcet, *Sur la Nécessité de faire ratifier la Constitution par les Citoyens* in *Oeuvres complètes*, XV, 203.

should find in the American system of conventions the proper method of constitutional amendment.[78]

The final word in the matter of conventions lay with the people. Although the legislative body might suggest constitutional changes, it was up to the citizenry to say whether or not such changes should actually take place;[79] that is, the business of conventions was entirely separate from that of the legislative body, and an important prerogative of the people.[80] Condorcet was rather meager in his details as to how the conventions should be convoked.[81] Moreover, he was somewhat contradictory as to when they should be summoned. Generally, however, he agreed that anywhere between ten and twenty years would be a good interval for

78.   Condorcet, *Discours sur les Conventions nationales* . . . in *Oeuvres complètes*, XVI, 214. Brissot was also enthusiastic about the conventional system of the United States. He found it excellent that the people had the right of both petition and referendum in constitutional questions. Brissot, *Discours sur les Conventions* . . . , pp. 18-19.)

79.   Condorcet, *Lettres d'un Bourgeois de New Haven* in *Oeuvres complètes*, XII, 57. Brissot had a similar view. The reform of a constitution could not be left to delegated powers because they would be least likely to be desirous of any change which might limit their own authority. Brissot, *Discours sur les Conventions* . . . , pp. 26-27.)

80.   Condorcet, *Première et seconde Lettres à M. le Comte de Montmorency, Député du Bailliage de Montfort l'Amaury* in *Oeuvres complètes*, XV.

81.   It seems that he finally agreed that the best way to convoke a convention was to have the initiative begin with the people in the primary assemblies. If a majority of the primary assemblies in a majority of the departments petitioned for constitutional amendments, then the way was cleared for the election of deputies to a Convention. (Condorcet, *Opinion sur la Nécéssité d'une Convocation extraordinaire des Assemblées primaires en 1792* in *Oeuvres complètes*, XVII, 359-362.)

conventions.[82] The main thing was that the people should have the legal right of altering their government to meet the political evolution of the time. Forming part of this right was their prerogative of accepting or rejecting any constitution which the conventional deputies might create. How could one expect the people to obey something which they had not sanctioned?[83]

In accordance with his belief that the people should rule themselves to the greatest possible extent, Condorcet advocated a single-house legislature. He said that this was the best way to destroy the inseparable abuses found in all human institutions.[84] Admirer of the constitution of Pennsylvania, which then provided for a sole chamber,[85] he thought that such a system would suit France. Answering critics who claimed that even a single chamber could be subverted to the tyrannical ends of a minority,[86] Condor-

82. Condorcet, *Des Conventions nationales. Discours dont l'Assemblée federative des Amis de la Verité a voté l'Impression le premier Avril, 1791* in *Oeuvres complètes*, XVI, 193.

83. Condorcet, *Discours sur les Conventions nationales prononcé à l'Assemblée des Amis de la Constitution, séante aux Jacobins le 7 Août 1791* in *Oeuvres complètes*, XVI, 222 *Sur la Nécessité de faire ratifier la Constitution par les Citoyens*, in *Oeuvres complètes*, XV, 221.

84. Condorcet, *Lettres d'un Bourgeois de New Haven à un Citoyen de Virginie* in *Oeuvres complètes*, XII, 13.

85. Refer to pp. 100-101.

86. One of Condorcet's critics was John Adams, latter President of the United States. He took exception to the remarks made by the philosopher in the essay *Lettres d'un Bourgeois de New Haven*. . . . Through a series of answering articles in the form of letters printed by the *Gazette of the United States*, published at Philadelphia in 1790, Adams attempted to refute Condorcet's reasonings. One letter was especially blunt. If the French philosopher's opinions on the legislative body were followed, said Adams, the French people would fail to obtain their desired liberty "as surely as emulation and rivalry are founded in human nature and inseparable

cet said this could be prevented by having all acts of the assembly referred to the people.[87] Moreover, the assembly would be limited in its powers by express laws.[88]

Although Condorcet always favored having a single house, he was not against having a second chamber of limited powers which would act more or less in an advisory capacity to the primary chamber. However, said he, this second body must not have powers either equal[89] to or greater than those of the first. It should be elected by the people in the same manner as the

from civil affairs." With a single house, sovereignty would certainly be exercised by a majority as tyrannically as any sovereignty ever exercised by kings or nobles. (Hazen, Charles Downer, *Contemporary American Opinion of the French Revolution* [Baltimore, 1897], pp. 153-155.)

87. Condorcet, *Lettres d'un Bourgeois de New Haven . . .* in *Oeuvres complètes*, XII, 113-114. "The people should be interrogated on the question of whether or not a measure is contrary to the natural rights of man." (Condorcet, *De la Nature des Pouvoirs politiques . . .* in *Oeuvres complètes*, XVI, 117.)

88. Condorcet, *Lettres d'un Bourgeois de New Haven . . .* in *Oeuvres complètes*, XII, 39.

89. "If there are two bodies with equal rights, there will be either a rivalry between them or condescension on the part of one which will render it useless. Besides, there is a chance that one house might become aristocratic, as happened in England." (*Ibid.*, XII, 117-118.)

Using figures, Condorcet illustrated the wrongs that might ensue from having two houses with equal rights. For example, if there was an upper chamber of 200 members and a lower of 1,000, 101 members of the first-named body (or a majority of said body) could thwart legislation favored by all the deputies of the lower branch plus ninety-nine of the upper (a total of 1099.) In other words, 101 men would be able to thwart the will of 1099. (Condorcet, *Examen sur cette Question: Est-il utile du diviser une Assemblée nationale en plusieurs Chambers?* in *Oeuvres complètes*, XV. 97.)

first but should have only suspensive and advisory functions. Such a suspensive body, made up of a few enlightened men throughly trained in law, might be a good thing. It would prevent hasty actions and mean more careful consideration of legislation.[90] By no means, however, should there be a superior chamber in which membership was based on either heredity or wealth.

As the French philosopher feared that an upper house might become aristocratic and tend towards inequality, so he feared that a strong executive might tend to infringe on the rights of the all-powerful people. To prevent this, he favored an arrangement in which the executive was strictly and solely an agency to administer the acts of the legislative body. Condorcet's executive would be plural, being composed of seven members.[91] Each member would be in charge of a certain department, such as that of war, treasury, or the like, and would be limited to the supervision of his own department. These administrators were to be elected by the people directly[92] and were to be responsible for their actions to the legislative body, which, according to Condorcet's preferences in government, was the predominant branch.

Justice, in the system of Condorcet, would be administered by judges elected by the people.[93] These judges could not hold office

90. Condorcet, *Examen sur cette Question* . . . in *Oeuvres complètes*, XV, 101-106.

91. Condorcet, *Sur l'Institution d'un Conseil électif* in *Oeuvres complètes*, XVI, 241-243.

92. When Condorcet used to word "directly," he generally meant that the processes of election began in the primary assemblies, those small governmental units in which democracy really functioned (refer to p. 256, note 12.) However, to explain the various methods of election as indicated by Condorcet would require far too much space in this monograph.

93. "They should be elected by those who will be judged." (Condorcet, *Lettres d'un Citoyen des États-Unis* . . . in *Oeuvres complètes*, XII, 155.) Condorcet praised justice in the United

for life; they were elected for a definite term and might be removed for dishonesty or inefficiency. There must be no special court for special classes; justice was something which should be applied equally.[94] Civil and criminal matters should, of necessity, be kept separate. A citizen, once tried, always had the right of appeal. District courts[95] of appeal, following the philosopher, would be composed of ten to twelve jurors, of whom six to eight, at least, should be lawyers.[96] The right of trial by jury was one of the citizen's fundamental rights, just as his right to participate in law-making was fundamental.[97]

The method of legislation favored by Condorcet was one which might be viewed as extremely democratic, and perhaps even impractical, today. Nevertheless, it was one in accordance with his policy of having the people rule themselves to the greatest possible extent. Moreover, it showed how the strongest of the branches of the government, the legislative, was but a servant of the citizenry and dependent on it for final legislative action.

States, where a citizen could not be judged by a special court or receive a judgment from a single judge without a right of appeal. He also lauded the right granted Americans of challenging juries. (*Loc. cit.*)

94. *Ibid.*, XII, 159. "All which tends to consecrate and increase distinctions among men is bad in itself."

95. Refer to p. 115, note 4.

96. Condorcet, *Sur les Tribunaux d'Appel* in *Oeuvres com plètes*, XV, 305. This stipulation that most of the jurors should be lawyers seems strange in the light of an opinion which Condorcet once expressed about legal gentlemen. Lawyers, he said, would not defend a poor man because the amount of their remuneration, if any, would be small. (Condorcet, *Lettres d'un Citoyen des États-Unis* . . . in *Oeuvres complètes*, XII, 157.)

97. "The right of concurring in the formation of laws is one of the rights of man in the state of society." (Condorcet, *Lettres d'un Citoyen des États-Unis* . . . in *Oeuvres complètes*, XII, 144.)

Condorcet wrote in 1789 that the most important part of any constitution which he might frame would be that describing the manner in which legislation would be referred to the people for their opinion and sanction.[98] His recommendations along this line resembled the provisions made for a referendum in the Constitution of 1793.[99]

It was Condorcet's belief that the legislative body should be regarded as a law-framing body. A good proportion of the deputies elected by the people would presumably be men elected for their qualities of leadership and for their intellectual attainments. Many would be trained in the law. However, instead of being able to dictate measures arbitrarily to the people, they were merely to recommend certain measures. The citizenry must have the final say. If a plurality of the citizens of all the districts voted against a measure, it was to be discarded.[100] Yet one ought to expect that the people generally would accept the advice of the legislative body, since its opinions would be viewed as those coming from a qualified group of specialists.

In the opinion of France's leading republican, the main part of law should relate to the regulation of economic affairs.[101] Keenly aware that political democracy was but a sham without control of certain economic forces, he advised, from the start of the Revolution, the initiation of laws which might prevent any harm accruing from the perhaps natural inequalities resulting from excessive differences of wealth.[102] During the early months

98. Condorcet, *Lettres d'un Bourgeois de New Haven* . . . in *Oeuvres complètes*, XII, 84.

99. Refer to pp. 265-266.

100. Condorcet, *Lettres d'un Bourgeois de New Haven* . . . in *Oeuvres complètes*, XII, 40-45.

101. Condorcet divided law into six sections. Four of these related to economic affairs; two concerned constitutional and military questions. (*Ibid.*, XII, 4-9.)

102. Inequality of riches was not contrary to natural law, said Condorcet. In fact, it was a result of one of the natural

of 1789, Condorcet was writing that one of the most urgent problems to be settled was that caused by bad laws favoring the capitalist at the expense of the small proprietor.[103] It was deplorable, said he, that everywhere one saw only very rich or very poor people. There were not enough members of the small-proprietor class, a class which Condorcet considered the healthy part of a free nation. Civil law, as it was then, made this state of affairs possible. If things continued to go on as they were going, thought the philosopher, the chances for republican equality would be rather slim.[104] However, while making the generalization that law must be concerned mainly with the regulation of economic matters, he was not very specific as to what these regulations should be. Moreover, the idea of government control was somewhat contradictory to his concept of free enterprise, a favorite concept with him. Still, he did have the courage to denounce economic evils along with political ones. He did make a few suggestions that had in mind the betterment of man's economic lot in society.

Wealth in itself was harmful only when its concentration in the hands of a few caused hardship to the many. The way to prevent the evils of riches was to see that there was a just distribution of them. Good laws ought to provide for a proper distribution.[105] A distribution increasing the number of small proprietors and land-

rights—that of having freedom and security in the enjoyment of one's property. Other natural rights were those of security and liberty of one's person and the right of equality. (Condorcet, *Idées sur le Despotisme* in *Oeuvres complètes*, XII, 232.) In a free, competitive system it was to be expected that a few, either by shrewdness or by other means, would accumulate more worldly goods than others.

103. Condorcet, *Lettres d'un Gentilhomme à Messieurs du Tiers-État* in *Oeuvres complètes*, XII, 300

104. Condorcet, *Lettres d'un Bourgeois de New Haven* . . . in *Oeuvres complètes*, XII, 79, 133-134.

105. Condorcet, *De la Nature des Pouvoirs politiques* . . . in *Oeuvres complètes*, XVI, 132.

owners would be the proper type.[106] Believing that any great fortune at all durable was a result of poor laws,[107] Condorcet hinted at legislation which would prevent any one individual from inheriting vast riches.[108] If a man died leaving a vast accumulation of worldly goods, these goods, instead of going to one relation (according to French law, to the oldest son), were to be divided amongst all relations in proportion to their needs. Such an arrangement might be one factor in helping to increase the number of small proprietors. Other factors would be a proper system of taxation and a proper attitude by the government towards commerce and industry.

A just tax, and one which was uniform and easy to collect, said Condorcet, was a land tax.[109] This was the only type of tax that the philosopher really favored. He advocated that every person in the state contribute to the support of the state in proportion to the amount of his lands.[110] Such a levy would naturally hit the large, wealthy landowners and favor the small. This was but simple justice, however, thought Condorcet. The effect of the land tax was to penalize those who sought to monopolize the earth's terrains, terrains created by God for the benefit of all.

Governments ought not to demand contributions from the poor.[111] Neither should they tax the physical necessities of

106. Condorcet, *Lettres d'un Bourgeois de New Haven* . . . in *Oeuvres complètes*, XII, 16.

107. *Ibid.*, XII, 130.

108. Condorcet, *Idées sur le Despotisme* in *Oeuvres complètes*, XII, 233.

109. Condorcet, *Lettres d'un Bourgeois de New Haven* . . . in *Oeuvres complètes*, XII, 98.

110. Condorcet, *De la Nature des Pouvoirs politiques* . . . in *Oeuvres complètes*, XVI, 120.

111. Condorcet, *Idées sur le Despotisme* . . . in *Oeuvres complètes*, XII, 235.

man.[112] All levies collected should be used solely for the public benefit; those exactions which were not so used were veritable thefts from the poor[113] and a general attack on the right of property.[114] Condorcet, an exponent of economic as well as political justice, wanted the main burden of taxes to fall on the rich. It was his complaint (this was written before 1789) that the burden in those countries where the people had no representatives actually fell on those least able to pay.[115]

While granting the fact that Condorcet wanted to eliminate poverty and to tax those most able to pay, it must be admitted there were some fallacies in his economic reasonings. A single land tax, paid in proportion to one's landed holdings, would by no means have hit all the wealthy. There were many rich men who counted their wealth in things other than land. Moreover, a single tax would probably not be sufficient to support the expenses of a state. Still, it appears that the philosopher's plan for a single tax was in reality not so much for the purpose of raising revenue as it was for the purpose of putting such a burden on the large landholders that they would be induced to divide up and sell their lands.

An advocate of the policy of *laissez-faire* in the distribution of agricultural commodities, Condorcet thought that one way to bring economic tranquility to France would be for the government to cease placing such hampers as tariffs on the free circulation of foods.[116] Commerce, like religion, said he, ought to be absolutely

112. Condorcet, *Note sur une Pensée de Pascal* in *Oeuvres complètes*, IV, 488.

113. *Loc. cit.*

114. Condorcet, *Lettres d'un Bourgeois de New Haven . . .* in *Oeuvres complètes*, XII, 8.

115. Condorcet, *Note sur une Pensée de Pascal* in *Oeuvres complètes*, IV, 488.

116. Condorcet, *Sur la Liberté de la Circulation des Subsistances* in *Oeuvres complètes*, XVII, 183.

free.[117] Under a system of free trade, agricultural products would naturally seek those markets where they were most urgently needed and where they would command the best price. Prices, believed Condorcet, perhaps with over-optimism, would be held down by the simple fact of competition. Several merchants trying to sell the same product in a district would, in attempting to under-sell their opponents, lower their prices on the product. The price lowering would be in favor of the consumer. Evidently, the idealist philosopher did not foresee that a policy of economic rugged individualism in a free competitive market might lead to the more powerful merchants' being able to freeze out the smaller merchants. The mighty ones could afford to depress prices far below cost. However, once competition was eliminated, there was nothing to prevent the successful merchants from raising them again. Perhaps Condorcet reasoned that this would be checked by the fact that no more than that which the people were willing to pay for goods could be expected from them.

It may be that Condorcet's political, economic and social principles were ahead of his time. It may be that some of these were impractical. Yet it would be an error to say that the democratic theories propagated by him did not contain the real essence of republicanism. Apparently, the appointment of the Girondin Constitutional Committee in October, 1792, headed by Condorcet, augured the happy conclusion of these theories as theories and their successful embodiment in a document which would be a practical proof of their worth. However, in the field of grim everyday politics the schemes of idealists, even when long cherished by the literati, sometimes receive a strange reception.

---

117. Condorcet, *Lettres d'un Bourgeois de New Haven* . . . in *Oeuvres complètes*, XII, 12.

Chapter VI

Partisan Issues Delaying Constitutional Discussions
(October, 1792 — February, 1793)

If the records are rather silent as to the activities of the Girondin Constitutional Committee between October, 1792, and February, 1793, certainly they are not silent regarding the events which occurred at the Convention for the same period. They are not only ample; they are also most illuminating. One clear-cut impression is to be gained from their study. This is that the primary and urgent task of giving France a republican charter was overlooked by many Conventionals in the excitement generated by partisan questions and by those questions regarding the fate of the king and the spread of the war. However, as we have learned, the Convention itself was responsible for delay in the creation of a constitution by decreeing at the very opening of its sessions that there would be certain postponements on constitutional questions. For one thing, there would be no debate — before the whole Convention — on constitutional questions for at least two months after the presentation of a plan by the constitutional committee. Then again, no deadline was set as to when the committee should complete its work. This would appear to be another example of the inefficiency of the idealistic but impractical Girondin leadership during the early phase of the Convention. True, the Girondins wanted to make sure that the republican constitution would be the product of great care and study. But then, there was really a need for haste in the establishment of a firm constitutional foundation for the fledgling republic. And the party of the opposition, the Mountain, made capital out of any weakness or uncertainty of decision on the part of the Girondins. Marat, for one, goaded them by requesting in his paper, *L'Ami du Peuple*, that the constitution be finished almost overnight.[1] The Girondin answer to Marat was sharp.

A notice inserted in the *Moniteur* (on October 14, 1792) condemned Marat's request for a quick completion of the constitution as one impossible of fulfillment and made simply to accuse the Girondins of delaying completion of the constitutional edifice. The obvious plan, said the notice, was to incite the Parisian populace against the representatives. In bringing about bloodshed and disorder, Marat hoped that there would be so much anarchy that a strong-arm government would be welcome.[2] Virtually punctuating the Girondin suspicions was an incident that occurred at the Convention a few days later.

Claiming to represent the forty-eight sections of Paris, a deputation appeared (on October 19, 1792) before the constituent body. The spokesman of the deputation said that the capital would deeply resent any measure passed which would create an armed guard for the Convention.[3] When the remarks caused an uproar amongst the deputies, he ominously added that Paris had made the Revolution and had given liberty to France. Paris would know how to maintain this liberty.[4]

Gensonné, a leading Girondin deputy, answered the petitioners by asserting that it was from the Paris Commune that the orders had come for all disorganizing moves. He then qualified this remark by saying that rather than have it believed that the

1. Refer to p. 174.
2. *Moniteur universel* (*Journal officiel de l'Empire français*, (196 vols., Paris, 1789-1863), October 14, 1792.
3. Refer to pp. 166, 172.
4. *Débats de la Convention nationale ou Analyse complète des Séances avec les Noms de Tous les Membres, Pétitionnaires ou Pérsonnages qui ont figuré dans cette Assemblée, précedée d'une Introduction* par Léon Thiessé (ed. by Léon Thiessé, 4 vols., Paris, 1828), I, 160. Hereafter to be cited as *Débats de la Convention nationale* (volume and page numbers).

petition represented the views of the whole Commune, the deputation should bury said petition in forgetfulness.[5]

It was becoming harder and harder, however, to excuse the various municipal agencies of the capital, especially when one of these agencies, the Revolutionary Commune, apparently was being used by Robespierre, Marat, and other Montagnard chiefs to harass, and possibly subvert, the authority of the Convention. Moreover, the exact legal status of the diverse municipal units since August 10, 1792, was anything but clear. When money allotted to city authorities was used to print unfavorable propaganda against the Convention and its measures, and to distribute this propaganda throughout the departments, it was time that these authorities were investigated, thought Barbaroux, Buzot, and other Girondin deputies.[6] As Conventional discussions (on October 25-26, 1792) regarding the municipal government of Paris succeeded only in confusing the deputies,[7] it was finally decreed that the Minister of the Interior, Monsieur Roland, would within three days give a report on the state of authority in Paris.[8]

Roland's report to the Convention (on October 29, 1792) was a detailed account of the administration of the capital since August 10. The crux of this report was that the Revolutionary Commune had for a time been necessary and useful. Now, implied

5. *Ibid.*, I, 161.
6. *Ibid.*, I, 181-187.
7. Kersaint, deputy of Seine-et-Oise, said that the discussions ought to teach the inhabitants of Paris how anarchical was their city's administration. They revealed that the capital had several governmental agencies, all of which were now rather uncertain as to their authority. Among these were the Directory of the Department of Paris and the Revolutionary Commune (established since August 10, 1792). Supposedly the Revolutionary Commune had a General Council, composed of representatives from the forty-eight sections, which democratically directed policy. In reality, the sectional representatives took their orders from the Montagnard leaders.
8. *Débats de la Convention nationale*, 1, 192.

the Minister of the Interior, there was no need for this extra-legal body. The city government should revert to the proper authority, the Department of Paris. Roland cited many instances in which the Commune had engaged in actions of doubtful legality. It had become the supreme judge of public safety; it paid no heed to the regular departmental administrators; dispatches from the Minister of the Interior were often ignored by the Revolutionary Commune; private property was confiscated; municipal officers were elected without the confirmation of the Department of Paris Directory; commissioners were sent to the other departments without notifying the Minister of the Interior, and almshouses and prisons were inadequately administered. On a smaller scale the sections and the National Guard units in Paris also suffered in their administration.[9]

As Roland's account approached its termination, the language became bolder. The Revolutionary Commune was accused of being despotic and so familiarizing the people with insurrection that this was becoming a daily habit. The character of the people was no doubt fundamentally excellent. Yet the Paris populace was being misused. A large part was intimidated or constrained while the other part was worked upon by flattery and inflamed by calumny.[10] As a climax, and apparently to connect the strife in Paris with the growing suspicions of dictatorship, Roland mentioned a letter which had been brought to his attention by the Minister of Justice, Garat. This letter, written by a Monsieur Marcaudier, alleged that there was a plot afoot to get rid of the so-called Brissotine-Roland group in the Convention. The plotters — whose names were not given — looked to Robespierre as the man who would be the salvation of France.[11] At the mention of his name, Robespierre arose and asked whether anyone wanted to accuse him formally. He did not have to ask twice. Louvet,[12]

9. *Ibid.*, I, 205-221
10. *Ibid.*, I, 222.
11. *Ibid.*, I, 223.
12. Louvet (de Couvrai), Jean Baptiste (1760-1797), was one

deputy from Loiret, jumped to his feet and said that he was more than willing to accuse the Montagnard chief.

Louvet accused Robespierre of perverting the Jacobin Club to his own guilty ends. Now all to be heard at its meetings, said he, was the basest flattery and adulation of the number-one leader of the Mountain. Such flattery was dangerous, thought Louvet. People should regard no one man as the sole salvation of a country. Blind faith in one individual might lead to a king, tribune, dictator, or triumvir; despotism masqueraded under any one of several titles. Louvet inferred that Robespierre was chiefly responsible for the September massacres.[13]

Another deputy, Jean Francois Delacroix, was even more bold in his accusations than Louvet. He charged that Robespierre, since August 10, 1792, had constantly humiliated the nation's representatives, whether of the Legislative Assembly or of the Convention. He was the real chief of the municipal powers of Paris and had planned to unify all the muncipalities of the nation under that of the capital, which he himself dominated. Robespierre probably would have taken the role of dictator at the time of the September massacres if it had not been for Pétion, Roland, and other men who were willing to play the part of Brutus against the new Caesar. Delacroix warned that public opinion was being prepared for a dictatorship. In this connection, it would be well to note the seditious works of Marat, Robespierre's *alter ego*. It was proposed by Delacroix that the constitutional committee investigate the possibility of a law banishing any man who created divisions by

of the more passionate Girondins. He was a proponent of vigorous and efficient action against the Robespierrists; if his recommendations had been followed, perhaps the Girondins would have been able to maintain the republic. His newspaper, *La Sentinelle*, became an important organ of the Girondins after August 19, 1792, and was directed against the authoritarian tendencies of the Montagnards. Subsidized by the Rolands, *La Sentinelle* had a wide circulation in the departments.

13. *Débats de la Convention nationale*, I, 231-234.

the use of his name. He also asked for the indictment of Marat and an investigation of Robespierre.[14]

The charges of Louvet and Delacroix seemed to have considerably flustered the Montagnard leader. Distracted by the roars of disapproval shouted at him, Robespierre finally made known that he would answer all accusations in a few days.[15]

Freedom of press being one of the fundamental liberties of a republic, the Girondins were somewhat embarrassed as to how they could stop the seditious-appearing writings of Marat and the inflammatory dispatches sent from the Revolutionary Commune to other French communes. The question of a departmental guard for the Convention had occasioned a great outpouring of Montagnard pamphlets to the departments. Dead set against any such guard, the leaders of the Mountain — above all, Marat — had sent thousands of brochures throughout France accusing the proponents of the guard of being federalists. Barbaroux, in an address to the Convention (on October 30, 1792), tried to settle the federalist issue once and for all. He also tried to emphasize the importance of the guard.

Aware, as were the majority of Girondins, that the word "federalist" was being used by Marat and others for propaganda purposes — and that an evil connotation was being attached to the word — Barbaroux asked the Conventionals precisely how many knew what the word meant. He then asked whether any of them had ever proposed such a government. Barbaroux answered for them. The answer, said he, was no. Those that were accused of favoring this type of administration had combatted it in their writings for at least ten years. Moreover, the inhabitants of southern France, where federalism was supposedly predominant, had made their deputies pledge that they would vote for the unity of the republic.[16]

14. *Ibid.*, I, 235-243.
15. *Ibid.*, I, 243.
16. *Moniteur universel, October* 31, 1792.

Attributing the charge of federalism to those ambitious ones in control of the General Council of the Revolutionary Commune[17] and the Paris sections, Barbaroux proposed measures that would completely break the Revolutionary Commune. The essence of these measures was that the General Council would be abolished and the sections would lose their permanent status. Municipal authority was to revert to the regularly elected Directory of the Department. Barbaroux also proposed that the Convention remain in Paris only as long as the capital was respectful towards it. All armed forces in the capital were to be at the service of the Convention, and the said Convention could be used as a court of justice to try conspirators against the state.[18]

Barbaroux's measures might have averted the plots of those seeking an authoritarian regime. Unfortunately, the fatal procrastination of many of the Girondins in taking decisive action manifested itself once again. Pétion asked that his colleague's proposals be adjourned. He supported a decree of Delacroix which meant only delay. On the advice of Pétion, the Convention set aside the propositions of Barbaroux and decreed those of Delacroix. Delacroix's measures were to the effect that at some time in the near future representatives from the General Council would appear before the Convention and render an account of their propagandizing activities. Moreover, any papers in possession of the Council would be subject to investigation.[19]

A remarkable example of naivete, or boldness, was witnessed by the Convention a few days after Barbaroux had delivered his speech against the factionals of Paris. A deputation from the sections came to the bar and asked why the people's representa-

17. The General Council presumably was made up of representatives from all the sections. Supposedly it combined legislative and administrative functions. It was considerably under the domination of Robespierre.

18. *Débats de la Convention nationale*, 1, 259-260.

19. *Ibid*, I, 261-263.

tives were surrounded by soldiers (many *Fédérés*[20] were still in Paris). Didn't the deputies trust the Parisians? With laughable audacity the spokesman of the deputation then asked that the sections be furnished with arms. They would never be used for ill-advantage, said he.[21] As the Conventionals had just previously been warned by a deputation of *Fédérés* that many of them had been designated by the tribunes to be assassinated, the amount of faith they placed in the sections' promises was very little indeed. They seem to have put as much faith in the sections' promises as they were to put in Robespierre's pleas of innocence a few days later — that is, not very much.

In answer to the accusations of Louvet and Delacroix, the Montagnard leader made sweeping denials at the Convention on November 5, 1792. If he had wanted to be a dictator, he never would have permitted the Convention to come into being. As to his relationship with that dictatorially minded individual, Marat, he had known him only since January, 1792. Robespierre denied his own influence over opinion at the Jacobin Club. The opinion of the Jacobins was that of the nation, he asserted, and was inspired by no one individual. Since August 10 he had served proudly as a member of the General Council of the Revolutionary Commune, an administrative group which reflected only the sentiments of the majority of the Parisians. Perhaps it was an illegal body. For that matter, the whole Revolution was illegal, said Robespierre with logic. Concerning the September Massacres in which the Council was seriously implicated, the chief of the Montagnards claimed that he had been too busy with other matters to attend the meetings of the Council just prior to and during the events of September 2-3. Robespierre excused the massacres. They had taken care of guilty ones who otherwise might have prevented a successful Revolution. With the Prussian enemy so close to Paris, one could not allow another enemy to

20.   National Guardsmen from the departments.
21.   *Moniteur universel,* November 5, 1792.

remain in the capital itself.[22] Robespierre concluded by defending the whole Revolutionary government in Paris. This government, meaning the Commune, was just and was supported by the populace. It would never have come into being if the authorities elected prior to August 10 had adequately fulfilled their duties.

At the motion of Barère, all charges against the head of the Mountain were dropped. In a pretty figure of speech, the member of the constitutional committee tended to underestimate the capabilities of Robespierre. If they were dealing with a really dangerous character, such as a Caesar, Sulla or Cromwell, said he, fears of a dictatorship might be justified. But as long as they were dealing with a petty leader of mobs, they had nothing to fear.[23]

Although Robespierre was exonerated, the Girondins continued to suspect him. They believed that the battalions of *Fédérés*[24] stationed in Paris would serve as a means of checking his ambitions and preserving the authority of the Convention. Needless to say, they regarded with alarm a proposal by Le Tourneur (on November 1792), reporter for the Committee of War,[25] to form the

22. *Débats de la Convention nationale*, 1, 274-290.

23. *Ibid.*, I, 296-297.

24. In lieu of a regularly established Conventional guard, the Girondins placed their faith for protection in the *Fédérés*, originally destined to fight on the frontiers.

25. The number of committees in the Convention varied. On an average, however, there were about twenty of these legislative groups. Among them were the Committees of Archives, Public Safety (at first termed General Defense), General Security, Decrees and Procès-Verbaux, Examination of Military Contracts, Clothing and Maintenance, Correspondence, Petitions, Finance, Legislation, Public Instruction, Accounts, and Naval and Colonial Affairs,

Beside the committees, the Convention appointed temporary commissions, such as the Commission of Twelve, appointed on May 18, 1793, and entrusted with the execution of all measures relating to the preservation of public tran-

Fédérés into battalions of the regular army and dispatch them immediately to the northeastern frontier. Buzot and Barbaroux said that they should stay in Paris; they were not needed on the frontier. They were, however, needed in the capital to maintain the unity of the republic. Buzot said that it was really the sections that wanted these troops sent away, and not the Minister of War, as claimed by Le Tourneur.[26] Parenthetically, Barère asked whether certain persons in Paris did not fear the *Fédérés*, whose patriotism and love of pure liberty was undoubted. He stressed the point that they were really needed in Paris to maintain law and order, especially since the king was about to be judged.[27] Despite the grumbling of Le Tourneur over the fact that the government was spending a good thirty sous a day on each *Fédéré*, which sum was usually wasted on the demoiselles of the city, the proposal to send the troops to the frontier was rejected.[28]

There were graver economic problems for the Conventionals to worry about than the squandering of thirty sous a day by each *Fédéré*. Economic matters were also subject to partisan dispute. The Minister of the Interior, Roland, reported to the Convention (on November 27, 1792) that the Paris Commune was selling grain at an inferior price in order to court favor with the populace and attract what he termed "undesirables" from other depart-

quility. This commission was dissolved on May 31. The first Committee of the Constitution (the Girondin), dissolved February 16, 1793, may be regarded as a temporary commission.

26. *Débats de la Convention nationale*, I, 241-344.

27. *Ibid.*, 352-353.

28. *Débats de la Convention nationale*, I, 351, 356. According to the report of the Minister of War to the Convention (on January 5, 1792), there were only 5,601 *Fédérés* in Paris. On the other hand, there were 110,542 soldiers of other categories (regulars and Parisian National Guardsmen). Thus, as far as numbers are concerned, the *Fédérés* could not be considered as much of a protection to the Girondins.

ments.[29] The next day a letter was read from Roland which voiced the suspicion that groups of armed men, motivated by those who controlled Paris, were being sent out to the departments to confiscate grain. The minister pleaded, to no avail, for a decree stopping illegal shipments of grain to the capital.[30]

Administration of army supplies was a knotty problem for the Conventionals, and seriously threatened the successful conduct of the war. A commission from the army, reporting on November 1, 1792, told of the poor and inadequate supplies being received by the soldiers. Shoes lasted only from six to twelve days; the soles were made partly of cardboard.[31] Deputy Cambon caustically remarked that it appeared that the Revolution had reached everyone but the financiers and partisans.[32] Treilhard commented that the conspirators were not only on the border, but were also the monopolizers and profiteers within.[33] A letter from General Dumouriez was read to the Convention on December 4. Pache, the Minister of War, was accused of failing in all his duties. Dumouriez asserted that at Brussels the officers of the volunteer forces had to take up a collection in order to pay their soldiers.[34]

The serious business of conducting a war was not to check the partisan struggle. Nor was partisanship checked by the imperative need to complete a constitution quickly. Despite the pleas of many serious-minded members, such as Jean Debry,[35] a supernumerary of the constitutional committee, that the Conven-

29. *Ibid.*, I, 430.
30. *Ibid.*, I, 459-460.
31. *Ibid.*, I, 265-408.
32. *Ibid.*, I, 266.
33. *Ibid.*, I, 407.
34. *Ibid.*, II, 13-13.
35. Debry, Jean Antoine Joseph (1760-1834), was one of the fortunate members of the Convention who lived to a ripe old age. He had the ability to change his political beliefs easily. He held rather important positions under Robespierre, the Directory, Napoleon, and, finally, the returning Bourbons.

tionals stop using up valuable time with false accusations and get down to the business of completing a frame of government, charges and counter-charges continued to be made. The session of December 7, 1792, is an example in point. Practically the whole session was wasted by some Montagnards vainly attempting to connect Monsieur Roland to a somewhat hazy royalist plot. A really impressive list of names was mentioned regarding this conspiracy: the Rolands, Fauchet,[36] Le Brun (Minister of Foreign Affairs from August 10, 1792, to June 21, 1793), Narbonne (former minister of Louis XVI), Talleyrand, and Madame Du Barry (former mistress of Louis XV). The facts of the case, as brought out, cleared the Rolands, Le Brun, and Fauchet. Supposedly, a certain Monsieur Viard had attemped to carry letters from a royalist group in London (headed by Talleyrand, Narbonne, and Madame Du Barry) to Roland, Le Brun, and Fauchet in France, whom the royalists believed would welcome their advances. If the latter group encouraged any correspondence with the French royalists in England, it would seem that it was only to expose their plots. After altogether too many hours spent discussing the case, the Convention decided that the only guilty one was Viard, an undisguised adventurer willing to sell his services to any side.[37]

Another example of unwise time-wasting, this time the Girondins being at fault, was the attempt (at the same time that the

36. Fauchet, Claude (1744-1793), a former abbé, was a supernumerary of the Girondin Constitutional Committee of 1793. Even before the Revolution he was quite rabid in his republican beliefs. A famous preacher, he lost one post because he had the nerve to speak of kings as tyrants. During the Revolution he held many important positions. As a deputy to the Convention, he associated with the Girondins because they appeared to be honestly endeavoring to make republicanism work in France. Shortly after their proscription, he too was arrested. He was guillotined by the Robespierrists on October 31, 1793.

37. *Débate de la Convention nationale,* II, 29-52.

king was being tried) by some deputies to have a democratic
member of the Convention, who had the misfortune of carrying the
blood of kings in his veins, ousted from his position as a representative of Paris. Louis Philippe Égalité (né Louis Philippe
Joseph de Bourbon, Duc d'Orléans),[38] father of the future King
Louis Philippe, and one of history's enigmatical characters, had
been born into the very highest ranks of the nobility. With the
coming of the Revolution, however, he had associated himself
with the more democratic elements. He welcomed the overthrow

38. Égalité, Louis Philippe Joseph de Bourbon, Duc d'Orléans
(1747-1793), had a frustrated career. Before the Revolution,
although one of the highest members of the nobility, he was
constantly ignored by Marie Antoinette and her encourage.
He was never given any notable position by the king. When
France took the side of the American colonies against the
British during the American Revolution, the Duc d'Orléans
tried to obtain an admiral's rank. Failing to receive such
a rank, he enrolled in the navy as a plain volunteer. As a
volunteer, he participated bravely in several engagements.
The French Revolution found the liberal *duc* associating
with what appeared to be the most violent democrats. At
the Contituent Assembly, at the Jacobin Club and finally at
the Convention, the *duc* (who had changed his title to plain
Citizen Égalité) was a quiet member of the Robespierrists.
This was the main reason, perhaps, why he was so violently
attacked by the Girondins. Yet, ironically enough, Égalité
was not to suffer at the hands of the Girondins. Indeed, his
fate was to be decided by his own colleagues. A few months
after the Girondin proscription, the Montagnards, evently
embarrassed by royalty in their own ranks, proscribed
Égalité too. The same act of accusation was used against the
abashed *duc* as had been used against the Brissotines. All
the dumfounded Égalité could say when shown the charges
was, "Really, this seems to be a joke!" It was no joke, however. The Duc d'Orléans' head was separated from his shoulders on November 6, 1793. (Kuscinski, A., *Dictionnaire des
Conventionnels* [Paris, 1916], pp. 239-242.)

of the king, for whose death he later voted, and happily witnessed the proclamation of a republic. Elected a Parisian deputy to the Convention — without the approval of Robespierre, it appears — he sat at the far left of the assembly hall with the Mountain. Perhaps this is one reason why he was a target of the Girondins.

Admitting that the Duc d'Orleans might be a good republican, himself, Buzot (on December 16, 1792) pointed out that the danger lay in his name and, yes, even in his popularity. If there were no longer any Bourbons left in France, there would be one less cause for division. Buzot, supported by Lanjuinais, proposed that the Orleans family be banished. The Montagnards regarded this Girondin proposal with suspicion. If one legally elected representative could be removed from the Convention, the precedent would be established for removing others. Side-tracking the issue, the Robespierrists said that since the tendency was to remove causes for division, then Roland (Minister of the Interior) and Pache (Minister of War) should also be removed. Ultimately, the question of the Orleans family became too embarrassing for both factions. At the session of December 19, it was agreed to suspend judgment on Égalité until the king's fate was decided.[39]

Since the opening of the Convention the problem of what to do with the deposed king had bothered the deputies. It was really a simple problem, whose solution could have been postponed until the all-important constitutional questions had been decided. Indeed, as Brissot had proposed early in October, 1792, the people could vote on the fate of the former monarch at the same time that they voted on a completed constitution.[40] The first and most important task of the deputies, however, was to complete a republican charter. The constitution would not only bring law and order, it would also mean the end of the Convention, which contained many troublesome and some suspect members. It appears that Robespierre felt that the question of the ex-monarch should take precedence over constitution-making. Speaking on December 1

39. *Débats de la Convention nationale*, II, 133-172.
40. *Ibid.*, I, 143.

and December 2, 1792, at the Convention, he asked that all other matters be put off until the lot of the ex-monarch had been determined.[41]

As it was the Montagnard minority that pushed the problem of the king forward, and as it was this minority that won practically all the ensuing arguments as to his disposal, it is interesting to compare its attitude with that of the Girondins. Durand-Maillane considered the victory of the Montagnards on the question of the king extremely important. It not only put off discussion of a constitution; it also enabled the forces of Robespierre to see how easy it was to embarrass and disorganize the Girondins. Winning this comparatively easy victory over the Girondins, thought Durand-Maillane, encouraged the Montagnard leaders to even bolder actions.[42]

Before discussing how the Montagnards and Girondins differed in their conception of law in regard to the king, it will be well to give the facts of the trial briefly. In the treatment of the development of French republicanism, however, the important thing about the judicial examination was that it revealed the distinct differences in political philosophy between the two main groups of the Convention. Sketchily, here are the facts of the trial.

By acclamation it was decreed (on December 2, 1792) that the Convention had the right to try the ex-monarch.[43] Two days later it was decreed that at every session the hours between eleven o'clock in the morning and six o'clock in the evening would be devoted to the case of the king. This schedule was to be maintained until the case was decided.[44] Jean Baptiste Lindet, reporter for the special commission appointed to list the alleged crimes of Louis XVI, gave his report on December 10. It contained an impressive list of charges against Louis; some of them, it must be admitted, were vague and without proof. The essence of the

41. *Ibid.*, I, 482.
42. Durand-Maillane, P. T., *Mémoires* (Paris, 1825), p. 51.
43. *Débats de la Convention nationale*, 1, 510.
44. *Ibid.*, II, 10.

report was that Louis through various intrigues, had tried to re-establish despotism and kill the democratic achievements of the Revolution.[45] Desèze, a capable lawyer — and quite brave, considering the opinion of many Frenchmen on kings — made a brilliant and seemingly unimpeachable defense of the royal defendant (on December 26).[46] Desèze was one of the three men appointed to defend Louis. Ignoring the legal reasonings of Desèze, of the 721 Conventionals present at the session of January 15, 1793, 683 voted that the former king was guilty of all charges.[47]

45. *Ibid.*, II, 71-95.
46. *Ibid.*, II, 193-252. Desèze began by congratulating the Convention for its republican attitude in giving the king a trial. Yet it was unfortunate, thought he, that the defense had been given only eight days to prepare a case really requiring eight months. Desèze's main defense was that, according to law, Louis, now being an ordinary citizen, could not be held for any alleged crimes which he might have committed as a king. Moreover, assuming that Louis was now king, which he was not, he would have to be tried according to the law of the Constitution of 1791. But the Constitution of 1791 no longer existed! France was now republican! Besides, even if there were existing laws by which the ex-monarch could be tried, it was a decided breach of republican legal procedure that the Convention should be accuser and judge at the same time. Having pointed out that the constituent body had no authority over Louis, the brilliant defending lawyer went ahead and answered all charges against the former king anyway. His chief contention was that most of the alleged crimes had been committed by Louis XVI's ministers and advisers.
47. *Débats de la Convention nationale,* III, 9. At the January 15, 1793, session, 683 out of a possible 749 members voted. Of the 66 deputies not voting, 8 were absent because of sickness and 20 were absent on special missions. This leaves 38 deputies unaccounted for. Perhaps it can be assumed that although they were present, they did not care to be on record as making a decision one way or the other.

The next day a vote was taken on the penalty to be imposed on Louis XVI. There were 726 deputies present at this session, a record attendance; of this number, 361, or exactly a majority of the 721 who cast ballots, voted unconditionally for the death of the former monarch.[48] Denied the right of any form of reprieve (either until the end of the war or until the completion of the constitution)[49] Louis XVI met, with the bravery usually characteristic of him, death by the guillotine on January 21, 1793.

As far as relations between the Girondins and Montagnards during the king's trial are concerned, it is worth noting that the members of the latter group always were in complete uniformity of views, while the members of the former group could not always seem to agree among themselves as to policy. The Montagnards showed the efficiency of a well-organized minority, while their opponents proved that they were filled with republican ideal-

48. *Ibid.*, III, 54-56. In the sentencing of Louis XVI to death, what precisely was the position of the 749 Conventionals? As far as can be determined, the stand of the 749 can be broken down into the following categories: 361 voted for an unconditional death penalty. This number included practically all the Montagnards and some of the Plain. 286 voted for banishment from France, either immediately or as soon as the war was over, 2 wanted Louis imprisoned (apparently for life), 46 voted for the death penalty only as a formality (Louis was to be reprieved and, as soon as the war was over or the constitution completed, finally pardoned), 26 voted for the death penalty with the condition that the sentence was to be delayed until there was further discussion about how the death of the king might affect public affairs, 23 deputies being absent (either because of sickness or special missions) could not vote, and 5 who were present refused to vote one way or the other.

49. The question of reprieving Louis XVI until the completion of a constitution was placed to a vote January 19, 1793. Of the 690 deputies present at this session of the Convention, 380 voted against such a reprieve. (*Ibid.*, III, 109.)

ism but deficient in organization. All the Conventionals did agree, however, with one possible exception, that the king could be judged, either by the Convention or by some other body.[50] Still, there was quite a difference between the way the leading Montagnards regarded the forms of law and the way the leading Girondins regarded them! Moreover, there was a wide difference of opinion regarding the concept of justice! Two leading members of the Mountain, Saint-Just and Robespierre, in speeches delivered on November 13 and December 3, 1792, respectively, revealed their ideas of justice.

Saint-Just[51] said that they did not have to consider justice in

50. The exception was Charles Morisson, a deputy from Vendée. He said that in the absence of any preexisting laws applying to the case of the dethroned king, Louis could not be tried by any court. Answering those, such as Robespierre and Saint-Just, who made the claim that Louis could be held accountable by natural law, Morisson said he respected this law. Yet, by ignoring the procedure of positive law, France, in the eyes of Europe, would be regarded as anarchical. (*Débats de la Convention nationale* . . . 1, 357-371.)

51. Saint-Just, Louis Antoine de (1767-1794), was one of the youngest and more bloodthirsty members of the Convention. Closely attached to Robespierre, he and the leading Montagnards after the fall of the Girondins practically ran France until July 27, 1794. He was one of the chief apologists for the necessity of a dictatorship with Robespierre in the key role. There were remarkable similarities between Saint-Just and Robespierre. Both had received excellent classical and legal educations. As youths, both were addicted to writing poetry and enjoyed the communion of literary fellowships. As Revolutionaries, they displayed the same austere, incorruptible manner; doubtless they really wished to better the lot of the people. And they believed that they knew better than anyone else what was best for the people. Before democratic and republican procedures could be allowed they would have to eliminate all opposition forces. The steps to genuine democracy must be slow and under pro-

the case of Louis XVI. A king was outside the law. Justice and law were not considered by the Romans when the Tarquins were driven out; neither were they considered when the English got rid of Charles I. Of course, history vouchsafes, with some qualification, the validity of Saint-Just's assumption. But definitions of law and definitions of justice are ever subject to Socratic searching! Yet, to Saint-Just, philosophical-legal concepts perhaps were reduced to the clarity of the zealot or crusader. Parading his knowledge of antiquity, Saint-Just said that Julius Caesar was judged with no other formality than that of twenty-three dagger thrusts.[52] Robespierre also referred to the fact that the Tarquins of Rome were not hailed before a court. There was no need to waste time trying Louis. Kings should not be judged; rather, they should be hurled into nothingness.[53]

The Montagnard leaders, then, believed, as did the Girondins, that the ex-king could be held accountable for his past actions as a ruling monarch. However, they would not have bothered with the formality of a trial, but would have arbitrarily executed him. Despite the opposition of Robespierre and Saint-Just, the king was given a trial and found guilty. It was in agreeing on a proper sentence that the Girondins displayed their usual tendency to procrastinate. There was no conformity amongst them as to what should happen to Louis XVI. They all thought that the death penalty would be too harsh and would have doubtful results, but they could not make up their minds as to an alternative sentence. Because of their vacillation, the Robespierrists, who never deviated from the stand that there could be only one sentence, and that death, were able to gather enough votes to assure the execution. The greater part of the Girondins favored referring the sentence

tective guidance all the way. The speeches of both Saint-Just and Robespierre were brimming with classical allusions and filled with assurances as to their great love of humanity.

52. *Débats de la Convention nationale* . . . , I, 372-379.
53. *Ibid.*, I, 499-504.

of the king to the people. However, the Montagnard leaders, appearing to fear trusting in the sovereignty of the people in this instance, were against a referendum.

Even before the conclusion of the trial Robespierre stubbornly maintained that there should be no referendum. His address of December 26, 1792, to the Convention contained arguments against appeal as well as denunciation of the Girondins. An appeal to the primary assemblies would light the fires of civil war, said he. Moreover, he described these local foyers of the people as being dominated by "prideful bourgeosie and aristocrats." He did not hide the fact that he also feared that once the primary assemblies were convoked, they might decide for new deputies. The reason why the Girondins did not want to execute the king, accused Robespierre, was that they would rather have him fall under a popular movement which could be blamed on the Montagnards. Decrying what he termed the oppressive use of their majority position, he warned that a minority had the right of propagating what it regarded as the truth.[54]

In contrast to the position of Robespierre and his group on referring the sentence of Louis XVI to the sovereign people, Girondin leaders generally favored a referendum. Even before the king was sentenced, Brissot thought that the fate of the ex-monarch should be left to the primary assemblies. A judgment by the people would be respected by all parties; foreign nations would be more likely to respect a decision coming from the whole nation.[55] After the king had been judged, Brissot made a plea for leniency; to execute Louis XVI, who had aided the colonists in the American Revolution, would be to court the disapproval of a sister republic, the United States. Besides, such an action would alienate the sympathies of the few friends that they already had in nations under the control of tyrants. Brissot had England in mind, especially.[56] Tom Paine also emphasized the bad effect which the

54. *Ibid.*, II, 298-315.
55. *Ibid.*, II, 353.
56. *Ibid.*, III, 100-102.

execution might have on public opinion in the United States and England. Indeed, it might cause nations now at peace with France to declare war on her. Louis was not worth the risk of further war.[57] Condorcet, who would have preferred having Louis tried by a special tribunal,[58] agreed with Brissot and Paine that to kill the king would give foreign nations the opinion that France was in a state of anarchy.[59] These three famous republicans and members of the constitutional committee were not afraid to leave the fate of the king to the people. True, they did differ in the manner of referral. Condorcet, for instance, had originally desired that Louis be tried by a separate body — rather than by the Convention — elected by the nation. Paine advocated that the king's lot should be settled by the succeeding assembly, which would, of course, be selected by the people. So, in principle, all agreed to let the people, in one way or another, decide as to the disposal of Louis Capet.

By far the best arguments for appeal were given by the two great Girondin orators, and also members of the Girondin constitutional committee, Vergniaud and Gensonné. At the same time that they were discussing the real meaning of sovereignty, they appeared to be pointing accusing fingers at Robespierre for his careless attitude towards republican forms. There was almost a prophetic note in their words uttered at the Convention.

All acts emanating from the representatives of the people were tyrannical, said Vergniaud (on December 31, 1792), if they were not submitted to the true sovereign, the people, for their approval.[60] In answer to the contention of Robespierre that to convoke the primary assemblies in the matter of the king would be to invite civil war,[61] Vergniaud remarked that this was a strange belief for

57. *Ibid.*, III, 96-98; *Moniteur universel*, January 23, 1793.
58. Condorcet, *Opinion sur le Jugement de Louis XVI* in *Oeuvres complètes* (21 vols., Paris, 1801-1804), XVIII, 86-134, *passim.*
59. *Débats de la Convention nationale*, III, 94-95.
60. Vergniaud, *Opinion sur le Jugement de Louis XVI* (Paris, 1793), p. 3; *Débats de la Convention nationale*, II, 321.
61. Refer to p. 243.

a Conventional. Certainly the head of the Mountain knew that the constitution was to be ratified by the people in their local assemblies. Well, if their judgment was to be trusted in one thing, it could be trusted in another.[62] Vergniaud was not afraid to state why he suspected Robespierre's haste in having the king executed. The apparent plan was to create more confusion in an already confused France. The execution would mean new enemies and more fronts to defend, with a corresponding increase in the difficulties accrued by the raising and supplying of large armies. In the ensuing difficulties, what was to prevent that so-called "virtuous minority" (the Montagnards) from bringing forth their "liberator" and "defender" (Robespierre) in the guise of a "necessary man"? If such a state of affairs came to pass, and Vergniaud prayed that they would not, perhaps the fate of the Girondins would be that of those Roman republicans, the Gracchi, who were murdered by the bewildered people that they sought to defend.[63]

Gensonné's opinions on sovereignty, proclaimed at the Convention on January 2, 1793, can be considered the official view of the constitutional committee. This committee, rarely heard from, undoubtedly felt that the debates over appealing the sentence of Louis called for some statements about the bases of the new constitution which was being prepared. As Gensonné explained, the principle of referendum had been thoroughly discussed by the committee. All members were one in agreeing that it was to form one of the chief bases of the republican frame of government. The people should learn to exercise their sovereign right of reviewing legislation; it was only by keeping close watch on the acts of their representatives that tyranny would be prevented.[64] Under the new

---

62. *Débats de la Convention nationale*, II, 326-327.

63. *Ibid.*, II, 328-336.

64. The people should learn to exercise their sovereignty at once. In the words of Gensonné: "Let us hasten! There is still time. Let us not lose a moment in placing in action the principles of sovereignty of the people. Liberty is lost if the general will does not raise itself above all the factions, and crush and dissipate all partisan strife." (*Ibid.*, II, 358.)

constitution the people would have the right of reviewing all legislation. It was only logical that they should now have the same right to review the case of the ex-monarch. Beware of that faction, said Gensonné, that was opposing appeal. Was it not a sure sign that the Robespierrists were but a dangerous minority when they feared to trust the judgment of all France? This faction, the one that reigned at the Jacobin Club and whose principal chiefs sat amongst them, should be regarded with the greatest suspicion. Above all, the country must beware of any individual who egotistically designated himself a "friend of the people" or an "incorruptible defender" of their rights.[65]

Disregarding the advice of deputies such as Tom Paine, who had argued that in so far as August 10 had figuratively killed Louis the king, there was no need to kill the insignificant being Louis the man, a weak majority of the Conventionals, swayed by the Robespierrists, voted away the life of the ex-monarch.

Although the execution of a man who had been an absolute monarch might be regarded as a challenge to the reigning despots of Europe, the fact that France had killed her king really served as but a climax to the many French developments which were worrying other European powers. One development causing anxiety in European capitals was the phenomenal success of the republican armies. The raw recruits, who in the early months of the war had run at the sound of the Prussian guns, now, under the leadership of competent generals such as Dumouriez and Kellermann, were vanquishing their opponents wherever they met them. Such victories against the Prussians and Austrians as those at Valmy (on September 20, 1792) and Jemmapes (on November 6, 1792) were convincing proof of the fighting spirit of the patriot troops. In the north, French armies had invaded Germany and taken several important towns on the Rhine. Soon after the battle of Jemmapes, all of the Austrian Netherlands were occupied. In the southeast, Savoy and Nice were first occupied and then annexed — France

65. *Moniteur universel*, January 4, 1793; *Débats de la Convention nationale*, II, 357-365.

having been at war with Sardinia since July, 1792. A concomitant of the advance of the French troops was the spread of republican propaganda. The dissemination of the principles of really representative government, principles which were anathema to all European monarchies, including the English, was viewed with greater alarm than the killing of the king.

Remarks of the Revolutionaries as to the aims of their war — or, better, crusade — were not of a nature to calm the nerves of divine-rights rulers. Appearing in person before the Convention (on October 12, 1792), Dumouriez boasted that liberty was triumphing everywhere; with philosophy as its guide, sacred liberty would overrun the world and, after crushing despotism and enlightening the people, would topple all thrones.[66] The aim of the French republicans was to separate the people from their enemies. In the words of the visionary Anacharsis Cloots, it was a time of "war against the castles and peace for the cabins." In enemy territory the only levies to be exacted, said Cloots, were those against a prince or his agents.[67] The rights and properties of defeated peoples should be respected, said Lasource. France, in antithesis to ancient Rome, was a deliverer, and not a conqueror. As a benevolent deliver, the French army should inform the inhabitants of occupied territory about such concepts as the rights of man and the sovereignty of the people.[68] In conformity with the proselytizing temper of the Conventionals was the famous proclamation passed on November 19, 1792. This announcement

---

66. *Moniteur universel,* October 13, 1792. A remark by General Dumouriez about the bloody engagements in the forests of the Argonne causes one to stop and reflect. He said that the Germans (Prussians) would have cause to remember that arid soil where "their impure blood served as fertilizer." (*Loc. cit.*) Apparently the memory of man is short. About one hundred and twenty-five years later, French republican armies, this time joined by Americans, were shedding, in the very same region, the blood of another German king's soldiers.

67. *Débats de la Convention nationale,* I, 167.

68. *Ibid.,* I, 177.

encouraged insurrection in all neighboring countries by offering the assistance of French arms to any peoples who wished to rid themselves of the shackles of despotism. As England at this time was having trouble with her own liberals as well as with her Irish subjects, this proclamation was not conducive to better relations between France and England.

If the English government finally joined the coalition of monarchical governments against France, it would seem that it was after some provocation by the latter power. It cannot be denied that France tried to encourage republicanism amongst the English people. For instance, a deputation from a London constitutional society was welcomed at the Convention on November 28, 1792. The spokesman for the deputation said that eleven similar societies were being formed throughout England; it was hoped that before long there would be a constitutional convention in the British capital.[69] Besides encouraging beliefs and organizations which would be subversive to the existing form of English government, French leaders boldly uttered statements at the Convention which where those of a nation about to embark on war against England. Of course, these warlike statements were made only a month before France declared war, in the main. By this time the attitude of the Britisth government was so unfriendly that it could be expected that soon England would be ranged with the enemies of France. However, speeches of such Conventionals as Kersaint, which struck at the very foundations of the British Empire, caused an irreparable breach between the two nations.

Kersaint, speaking at the Convention on January 1, 1793, proposed that France strike at the colonial possessions of England as well as those of her economic satellites, Holland, Spain, and Portugal. Since England was dependent on trade for her very life-blood, she would soon be brought to her knees. As for the British fleet, France need not worry. The fear of invasion would keep it bottled up at home. Once the British, Dutch, Spanish, and Portuguese colonial markets were won over, they would be opened

69. *Ibid.*, I, 448-453.

up to all the nations of the world, with the exception of England. With naiveté Kersaint said that this economic strangulation was not for the purpose of hurting the English people. It was aimed at the small aristocracy of wealth which controlled British politics.[70]

Brissot, reporting for the Diplomatic Committee on January 12, 1793, was quite caustic in his comments about the English government. The only reason it had remained neutral as long as it had was because of the profits to be gained by trading with all sides. Now that the River Scheldt was opened to commerce,[71] to the advantage of the Austrian Netherlands (now occupied by the French) and to the disadvantage of the exclusive trading rights of Holland and England, the British administration feared reduced profits. Brissot looked upon the refusal of the English government to send an ambassador to France (one had been recalled on August 17, 1792), and its suspicious ordering of troop movements, as warlike acts.[72] Largely on the basis of Brissot's report,[73] that

70. *Ibid.*, II, 339-351.
71. This river had been closed by the Treaties of Westphalia, ending the Thirty Years War in 1648.
72. *Débats de la Convention nationale*, II, 452-478.
73. According to a document discovered rather recently—historic-ally speaking—Brissot had first read this report to David Williams, the English philosopher, then residing in France. As Williams thought some of Brissot's remarks too bellicose, the latter agreed to change them. However, Brissot gave this report to the Convention as he had originally conceived it. Williams, in the document, made the claim that Le Brun, French Minister of Foreign Affairs, had asked him to deliver a letter to Lord Grenville, British Minister of Foreign Affairs. The purpose of this letter, which Lord Grenville refused to receive, said Williams, was to try and bring about friendlier relations between two governments. Thus, some French leaders, while publicly revealing a belligerent manner towards England, were privately seeking peace ("Un Document inedit sur la Gironde: David Williams," *Annales historiques de la Revolution francaise* [September-October, 1938], fifth year, No. 89, pp. 417-418.)

the spread of conflict seemed inevitable in the face of the many hostile acts of the British,[74] war was finally declared on England and her political and economic ward, Holland, on February 1, 1793.

On the same day that France declared war on England, William Pitt the Younger, the English Prime Minister, made a speech before the House of Commons in which he accused the French of having disturbed the peace of Europe. It was England's duty, as well as an obligation of honor, to join the Allies and save Europe from being dominated by France.[75] Now the great power of the British Empire was added to that of the other monarchies which sought to stifle the over-expansion of French republicanism. When, about one month later, Spain and the Holy Roman Empire joined the coalition of England, Austria, Prussia, Holland and Sardinia, France was at war with all her neighbors. Thus, in addition to the many trying internal problems resulting from factional strife, the Convention faced the equally, perhaps more trying problem of ever-expanding warfare.

Partisan controversies, the trial of the king, and questions of war, then, were the many issues which had occupied the Convention since the appointment of the constitutional committee in October, 1792. Since most of the committee members were also active leaders in the Convention, it was to be expected that these issues would distract them from their task of quickly finishing the constitution. Distractions were probably the chief cause for re-

74. Among the hostile actions enumerated were that England had flooded France with forged *assignats*, prevented grain from reaching French ports, sheltered many royalist emigrants, and made an alliance with the Dutch *stadholder* against France.

75. Several days later Pitt, in a speech before the House of Commons, was a little more specific as to why England must fight France. The English, said the Primer Minister, saw in their true light "those detestable principles which, having ruined France, will not be long in ruining all Europe if their propagation is not checked." (*Moniteur universel*, March 1, 1793.)

tardation. Perhaps another cause, however, was the painstaking care taken in forming a charter which might mean so much to the successful future of French republicanism. Certainly, careful and thorough execution had always characterized the work of the principal author of the Girondin Constitution of 1793, the *philosophe* Condorcet. The long-overdue constitution, which Condorcet began to read on February 15, 1793, to an expectant and rather anxious Convention, represented no variation from the standard of work that the philosopher had always maintained.

Chapter VII

Rejection of the Girondin Constitution; Proscription of Its Authors

For some months before the Girondin Constitution of 1793 finally emerged from committee, the thinking French public had reason to be well prepared in the elements of republican constitutionalism. Besides the constant reminder that the Convention was going to prepare a charter which would be a panacea for all governmental ailments, most of the leading newspapers carried advertisements relating to books about the organization of representative government. For example, of three books advertised in the *Moniteur universel* of November 9, 1792, two were about constitutions and one was the Bible. It was significant that, according to the titles, one of the two constitutional works claimed to contain the articles of government of the Spartans, Athenians, and Romans; the other contained the charters of the thirteen states of the United States!

The great effect that the examples of the United States and antiquity had on the cause of French republicanism needs no stressing.[2] Their effect on Condorcet, combined with that of the Anglo-French philosophers and publicists, was enormous. The document that Condorcet presented to the Convention on February 15, 1793, was in a way, a synthesis of what the philosopher thought was best in the practical systems of antiquity and the United States, and in the theoretical systems of the philosophers.

Before commenting on the constitution proper, it is well to review part of the remarkable survey, entitled *Exposition des Principes et*

1. *Moniteur universel* (*Journal officiel de l'Empire français*), (196 vols., Paris, 1789-1863), November 9, 1792.
2. Refer to chapters I and II of this monograph.

des Motifs du Plan,[3] with which Condorcet prefaced its intended reading.[4] In this survey, not only are the main points of the charter explained; also sharply delineated are the democratic intentions which motivated the Girondin committee. Indeed, in appreciating the uniqueness of the Girondin frame of government, more can be gained from reading Condorcet's exposition, perhaps, than from simply reading the constitution itself. Certainly, the latter should not be read before one has studied the exposition.

Condorcet's survey was opened with a reference to the important and complicated problem that the committee had had to resolve. Their (the committee members')[5] task had been to frame a cons-

3. Among the many reproductions of this exposition, which were printed shortly after Condorcet's reading of it at the Convention, by far the best is that found in the *Moniteur universel* of February 17 and February 18, 1793. The *Moniteur's* copy was used by the writer. The title, however, was taken from the copy found in No. 151 of the *Journal des Débats;* here the full title was *Extrait de l'Exposition des Principes et des Motifs du Plan présenté à la Convention nationale par Condorcet, au Nom du Comité de Constitution.*

4. Although Condorcet had the intention of reading the whole constitution to the Convention, according to vol. VI, p. 246, of the *Procès-verbal de la Convention nationale* (72 vols., Paris, 1792-1795), he never got beyond reading the exposition, the Declaration of Rights, and a few Titles of the constitution proper. Fatigue, due to a weakened physical condition, prevented him from ever finishing. According to some accounts, even on the first day of reading, Barère had to relieve him. Cited by Alengry, Franck, *Condorcet: Guide de la Révolution française, Théoricien du Droit constitutionnel et Précurseur de la Science sociale* (Paris, 1904), p. 238. The following day (February 16), Gensonné continued the reading, Condorcet still being indisposed. However, rather than be bothered with listening to the whole constitution, the Convention cut Gensonné short and decreed that the project be printed so that all the deputies could read it for themselves.

5. Although there can be little doubt that Concorcet was the

titution which, founded on principles of reason and justice, would assure the people the greatest possible enjoyment of their natural rights. Their constant endeavor had been to so combine its various parts that any necessary bending of the individual will to the general will would in no way change the principle of equality among citizens or limit the people in their rights of sovereignty. This was a roundabout way of saying that the aim was to protect the people from any possible encroachments of their own government. Condorcet well realized that even a republican frame of government, if not carefully formed, could be subject to misuse. To prevent any one individual from having too much power for too long a period had been one of the guiding principles of the committee, said the philosopher. Highest authority could not be entrusted to any individual for a long space of time without conferring on the favored one an influence attached to his person rather than to his functions. Such an unwise bestowal of authority would be tantamount to giving an ambitious being the means of threatening public liberty. However, just because the Girondin committee was against over-concentration of power in the hands of one man, it was not to be implied that the committee was against an adequate central control or that it favored a loose federation.[6]

Special pains were taken by Condorcet in his preliminary survey to show that his Girondin associates were not federalists. By geography (there were no great natural obstacles) and tradition (the country had long been governed by a single agency — a king), France was destined to absolute unity. Moreover, now that an ever-growing coalition of the absolute powers threatened the borders of their country, there was need for even stronger unity. Time should not be foolishly wasted in debating the issue of who

principal author of the Girondin constitution (refer to chapter V, *passim*) he, for courtesy's sake, always spoke in the plural when discussing any of the work regarding it. Of course, even though he was the author, other committee members probably helped him formulate his ideas.

6. *Moniteur universel*, February 17, 1793.

was a federalist and who was not, when the country faced the dreadful perils of war. Did the thirteen original English colonies of America, which during their struggle for independence formed a weak federation of states, stop to argue the pros and cons of their form of union? Let all Frenchmen agree that France would be a republic, one and indivisible.[7] Having expressed his own and his associates' wish to maintain the unity of their country and the sovereignty of its people, Condorcet now explained, in broad terms, the system of government that it was believed would best carry out these objectives.

Although a government having completely democratic operation might be impractical, agreed Condorcet, still one could be formed which would at least approach this ideal. He believed that the committee's project came close to the ideal. It guaranteed the people the greatest possible participation in their own administration and strictly limited the amount of delegated authority. In this project, which has come to be known as the "Girondin Constitution of 1793," government was a simple, everyday affair — something tangible, something democratic — personally and sympathetically concerning the lives of all Frenchmen, no matter how humble their station. The delegated authorities were carefully restricted in their powers and were actually but servants of the people, who were to keep the closest check on them. According to the Girondin project, the various government agencies were not to be viewed as something in which membership would place an individual above the common herd. Obsequiousness to any person holding a position of delegation should not be encouraged. In the governmental solar system, the people formed the all-important life-giving center, around which, and dependent on it, revolved the diverse administrative agencies. Condorcet, in his exposition of the constitution, sought to show how the whole organization of this democratic charter was aimed at jealously preserving the sovereign rights of the citizenry.

One of the cornerstones of the Girondin constitution, and in

7. *Loc. cit.*

line with the democratic reasoning that people should rule themselves to the greatest possible extent, was the provision whereby
an ordinary citizen could either call for a referendum on old
legislation or petition for the initiation of new. In that the right
of referendum was, under the constitution, a recognized sovereign
right of the people, said Condorcet, it was only natural to expect
that this same constitution should be submitted to all Frenchmen
for approval. The philosopher, who must have been aware that one
of the first acts of the Convention had been to decree just such a
referendum,[8] thus manifested his suspicion that the Robespierrists
might attempt to prevent a plebiscite on the constitution. Doubtless,
Robespierre's speech during the debates on the fate of the king,
in which the Montagnard leader had said that to refer the judgment of the ex-monarch to the people would invite civil war,[9] had
alarmed Condorcet. His remarks, that in times of doubt and
uncertainty it was more necessary than ever for representatives to
affirm the rights of the citizenry,[10] might be considered his answer
to Robespierre. The venerated associate of the Girondins, in a few
general introductory remarks about the purposes of the primary
assemblies as visualized by the committee, made still further
thrusts at the principles of the Mountain.[11]

It was recognized that the primary assemblies, the smallest
units of governmental structure, were in direct contact with the
people. It was in these small cells that the people would really
learn to appreciate their rights and duties as French citizens.
Realizing their importance as parts of a really democratic system
the Girondin committee had voted to retain these units, with some
modifications due to the increased suffrage.[12] The primary assem-

8.   Refer to p. 165.
9.   Refer to p. 243
10.   *Moniteur universel*, February 17, 1793.
11.   It should be emphasized again that the synonymous expres
        sions "Mountain," "Montagnards" and "Robespierrists" are
        for the sake of variety, used interchangeably.
12.   In legislation enacted by the Constituents in 1789, the number
        of primary assemblies—which were then viewed simply as

blies had come into existence at the start of the Revolution. Besides their instructional importance, they were valuable as politico-social centers. Instead of going to what Condorcet termed "wildcat reunions," where demigods encouraged strife and disunity, the citizenry could meet in recognized assemblies and discuss its political problems and their remedies in an atmosphere conducive to unity and good government. Scarcely trying to veil his vexation over the unruly attitude of Paris and its extra-legal government, Condorcet said that only by firmly supporting the lawful groups could the illegal bodies be discouraged. However, even amongst the lawful groups, no one group — even though favored by its

electoral bodies—was determined according to the following rules: One primary assembly was allowed for each piece of territory that contained a population of not more than nine hundred "active" male citizens. An "active" citizen was one who paid a yearly tax equivalent to the average wage for three workdays in 1789. (The distinctions of "active" and "passive" citizens, however, were wiped out in August, 1792.) Two assemblies were permitted for a territory having a population of between nine hundred and fifteen hundred active male citizens. Regions with over fifteen hundred active citizens were permitted three primary assemblies. (Sagnac, P., *La Révolution, 1789-1792* in *Histoire de France contemporaine depuis la Révolution jusqu'à la Paix de* 1919 [ed. by Lavisse, Ernest, 10 vols , Paris, 1920-1922,] I, 164, note 2.)

By the Girondin Constitution of 1793, the number of primary assemblies was to be determined according to population. However, now that the distinction between "active" and "passive" citizens had been removed, there would be a much larger number of primary assemblies than the number constituted in 1789. Instead of one primary assembly for every nine hundred male individuals paying a certain tax rate, there would be one for every section of territory that contained not less than four hundred and fifty or more than nine hundred males of voting age, regardless of the citizens' financial status. (Title III, section I, article I of *Constitution française telle qu'elle a été lue à la Convention nationale, le Vendredi 15 Février 1793* [*Paris*, 1793].)

location, such as that in a big city — should predominate over others.[13]

Government, then, according to the Girondin project, was to be for the most part centered in the people, who were to participate in its functions directly through their primary assemblies. In creating a frame of government in which the citizenry acted so directly, Condorcet showed the influence of Jean Jacques Rousseau.[14] In some respects, Rousseau was indeed the master of the Girondons.[15] Since the Girondin Constitution of 1793 was so closely based on the fundamental axiom of *The Social Contract* that sovereignty lay with the general will, in discussing the project of the Girondins it is logical to center the whole discussion around the guaranteed rights of the people and the manner in which they exercised their sovereignty. In the examination which follows, the main sources depended upon will be the Girondin charter itself[16] and Condorcet's version of it in the *Moniteur*, the latter source being a valuable supplement to the former.

Amongst the rights of free men which introduced Condorcet's plan of government,[17] there were some whose liberalism was

13.   *Moniteur universel*, February 17, 1793.
14.   Refer to pp. 19-30.
15.   Combes de Patris, Bernard, *L'Ésprit financier des Girondins* (Paris, 1909), p. 31.
16.   *Constitution françoise* (sic), *telle qu'elle a été lue à la Convention nationale, le Vendredi 15 Février 1793* (Paris, 1793.) Hereafter, instead of repeating the whole title, the constitution will simply be referred to by the titles (within the constitution), sections, and articles.
17.   To avoid the constant repetition of the phrases "Girondin Constitution of 1793," "the Girondin frame of government," or "the Girondin charter," these phrases are sometimes alternated with "Condorcet's charter," "Condorcet's project," or "Condorcet's frame of government." This is not an incorrect interchange, as all evidence seems to point to the fact that the philosopher was the author of the Girondin Constitution of 1793. In the substitution of the word "charter" for "constitu-

extraordinary for the eighteenth century. Some of these, in certain parts of the world, would be considered liberal even today. Such rights as freedom of speech, press, and religion, and such guarantees as those relating to one's person and property were naturally listed.[18] They were but adaptations of the federal and state Declarations of Rights of the United States. The rights which might be considered unusual were the following: The people had the right — through the initiative and referendum — to concur in tax legislation.[19] It was the duty of society to provide an education for all its members.[20] One of society's most sacred obligations was to provide for a system of public relief.[21] Men gathered in society should have some legal means of resisting oppression. There was oppression when officials were discriminatory or arbitrary in the administration of laws. In every free government the means of resistance should be regulated by the constitution.[22] The people always had the right of changing their constitution. One generation had no right to subject future generations to its laws.[23]

tion," it is recognized that the former word is not altogether synonymous with the latter. Moreover, the words "government" and "administration" are recognized as not being completely synonymous. Apparently it is one of the lacks of the English language that there are few synonyms that can be substituted for either "constitution" or "government."

18. These ordinary rights and guarantees were found in the first twenty-one articles of the *Déclaration des Droits naturels, civils, et politiques de l'Homme*, which preceded the constitution proper.

19. *Ibid.*, article XXII.

20. *Ibid.*, article XXIII.

21. *Ibid.*, article XXIV.

22. Ibid., articles XXXI-XXXIII. Condorcet probably got the idea of men having the right to resist the oppression of their government through legal means from his friend d'Holbach. Refer to p. 57.

23. *Ibid.*, article XXXIII. This right is taken almost literally from Rousseau. Refer to p. 29.

Title I of the constitution proper related to the division of territory in the republic. As Condorcet explained in his preliminary survey, the democratic motive for the territorial arrangement decided upon was to enable all citizens to participate easily in their own government without any burden to themselves. The French territory was divided into *departments* and *large communes*; former district divisions were abolished.[24] The large communes were subdivided into *rural* and *municipal sections* (for the city districts). *Sectional assemblies*, corresponding in functions to the primary assemblies, were established for the municipal sections.[25] Communes were limited in area by the rule that their size would be such that all their inhabitants would live within two and one-half miles from the center of the communal capital.[26] Thus, those citizens living on the outskirts of the commune would be able to go to the capital, vote, and return home all in one day.[27]

Rules for citizenship were liberal enough. Any male (native or foreign born) over twenty-one years of age, who had resided in France for a year and who had his name inscribed on the rolls of some primary assembly, was automatically a French citizen.[28] The only requirements necessary for voting were that one had to be a French citizen and to have had the same residence for three successive months.[29] Condorcet, in his introductory explanation, stated that the opinion of the constitutional committee was that the voting privilege should not belong to landholders alone. For the first time in history, boasted Condorcet, the complete equality of

24. Refer to p. 115, note 4.
25. As far as can be learned, Condorcet considered that, function-
     ally, the sectional assemblies and primary assemblies were
     one and the same thing. Presumably, the detailed discussion
     relative to the latter in the Girondin project can also be applied
     to the former.
26. Title I, articles I-VII of the *Constitution françoise* (*sic*).
27. *Moniteur universel*, February 18, 1793.
28. Title II, article I.
29. Title II, article III.

nature was recognized.[30] The right to vote was denied to women, children, criminals and the insane.[31] To hold any public office in France, one need be only a French citizen.[32]

In keeping with their importance, the primary assemblies were given fuller treatment than any other subject in the constitution. It was necessary that the organization of these units, in which the people directly exercised their sovereignty, be carefully explained. According to Title III, section I, article I, their size would be regulated by the rule that none would have fewer than four hundred and fifty or more than nine hundred members. In order to conduct the business of the meetings and to keep the official records, each primary assembly was to have a bureau, the members of which were elected by the whole assembly. These bureaus, renewed every time there was a new convocation of the assembly, were to be composed of a president, three secretaries, and vote-tellers.[33]

Section II of Title III enumerated the functions of the primary assemblies. They were to be convoked in order to perform the following acts: 1. To hold any elections stipulated by the constitution. 2. To accept or reject either a new constitution or any changes that might be made in the old. 3. To accept or reject a petition of one of their members demanding a national convention. 4. To carry out the processes of either referendum or petition.[34]

By far the most complicated section in the whole constitution was that which discussed the rules for the election of all departmental officials and national deputies by the primary assemblies. However, if the election rules seemed a trifle involved, it was only to make sure that they would be democratic. Condorcet's idea was to have the people elect officials as directly as possible. With this in mind, he made no provision for the old system of electoral

30. *Moniteur universel,* February 18, 1793.
31. Title II, article V.
32. Title II, article IX.
33. Title III, section I, articles I-XI.
34. Title III, section II, articles I-III.

assemblies.[35] Electoral assemblies, said he, might tend to support local officials against the central authority and cause disunity.[36] By reducing the election procedure to its simplest form, one finds that for all elections there were two main steps. First, a preliminary list, called a *presentation list*, was formed. Secondly, the preliminary list was reduced to a *definitive list*. Some explanation of these two lists is necessary.

Citizens gathered in their primary assemblies inscribed on their ballots a list of names equal to the number of positions to be filled. The ballots of all the primary assemblies in each department were collected by each departmental administration. From these ballots the administrations drew up a reduced list, consisting of the names of those who had received the greatest number of votes, equal to three times the number of posts to be filled. This was the presentation list. It was then sent back to the primary assemblies, along with ballots containing two blank columns. In the first column the citizens, choosing from the presentation list, indicated for their first choice a number of names equal to the number of offices to be filled. In the second they indicated a like number of names for their second choice. The ballots were then sent again to the departmental administration and tabulated. The tabulation of the first column of all the ballots was first made. Those candidates who received an absolute majority of all the first-column votes for the position for which they were running were considered elected to that position. If, for a particular position, there was no candidate who received an absolute majority in the tabulation of the first-column votes, then recourse was had to the second column. The person who received the most votes in the addition of the two columns was elected. Supernumeraries were selected from the same columns after the regular candidates had been elected.[37]

In recording the votes on national measures, such as a consti-

35.   Refer to p. 115, note 7.
36.   *Moniteur universel,* February 18, 1793.
37.   Title III, section III, articles I-XXV.

tutional change, a ladder system was followed. First, the results of all the primary assemblies of a department were recorded by the departmental administration. The results gathered by all the departmental administrations were then tabulated by the national legislative assembly.[38]

Title IV related to the departmental and communal administrations. Every department would have an *Administrative Council* of eighteen members, of whom four would form a *Directory*. The departmental administration would hold office for two years. Its duties were to allot and collect taxes and supervise the communes. The large commune's administration consisted of twelve men besides the mayor, subordinate to the administration of the department. The municipal sections were to have a secondary agency entrusted to a single citizen. The reunion of the secondary agencies of each section with the communal administration formed the *Council General* of the commune.[39] Departmental and communal administration were subordinate to the *Executive Council of the Republic*.

By the Girondin Constitution of 1793, the executive power was strictly limited. Condorcet, in writing the rules for the executive head, showed how much he had profited from what Rousseau and Mably had had to say about one man's holding too much power.[40] Moreover, in creating an executive of seven heads, he proved that he was still an admirer of Pennsylvania's first state constitution.[41]

Title V, section I, article I of the constitution said that the Executive Council would be composed of seven ministers and a secretary. The seven ministerial posts were: Legislation, War, Foreign Affairs, Navy, Taxation, (Agriculture, Commerce, and Manufactures)[42] and, finally, (Public Works, Public Aid, Public

38.   Title III, section V, articles I-XIII.
39.   Title IV, sections I-II.
40.   Refer to pp. 19-43.
41.   Refer to p. 101.
42.   This was all one cabinet post.

Establishments, and Arts).[43] As far as authority was concerned, all ministers were equal. There was no president. Every fifteen days the Executive Council would be presided over by one of the ministers. The main functions of the Council were: 1. To see that all new laws and decrees of the Legislative Corps were received and understood by the departmental administrations and courts. 2. To see that all laws and decrees were properly executed. 3. To superintend all the various administrative officials and recommend their removal by the Legislative Corps when this was necessary. 4. To supervise the land and naval forces. 5. To recommend to the Judiciary Censors[44] the removal of any dishonest or inefficient judge.[45]

The Executive Council could not make laws or interpret or modify those which had already been passed.[46] It could not interfere in any way with the business of the Courts or that of the National Treasury.[47] In other words, the Executive Council was but a superior administrative and advisory body.

Members of the Council were elected by all the people in a manner somewhat similar to the one already explained.[48] Each member was named on a separate ballot. For the seven positions, there would be seven ballots altogether. All the ballots cast in each

43. This was also all one cabinet post.
44. Refer to p. 268.
45. Title V, section I, articles I-XVII.
46. Title V, section I, article VI.
47. Title V, section I, articles VII, XVIII. In his preliminary survey Condorcet explained why the handling of public funds was not entrusted to the executive. He stated that executives tended to become arbitrary when, besides holding office for an indefinite term, they were able to make lucrative appointments. One could learn from history, said Condorcet, of the misfortunes which nations had suffered by allowing their rulers to hold the purse strings: "A long and painful past history would prove that oftentimes gold demanded of nations for the defense of their liberty was too often used to enslave them." (*Moniteur universel*, February 17, 1793.)
48. Refer to pp. 261-262.

primary assembly of a department were sent to the departmental administration. From these seven ballots, the departmental administration of each department drew up lists of presentation carrying the names of the twenty-one candidates who had received the most votes. The lists of presentation of all the departments were sent to the Legislative Corps, which drew up a definitive list of thirteen candidates, printing these thirteen names on ballots and distributing them to all the primary assemblies. From these thirteen names the people selected the seven ministers.[49]

Ministers were elected for only two years and could be re-elected.[50] If the ministers were corrupt or inefficient, the Legislative Corps could, with the aid of the National Jury,[51] remove them.[52] Moreover, their removal could be brought about by recall measures originating with the people in the primary assemblies.[53]

All financial matters of the French Republic were to be handled by the *National Treasury* and the *Bureau of Accounts*. There were three members in each of these financial branches of the government, elected by the people in the same way as the ministers of the Executive Council. The term of office for the members of each branch was three years. No money could be withdrawn from the National Treasury without the sanction of the Legislative Corps. The amount of money allotted for each transaction was determined by the Bureau of Accounts.[54]

Indicative of the influence of Pennsylvania's first state constitution on Condorcet was the legislative arrangement. The *Legislative Corps* was to consist of a single House. The number of deputies per department was determined by the proportion of one deputy for every fifty thousand inhabitants. They were elected in the manner already described,[55] for a term of two years.

49. Title V, section II, articles I-XXII.
50. Title V, section II, article XX.
51. Refer to p. 268.
52. Title V, section I, articles XXI-XXX.
53. Title VII, article I.
54. Title VI, articles I-XIII.
55. Refer to pp. 261-262.

Purely a legislative body, and nothing else, the Legislative Corps prepared two types of measures. These were called *Laws* and *decrees*. Laws were distinguished from decrees by their generality and indefinite duration. Decrees had only local application and had to be renewed at definite intervals. Such acts as those concerning criminal and civil legislation, taxation, public domains, and mintage were termed laws. Decrees related to such matters as the annual determination of the size of the army and navy, the amount of funds necessary to maintain the armed forces for a year, declarations of war, ratification of treaties, and rules governing the conduct of public officials.[56] Laws had to be submitted to the people gathered in their primary assemblies. The people could either pass or reject a law. A law rejected by a majority of the primary assemblies was considered void. Even decrees could be declared void, through the people's right of censure.

The most distinctive feature of the constitution was that part entitled *The People's Censorship of the Acts of the National Representation and Their Right of Petition.* It was within the power of the ordinary citizen to have a new law passed, an old law abrogated, an official recalled, or any other political act undertaken by the Legislative Corps. In other words, the citizen had the right of petition, referendum, and recall. To start the governmental machinery in motion in order to effect the adoption of any of these acts, the citizen had simply to gather fifty signatures demanding the convocation of his own primary assembly. If a majority of all the members of the citizen's assembly favored his particular act, then all the primary assemblies of the same commune would be convoked. If they also agreed, then all the primary assemblies of the department would be summoned. If there was still a majority in favor of the proposition, it would be sent to the Legislative Corps, which could sanction or reject it. However, if another department agreed to the proposition, all the primary assemblies of the republic would have to be convoked. If a majority of these assemblies adhered to the act, the Legislative Corps

56.   Title VII, sections I-II.

would then disband and a newly elected Assembly would legislate according to the will of the original humble petitioner.[57]

An ordinary citizen could also bring about the calling of a constitutional convention. If, by a method exactly similar to that used in exercising censure, he could get a majority of all of the primary assemblies of his department to agree that a new constitution was necessary, then the Legislative Corps would have to summon all the primary assemblies of all the departments. If a majority of these also agreed, a convention would be elected without delay by all the French citizenry. However, whether it was petitioned or not, a convention would meet regularly every twenty years in order to make any necessary alterations in the constitution. Every new constitution and any changes in the old had to be referred to all the people for their sanction.[58]

According to the constitution, the judiciary was rigidly separated from the executive and legislative branches of the government. All judges were elected by the people and were paid a fixed salary. The agencies for the fulfillment of civil justice were: *justices of the peace* (one per commune), *arbiters* (chosen by the litigants themselves from supposedly impartial persons), and a *civil jury* (one per department, the members of which were drawn from a panel elected by the primary assemblies of the department). Litigants in civil cases tried first to settle their differences by arbitration (with the aid of the justices of the peace). If this failed, they then had recourse to the department civil jury.[59]

Jury trial was absolutely necessary in all criminal actions. The accused had the right to challenge any of the jurors selected. Moreover, he had the right of legal counsel. No person, once

57. Title VIII.
58. Title IX. Doubtless Condorcet had in mind the many vexations suffered by the existent Convention at the hands of the Paris populace, when he wrote article II. By this article the convention would always have to meet at least fifty leagues away from the capital.
59. Title X, sections I-II.

acquitted of a charge, could be tried over again on the same charge. Criminal tribunals — there were to be seven of them — existed solely for the purpose of passing sentence on those persons convicted of a crime.[60]

Supervising the whole judicial system in each department were officials called *Judicial Censors*. These censors were elected by all the primary assemblies of each department for a term of two years. There could be between four and seven censors. How the number was to be determined was not stated by the constitution. The duty of the censors was to see that proper legal forms were followed in all trials.[61]

All crimes of treason were tried by a *National Jury*. The members of the panel from which the jury was selected were elected by the primary assemblies of the republic in the manner prescribed for primary assembly elections.[62] Three panel members were allowed for each department.[63]

Civil liberty was guaranteed by Title X, section VI, of the constitution. The articles of this section were somewhat of an enlargement of the Declaration of Rights. They explicitly stated just how far the law could go in taking action against an individual's person or property.[64]

The armed forces of the republic were to be composed of all citizens capable of carrying arms. They could be used to defend the country against interior as well as exterior enemies. They were directly under the Executive Council. Their use, however, was to be carefully supervised by the Legislative Corps. Armies were expected to obey. They could not take any initiative in an executive, legislative, or judicial way without the sanction of the Legislative Corps. Commanders-in-chief were limited as commanders to only one campaign at a time. Regardless of whether

---

60. Title X, section III.
61. Title X, section III.
62. Refer to pp. 261-262.
63. Title X, section V.
64. Title X, section VI, articles I-XVI.

the campaign might be over or not, they were replaced at the end of a year. Commanders of the National Guard were to be named yearly by the citizens of each commune.[65]

Taxes were fixed every year by the Legislative Corps. The amount of direct taxes a person had to pay was determined by his income. Taxes could never be levied to such an extent that they would lower the standard of living of the people below a decent subsistence level. Moreover, they must not in any way threaten a person's property or business.[66]

Wars of conquest were denounced by the constitution. No foreign territory would be annexed by France without the consent of the people of the territory. Moreover, France would respect all institutions of foreign countries as long as these institutions had the support of the people of the respective countries.[67]

With the title relating to France's relations with other nations, the Girondin Constitution of 1793 was concluded. Perhaps it was somewhat obscure and incomplete in parts. Yet it was a remarkable step forward as far as man's progress towards governing himself is concerned. This democratic charter endeavored to make government something that was directly participated in by all the people. It tried to establish entire equality among all men. Condorcet, the author of the Girondin frame of government, hoped that it would end factional disputes in France and bring about complete unity. Still, he feared that certain individuals would endeavor to destroy this attempt to organize a democratic form of government.

Beware, said Condorcet, of those ambitious men who were now everything as heads of factions but would be but ordinary beings once France had an orderly constitutional government. It was to be expected that they would try to retard and even prevent the passage of the new constitution.[68] Certainly there was considerable prophecy in the philosopher's words!

65.   Title XI.
66.   Title XII.
67.   Title XIII.
68.   *Moniteur universel*, February 18, 1793.

As soon as the Girondin project was presented to the Convention, the constitutional committee, in conformity with the decree which had established it, was dissolved. According to another decree, passed several months before, discussion in the Convention over the constitution was to be postponed for two months after the committee had presented its project. This decree was closely adhered to. There were no serious discussions about the constitution until the middle of April, 1793. Yet as soon as Condorcet's project was made public it was subject to rather caustic criticism by the Montagnards in their speeches at the Jacobins and in various newspaper articles and pamphlets written by them. They were disposed, in advance, to find fault with any plan emanating from their opponents.[69]

Jacques Coupé, deputy from l'Oise to the Convention, wrote a pamphlet in which he remarked how mournfully Condorcet's plan had been received at the Convention. Speaking in generalities, he claimed that the Executive Council of the constitution was a seven-headed king, an aristocratic arrangement. The voting system was impractical and open to intrigue. Finally, sovereignty did not really lie with the people![70] Jeanbon Saint André, deputy from Lot, in a letter to Hérault de Séchelles, deputy from Seine-et-Oise, spoke of the project as being one which was "the unfortunate child of eight or nine Brissotine fathers" (the Girondins were usually spoken of by contemporaries as "Brissotines," after their leader). "Its essential vice, then, in the eyes of many," said Saint-André, "was simply its origin."[71]

It was at the Jacobin Club that the Robespierrists gave free

69. Frayssinet, Marc, *La République des Girondins* (Toulouse, 1904), p. 239.

70. Coupé, J. M. *À ses Commettants sur le nouveau Projet de Constitution* (place of publication and date of publication are not indicated), pp. 1-3.

71. Saint-André to Hérault de Séchelles, February 16, 1793, as quoted by Lévy, L., *Le Conventionnel Jeanbon Saint-André* (Paris, 1901), p. 233.

scope to their opinions about the Girondin plan. Francois Anthoine, a deputy from Moselle to the Convention, criticized the composition of the constitutional committee. The Jacobins should immediately draw up their own plan and have one of their members submit it to the Convention within fifteen days. Georges Couthon[72] supported this proposal. Condorcet's project, said he, was a strange combination of confusion and intended viciousness. The system of election was too complicated, and the Executive Council, being elected by all the people, would have too much power. One Jacobin brought up the old refrain of federalism. The constitution was really planned, said he, to fool the people and give them a federative government. The Jacobins finally decreed that they would add more members to their own constitutional committee[73] and quickly draw up what, in their own opinion, was a suitable frame of government. This frame would then be presented to the Convention. A decree, aimed at building up public opinion against the Girondin project, was passed on February 20, 1793. It stipulated that an address would be sent to all the departmental Jacobin Clubs with the intention of pointing out the evils of the Girondin constitution.[74]

Shortly after the constitution's presentation, the Robespierrists made one rather feeble attempt at the Convention to cast suspicion on it. Amar, deputy of l'Isere, seconded by Marat, said (on February 20, 1792) that there were some copies of the committee's project being circulated that had provisions for a two-house rather than a single-house legislative body. The committee was at fault

72. Refer to p. 163, note 27.
73. Refer to p. 187, note 8. The members added were Dubois de Crancé, Collot d'Herbois, Anacharsis Cloots and Couthon. The results of the work of the Jacobin constitutional committee, if any, appear never to have been presented to the Convention.
74. The Jacobin criticism of the Girondin Constitution of 1793 is to be found in Aulard, François V. Alphonse, ed., *La Société des Jacobins: Recueil de Documents pour l'Histoire du Club des Jacobins de Paris* (6 vols., Paris, 1891-1892), V, 29-38.

in not telling the Convention about these provisions. Barère spoke up for the committee. It was unfortunate, said he, that certain individuals should seek so soon to destroy a really democratic constitution by baseless accusations. The committee, as was well known, had never favored two houses. There had been some talk of dividing the single house into sections, however, for the purpo͟s of legislation. A few members of the committee had favored ͟his. If their views had been placed in an appendix of some of the printed copies of the constitution, it was only for the purpose of enlightening the Convention about dissenting opinions. Barère concluded his remarks by saying that he was honored to have his signature attached to a constitution which really guaranteed the sovereignty of the people and gave them the right to resist oppression. Measures like these would prevent the people from being subjected to any faction, said Barère, with over-optimism.[75]

It was rather difficult for the Montagnards to continue alleging that aristocratic tendencies, vague evils, and federative characteristics were incorporated in the committee's constitution once it had been printed and widely distributed throughout France. The people were able to read this democratic charter for themselves; they could see that the allegations of the Mountain were exaggerated, to say the least. However, to the Montagnard mind, the source of the constitution was suspect. Petitions against the Girondins were read at the Jacobin Club almost regularly. Girondin leaders were accused of working against the capital in pursuit of their federalist aims. On March 4, 1793, Monsieur Roland, a leading Girondin and ex-Minister of the Interior, was charged in a petition with having calumniated Paris in the eyes of Europe so as to be able to destroy French liberty.[76]

Seemingly, the Montagnards wanted no part of a constitution believed to be authored by the so-called Brissotines. At the Jacobin Club it was proposed to delay the beginning of a constitutional regime by postponing constitutional government until

75. *Moniteur universel*, February 22, 1793.
76. Aulard, ed., *La Société des Jacobins*, V, 66.

the war was over. It was not right to pass on articles of government, it was claimed, when those who had the most right to concur (the soldiers) in their formation were not able to do so.[77] The genuineness of this concern for the soldier vote appears doubtful. Within a few months many servicemen would vote on the republican constitution which finally came out of the Convention. But then, on the grounds of a national emergency, the Robespierrists would postpone constitutional government indefinitely.

Condorcet and Brissot felt that the forces of Robespierre would do everything they could to delay action on the constitution. Condorcet wrote in the *Chronique du Mois* (sometime in March, 1793) that certain turbulent forces did not want regular constitutional government, as this would mark the end of their power.[78] These forces were led by dangerous demigods who had the art of stirring up masses by leveling false charges at opponents.[79] Brissot wrote (on March 24, 1793) to the members of a political club at Bordeaux that it would be hard for them to imagine the efforts being employed by certain individuals to put off passage of a democratic frame of government.[80]

The desertion of General Dumouriez, a former minister in a Girondin cabinet, to the enemy in March, 1793, did not help the Girondins any. The Mountain was quick to make political capital out of this ocurrence. Some of the Girondin leaders, especially Brissot, were accused of being traitors because a man once associated with them had turned out to be disloyal. Until the Girondins were finally proscribed in May and June, 1793, the

77. *Ibid.*, V, 83.
78. As cited by Alengry, Franck, *Condorcet: Guide de la Révolution française, Théoricien du Droit constitutionnel et Précurseur de la Science sociale* (Paris, 1904), p. 254.
79. Condorcet, Marquis de, *Ce que les Citoyens ont Droit d'Attendre de leurs Réprésentants* in *Oeuvres complètes* (21 vols., Paris, 1801-1804), XVIII, 415.
80. *J. P. Brissot: Correspondance et Papiers* (ed. by Perroud, Cl., Paris, 1912), p. 318.

Robespierrists were to remind the Paris populace constantly of their opponents' one-time connection with Dumouriez.[81]

Taking a brief time-out from partisan squabbles, the Conventionals finally got back to the constitution in April. On April 4 a new type of constitutional committee was appointed. This was called the "Committee of Analysis" or "Commission of Six."[82] Its function was to examine all the constitutional projects, including Condorcet's, that had been sent to the Convention since October, 1792.[83] This was a huge task, as more than three hundred of these projects had already been sent and more were arriving all the time. The committee, however, divided up the work among its members.[84] In this way it was able to analyze a large number of the projects.[85] The committee, as far as can be learned, made

81.   Durand-Maillane, P. T., *Mémoires* (Paris, 1825), p. 88.

82.   Its members were Jean de Bry, Mercier, Valazé, Barère, Lanjuinais and Romme.

83.   The decree of October 19, 1792, had invited all interested people, foreigners as well as Frenchmen, to send their opinions about constitutional matters to the Convention.

84.   *Archives parlementaires, 1787-1860: Recueil complet des Débats des Chambres françaises* (ed. by Mavidal, Jérôme; Laurent, Émile, and others; series I, 1787-1799, 82 vols., Paris, 1879-1913; series II, 1800-1860, 137 vols., Paris, 1862-1913), series I, vol. LXII, p. 120.

85.   Historians have never attempted to study thoroughly all the constitutional projects presented to the Convention. In 1932 a Monsieur Francois Galy wrote a law thesis in which he analyzed only twenty-five out of at least three hundred projects. (Galy, François, *La Notion de Constitution dans les Projects de 1793*, Paris, 1932.)

    In studying the many projects, one notes that they are all outstanding for their prevailing spirit of liberalism. Moreover, it is noted that many are alike in asking for similar things: a plural and weak executive, a single-house legislative assembly, jury trial, referendum, petition, universal suffrage, public works, aid for the sick and aged, *etc.*

relatively few reports to the Convention. Sometimes the Convention followed its recommendations; generally it did not.

Serious debates over the constitution, if one can term debates frequently relapsing into partisan strife as serious, began on April 15 and ended on May 29, 1793. Of course, the constitution was very much of a partisan question. And in the Robespierrists'

Their liberal tendencies can be attributed largely to the influence of the philosophers and the institutions of the United States. Selecting one project at random, that of Guy-Kersaint, one finds that he attributed the Revolution in France to both these factors. Rousseau's *Social Contract* was such a wonderful work that it should be used in the schools as a textbook, said Guy-Kersaint. (Guy-Kersaint, A., *De la Constitution et du Gouvernement qui pourraient convenir à la République française* (neither place nor date of publication is given), p. 10. Lanthenas, a member of the Girondin Constitutional Committee, said that before the American and French Revolutions the philosophers had outlined those democratic principles that they were now putting into practice. (Lanthenas, F., *Motifs de faire du 19 Août un Jubilé fraternal* [Paris, 1793], pp. 9-10.)

Many of the projects stressed that it was society's duty to provide work for the unemployed, take care of the sick and needy, and prevent the spread of poverty. In this respect there were no projects more liberal than those of Robespierre. However, Robespierre's sincerity is somewhat suspect. As Aulard explains, the Montagnard leader obviously had to make his projects ultra-democratic in order to overshadow the sincerely democratic projects of the Girondins. (Aulard, *Histoire politique*, p. 291.) Still, Robespierre's statements are interesting. For example, he said, "Aid to the indigent is a debt of the rich towards the poor." (Robespierre, Maximilien, *Déclaration de Droits de l'Homme et du Citoyen* [Paris, 1793], p. 5.) He also said, "The first object of every constitution is to defend the individual against the government itself." (*Discours sur la Constitution* [place and date of publication are not indicated], p. 4.)

scheme of things — which may or may not have been to the people's advantage — the opponents and their constitutional work had to be destroyed. In so far as Robespierre and his supporters claimed to be liberal democrats, however, who only carried out the people's will, they could not openly oppose constitutional government. So, it appears, they worked out the following stratagem: 1. To turn public opinion against the Girondins by accusation. 2. To delay any progress on the constitution until the leading Girondins were ousted from the Convention. 3. As part of the plan of delay, and also to show that they were really more liberal than their opponents, to propose constitutional articles that seemed to be more socialistic.

Less than a week before the constitutional debates actually opened, the Convention witnessed a strong attack against the Girondins which had all the appearance of being purposefully planned by Robespierre. The session of April 10, 1793, was interrupted by the reading of a petition from the Halle aux Blès section of Paris. It boldly asked for the indictment of Girondin deputies whom it said were unworthy of their positions. At the same session Robespierre gave a long diatribe in which he specifically asked for the indictment of Brissot, Vergniaud, Gensonné and Guadet. He accused these republicans of being royalists and of being in league with the tyrants of Europe. He also accused them of trying to arouse the departments against Paris. The Girondins' answer to the petitioners and to Robespierre proved that they suspected their opponents' intentions. In answer to the first accusation, Pétion and Guadet said that the petition was but another example of artificial public opinion directed against the Convention. It appeared to be part of the plan of those who wished to dissolve the Convention.[86] In answer to Robespierre, Vergniaud and Guadet both gave long, detailed speeches in which they endeavored to refute the Montagnard chief's remarks. They warned that the Convention had better not sit idly by and allow its deputies

86. *Moniteur universel*, April 12 and April 13, 1793.

to be recklessly accused.[87] By his own admission, Robespierre could not produce one shred of written evidence to support his charges.

A few days after Robespierre had made his accusations against the Girondin leaders, the Committee of Analysis made its first report (on April 15, 1793). Lanjuinais, the reporter, said that the committee had agreed that a declaration of rights should be decided upon before the constitution was discussed. The rights of man were the "rules of the social pact," while the constitution was but a framework guaranteeing the social pact.[88] Robespierre agreed with the committee. He cited Rousseau as saying that a declaration of rights was the basis of every constitution. Before framing a constitution, careful preparation should be given to such a declaration. Perhaps it is significant that Robespierre made these remarks after Buzot had said that it was imperative that they give the people some sort of a constitution at once, without bothering with a declaration. To delay might mean the end of the republic.[89] The Convention adopted the committee's recommendation, however. It decreed that a declaration of rights would be debated first. Furthermore, it decreed that henceforth Monday, Wednesday, and Friday of every week would be days allotted to constitutional discussions.[90]

Romme, in the name of the Committee of Analysis, presented (on April 17, 1793) a précis of various declarations of rights that had been examined. In regard to the constitutional committee's declaration (Condorcet's), it found that the phraseology used was

87. *Moniteur universel,* April 13 and April 14, 1793; Vergniaud, Pierre, *Réponse de Vergniaud Deputé de la Gironde aux Calomnies de Robespierre* (Paris, 1794), *passim.*

88. Lanjuinais, J. D., *Rapport présenté à la Convention nationale au Nom de la Commission des Six sur l'Ordre à suivre dans la Discussion de la Constitution* (place of publication and date of publication are not given), p. 3.

89. *Archives parlementaires,* LXII, 122.

90. *Ibid.,* LXII, 126.

not quite democratic enough. For instance, article XVIII stated that all men had the right to dispose of their goods, capital, income, and industry in any way they saw fit. Romme said that this article should have also stated that workers had the right to dispose of their salaries as they saw fit. The word "capital" should be left out, as this word "recalled a type of industry that dishonored the social order."[91] The Committee of Analysis proposed its own declaration, which was far more wordy and actually not any more liberal than the one of Condorcet. It was interesting, however, in that it had one section entitled the "Rights of Nations." One article of this section stated that if the sovereignty of any one nation was threatened by an aggressor nation, then all others would take up arms against the aggressor.[92]

The Convention gave priority to Condorcet's declaration rather than that suggested by the Committee of Analysis. It was decreed (on April 17, 1793) that thenceforth Condorcet's plan would serve as the point of departure in all constitutional debates. Salle and Isnard, two Girondin deputies, reiterated the need of haste in fiinishing some sort of a constitution. It was the only way to prevent an impending tyranny.[93] They did no say from whence the tyranny might come. The Convention, however, adhered to its program to discuss a declaration first. In a surprisingly short time a declaration in many respects similar to that of Condorcet was voted by the Convention. There was some debate on a few of its articles.

One Montagnard deputy (on April 17, 1793) asked that the declaration be preceded by a preamble which would recognize a Supreme Being. Louvet, a Girondin deputy, commented that the existence of God did not need the recognition of the National

91. *Ibid.*, LXII, 286.
92. Romme, G., *Troisième Partie du Rapport fait au Nom de la Commission des Six sur la Déclaration des Droits dans la Séance du 17 Avril 1793 l'An 2 de la République* (Paris, *1793*), pp. 5-14.
93. *Moniteur universel*, April 20, 1793; *Archives parlementaires*, LXII, 277.

Convention of France. There were a few Girondin deputies who wished to limit the right of freedom of the press. Obviously with Marat in mind (his sheet *L'Ami du Peuple* had long been crying for a dictator), they said that freedom to spread seditious writings should not be permitted. Robespierre reminded the Convention that freedom of the press was a necessary aid in exposing any plots against the state. Pétion, a leading Girondin and a member of the constitutional committee, said that the right of men to be unrestrained in their expression was incontestable. The committee's article on the press, which granted complete freedom for any individual to print what he pleased, was finally adopted unchanged.[94]

After considerable debate over the article relating to freedom of religion, it was decided to omit any reference to religion in the Declaration. Barère, the constitutional committee's spokesman, said that the intent of the article had been to allow a person to worship anything he pleased — even a rock, if the person so wished. Gensonné, another member of the committee, said that in so far as religion was to be treated in the section of the constitution relating to civil liberties, perhaps there was no need for repetition in the declaration.[95] Discussion over the article was adjourned indefinitely.

Final debates over the constitutional committee's declaration of rights took place on April 22, 1793. The thirty-three articles of the committee's declaration were condensed into thirty articles. There were a few slight changes made in their phraseology. Articles XXIV (which stated that public aid was a sacred debt of society) and XXI (relating to men's right to resist oppression) provoked debate. Oudot, deputy from Côte-d'Or, in his comments about the first, said that "it was time that the rich ceased to regard aid to the poor as something dependent on their personal generosity." The committee did right in recognizing, for the first time in history, that the elimination of poverty was one of the fundamental duties of the state. Boyer-Fondfrède, a sole protester, said that if the state

94. *Moniteur universel,* April 20 and April 21, 1793.
95. *Ibid.,* April 21, 1793.

was to aid the poor, all incentive to work would be killed. Article XXIV was finally adopted as originally drawn up by the constitutional committee. Article XXI was changed in its wording from "Men united in society should have a legal means of resisting oppression" to "Men in every free society should have a legal means of resisting oppression. When this means becomes insufficient, then insurrection is the holiest of duties." Robespierre was against this article. He said that it was absolutely impossible to determine when oppression began. In other words, it was his opinion that insurrection should be a matter of the people's intuition. Legal resistance to tyranny was a joke. Gensonné and Vergniaud summed up Girondin beliefs when they said that a constitutional method of opposing the government would prevent violent revolts and thus safeguard liberty.[96]

With the decreeing of the article relating to the lawful right of the people to oppose governmental oppression, the constitutional debates over a declaration of rights were temporarily concluded. This first declaration, decreed by the French Republic on April 22, 1793, was quite similar to that of the constitutional committee. In fact, it can be said that with a few slight changes in wording, it was but a reshuffling of the committee's project.

Robespierre showed his dissatisfaction with the declaration decreed by the Convention by presenting one of his own two days later. According to Aulard, the extreme liberalism of Robespierre's declaration was not to be attributed to his desire to effect a radical reform of society. Rather, it should be considered an act of political strategy. The Girondin declaration was so democratic that in order to make it less popular, and to make it appear moderate, it was necessary to have recourse to socialism.[97] The unusual articles of the Mountain chief's project were: XIV. Those who have a superfluity of wealth have an obligation to fulfill towards those who lack necessities. XV. When a citizen has given up his daily work to participate in elections, the state should give him adequate

96. *Archives parlementaires*, LXIII, 113-116.
97. Aulard, *Histoire politique*, p. 291.

remuneration. XXXI. To impede, by legal forms, the right to resist oppression would be the last refinement of tyranny. In every free state law ought to defend, above all, public and individual liberty against the abuse of authority by those who govern. Every constitution which does not suppose the people good and the magistrates corruptible is vicious. (This was one of the many principles from Rousseau that Robespierre was fond of repeating.) XXXVII. Kings, aristocrats, tyrants, whoever they might be, are slaves that have revolted against the sovereign of the earth — the people.[98]

All the liberal professions of Robespierre in his declaration seem to prove meaningless in the light of his later authoritarian actions. But then again, like some more-recent totalitarians, he believed that an idealistic platform for man's betterment was something that could be returned to once the people were ready for such a return. Probably he was sincere in wanting to improve the lot of the mass of the French people.

The same day that the Montagnard leader offered his declaration (which was ignored), the Committee of Analysis gave a report on the various types of territorial division found in the many projects which they had examined. None of these projects had divisions which would compare in efficiency to those of the constitutional committee, said the reporter of the Committee of Analysis.[99] As soon as Robespierre heard this favorable remark about his opponents' constitution, he quickly jumped to his feet and began to criticize it severely for not strictly defining property rights. Continuing in what appeared to be an irrelevant way, he said that the Girondin constitution was not made for men. It was made for the rich, monopolizers, stock-jobbers and tyrants![100] Either intentionally or in ignorance, he wrongfully stated that the constitution did not provide for a progressive income tax. While convinced that equality of goods was a chimera, Robespierre

98. *Moniteur universel,* May 5, 1793.
99. *Archives parlementaires,* LXIII, 193.
100. *Moniteur universel,* April 25, 1793.

nevertheless said that he thought rigid restrictions on property rights should be placed in any declaration of rights.[101]

Saint-Just, a right-hand man of Robespierre, immediately followed his leader in criticizing the Girondin frame of government. His main criticisms were that the system of election, being long and complicated, would keep the poor hard-working people from the polls. Besides, the Executive Council, in that it was elected by the whole republic, would have too much prestige. It would eclipse the Legislative Corps, where all real authority should lie.[102] Robert, a Parisian deputy, made practically the same comment as Saint-Just. It was an eternal call to anarchy to have both the Legislative Corps and the Executive Council elected by all the people. There was apt to be tragic rivalry between them.[103]

Vergniaud answered Robespierre's criticism in a long speech at the Convention on May 8, 1793. He agreed with the Montagnard leader that riches usually led to corruption. Rousseau and Montesquieu had taught them that equality in a democracy vanished with the introduction of luxuries. However, the constitution proposed by the constitutional committee was not made for the rich. It was made chiefly for the nineteen million ordinary people of France — the small farmers. The constitution would prevent gross inequality in wealth; at the same time, it would guarantee property. If property was not guaranteed, liberty would be lost. The constitution must be hastily concluded, said Vergniaud. It was the only way to prevent factionalism and bring order out of the chaos threatening France. It was the only way to check those men who, in the name of liberty, aimed at establishing a tyranny.[104]

Robespierre gave another speech against the committee's constitution on May 10, 1793. He seemed to be purposely ignoring

101. *Loc. cit.*
102. *Moniteur universel*, April 25, 1793.
103. *Ibid.*, April 27, 1793.
104. *Ibid.*, May 11, 1793; Vergniaud, Pierre, *Opinion prononcée à la Convention nationale le 8 Mai 1793, l'An deuxième de la République* (Paris, 1793), *passim.*

its provisions when he proposed as original ideas principles that were already found in the constitution. For instance, he stated that the people should have some way of being able to express their dissatisfaction with functionaries.[105] The provisions for recall happened to be quite explicit in the Girondin constitution. Robespierre, however, refused to recognize their existence.

Meanwhile Condorcet, the author of the Girondin constitution, was becoming ever more anxious over the way the Convention was procrastinating in voting a frame of government. When the Committee of Analysis appeared to reject his project by having the Convention adopt a new plan of discussion (on May 13, 1793) which did not have his constitution as a point of departure,[106] he decided to intervene. He saw that the Robespierrists were seeking to prevent the formation of a republican regime by their political adversaries, the Girondins. As long as Robespierre and his followers were members of the Convention, not much progress along constitutional lines could be expected. In order to prevent the protraction of useless debate, Condorcet proposed that the Convention definitely finish a constitution and have it sanctioned by the people before November 1. If France did not have a charter by this date, a new constituent body should be elected.[107] This proposal was decreed.

It may be that the Robespierrists felt that Condorcet's proposal would mean that their opponents would pressure the Convention into completing a constitution quickly. Moreover, even if they could delay the passage of a constitution by filibuster tactics, their own power would end with the calling of a new constituent body in November. Thus, there is a strong possibility that the suggestion

105. *Moniteur universel,* May 12, 1793.

106. *Ibid.,* May 14, 1793.

107. *Ibid.,* May 14, 1793; Condorcet, Marquis de, *Discours sur la Convocation d'une nouvelle Convention nationale, en Cas que la Constitution ne soit pas finie à un Temps déterminé,* in *Oeuvres complètes* (21 vols., Paris, 1801-1804), XVIII, *passim.*

of the philosopher forced the hand of authoritarian-minded individuals. There were to be but a few more free sessions before the Robespierrists, by their coup d'état of June 2, would finally kill France's first trial at republican government.

The few remaining sessions of a free Convention, when not disturbed by confusion resulting from the visitations of sundry delegations from the Parisian populace,[108] were devoted to acrimonious debates between the Girondins and Montagnards over the question of how the territory of France should be divided for purposes of administration. The Montagnards, in condemning the system of large communes found in the Girondin constitution, repeated the old refrain of federalism. The large communes would have a tendency to adopt a separatist attitude towards the central government, said Collot d'Herbois.[109] Saint-Just said that with the country divided into many municipalities, it would be easier to tyrannize the people.[110] Saint-Just and a deputy by the name of Guffroy even wanted the departmental divisions abolished. Guffroy cited Jean Jacques Rousseau as saying that dividing the territory of a country for administrative reasons might mean that parts of the country would become dominated by masters with separatist notions.[111] Buzot, a Girondin leader, also quoted Rousseau. His version of the great philosopher's ideas on the subject was to the effect that liberty could not long exist in a large city where a mass of men tried to dominate all around them. It would be impossible for Paris to remain the seat of government if she

108. Because of constant interruptions by a mob of riotous women in the galleries, Buzot had to discontinue a speech relating to the constitution (on May 20, 1793). He designated the women as hare-brained females who, because they were bribed or because they were ignorant, tried to hinder a government working for their welfare. (*Moniteur universel,* May 22, 1793.)

109. *Ibid.,* May 24, 1793.

110. *Ibid.,* May 25, 1793.

111. *Ibid.,* May 23, 1793.

continued to be dominated by anarchists, as she now was. France ought to imitate the United States. The republic across the sea had decided the question of where the capital should be by legislating the building of a new city, Washington, to house the government.[112]

Progress on the constitution was proceeding at a snail's pace. By May 29, only the Declaration of Rights and six articles relating to the territorial distribution of France had been decreed. The Convention sessions were becoming more turbulent and disorganized every day. It was very apparent that the Girondins would have little chance of having their whole constitution passed by a Convention which seemed unable to check the harassing tactics of the Robespierrists. The Girondins must have had a somewhat hopeless feeling when (on May 29, 1793) the Convention decreed that the Montagnard-packed Committee of Public Safety[113] would create a frame of government in the shortest possible time. To aid the committee, the following men would be associated with it: Hérault de Séchelles, Ramel, Saint-Just, Mathieu and Couthon.[114] Evidently the Montagnards, by their clever use of filibustering tactics, had made the disorganized and weak members of the Plain[115] believe that the Girondins would never be able to put their constitution into action. At any rate, they voted with the

112. *Ibid.*, May 24, 1793.

113. The Committee of Public Safety was an executive body created by the Convention on April 6, 1793. It was composed of nine members whose duties were to supervise and accelerate the execution of administrative matters. In urgent matters it had almost absolute powers. During the control of Robespierre the Committee of Public Safety was practically the only governing body of France. Of course, it then seemed to take orders generally from Robespierre and his young protégé, Saint-Just.

114. The members of the Committee of Public Safety were Barère, Delmas, Berlier, Cambon, Danton, Jean de Bry, Guyton-Morveau, Treilhard and Delacroix.

115. Refer to p. 156.

Montagnards to turn the constitutional problem over to the Committee of Public Safety.

Now that the Robespierrists had figuratively thrown the Girondin constitution out, they decided to rid themselves of the some twenty Girondin leaders as well. When the Girondins began to investigate the conduct of the municipal government of Paris, the Robespierrists became all the more interested in getting rid of their hated adversaries. A special Conventional Commission of Twelve (composed mainly of Girondins) had revealed what were alleged to be subversive activities going on in the capital. Certain sections, dominated by questionable characters, were plotting "to save the country" from the federalists (Girondins).[116] One city official and prominent Jacobin, Hébert, was so implicated that the commission had him arrested. Because of the pressure of the Montagnards, the Convention soon had him released, however. The arrest of Hébert was termed an arbitrary act by the Robespierrists. Perhaps it was. Supposedly to prevent further arbitrary acts, an extra-legal group composed of some members of the General Council of the Revolutionary Commune and commissioners from the forty-eight sections[117] demanded the arrest of all the members of the Commission of Twelve as well as that of the twenty-two leading Girondins in the Convention.[118] Marat told the extra-legal group that he would see the "good members" of the Convention decree the arrest.[119] In order to make the "good members" see the necessity of arresting some of their colleagues, the Robespierrists had the Convention surrounded by 70,000 National Guardsmen.[120] Deputies were not able to leave the Convention until they passed the desired

116.   Meillan, Arnaud, *Mémoires* (Paris, 1823), p. 36.
117.   According to Durand-Maillane, the sections were controlled by a small group of terrorists. Decent people were afraid to attend the meetings of the sectional General Councils, claimed he. (Durand-Maillane, Pierre, *Mémoires* [Paris, 1825], p. 111.)
118.   Meillan, *op. cit.*, p. 45.

decree.[121] The decree was passed by a small number of apparently coerced representatives on June 2, 1793.

By the Conventional act of June 2, 1793, indictments of arrest were issued against all the leading Girondins — Brissot, Vergniaud, Gaudet, Gensonné, Buzot, Barbaroux, and some sixteen others. The name of Condorcet was omitted from the original proscription list. Perhaps the Robespierrists still had too much respect for the name of the last of the *philosophes* to include it on the proscription list. He was left alone for several weeks. However, when he dared to criticize the constitutional work of the Montagnards, and accused the Convention of being under the thumb of terrorists, he too had an indictment of arrest issued againt him.

119. Tourneaux, Maurice, ed., *Procès-verbaux de la Commune de Paris 10 Août 1792-1er Juin 1793* (Paris, 1894), p. 151.

120. Meillan, *op. cit.*, pp. 52-53. Of the 70,000, said Meillan, probably only about 5,000 had any idea why they were told to surround the Convention. Henriot, a Robespierrist and the commander of the Paris National Guard, arranged the 5,000 elite troops immediately around the Convention. The 65,000 others were kept in the background and were only for the purpose of fooling the deputies into thinking that thousands were behind the coup d'état, says Meillan.

121. Durand-Maillane was secretary of the Convention at the time of the coup. The deputies were locked in, said he. They could not get out until the proscription decree was passed; even those unfortunates who "had urgent needs to satisfy" had to endure the pangs of nature's call. (Durand-Maillane, *op. cit.*, p. 123.)

122. One of the more noteworthy pamphlets was that of Jacques Billaud-Varenne, entitled *Discours sur les Députés de la Convention mis en État d'Arrestation par son Décret du 2 Juin prononcé dans la Séance du 15 Juillet* (Paris, 1793). In this brochure the old charge that the Girondins were federalists was repeated (see p. 16). By implication, a federalist could be regarded as a royalist as well, even though these two nouns would seem to be contradictory in meaning. Brissot said the

Many of the proscribed Girondins had managed to avoid immediate arrest by not attending the session of June 2. Some fled to the departments and tried to arouse them against Paris. This was of no avail, however, as they were constantly hounded by Robespierre's men and could not properly organize resistance. Moreover, the departments, through local Jacobin Clubs, were effectively propagandized by pamphlets[122] from the now Montagnard-controlled Convention, accusing the Girondins of being royalist and of being in secret correspondence with the enemies of the republic. Almost all of the proscribed Girondin deputies were to meet violent deaths, either by their own hand (suicide) or at the hands of the Robespierrists.[123]

Perhaps it can be said that the proscription of such men as Condorcet and Brissot and their supporters meant the end of France's first real republican party. The record would certainly indicate that these men, in their writing and political activity, had long promoted republican principles. If one grants, that they were sometimes impractical and seemingly more at home

word "federalist" was used to incite the people of Paris against him and his associates. For instance, when Condorcet wished to convoke the primary assemblies in order to elect a new convention (refer to p. 283), the Montagnards loudly shouted that such a proposal could come only from federalists. (J. P. Brissot: *Mémoires* [ed. by Perroud, Cl., 2 vols., Paris, 1911], II, 340.)

123. Brissot was guillotined on October 31, 1793. An indictment was not issued for Condorcet's arrest until July I, 1793. By going into hiding, he managed to elude arrest for a time. However, he was eventually captured and imprisoned. He died in jail under rather mysterious circumstances on March 29, 1794. The report of the doctor who examined the body was that he had committed suicide. The other member of the trio of famous French republicans, Tom Paine, was not imprisoned until January, 1794. He was incarcerated for only a short time, however, Once released, he halfheartedly renewed his duties as a deputy.

in the realm of theory than in the field of everyday politics, the question then might be raised, it is true, whether or not they were flexible enough to adapt themselves and their principles to revolutionary contingencies.

The Montagnards were to produce a constitution quickly enough, and they were to give the people the privilege of voting on it. They could not do anything else very well. France had been awaiting a republican charter for some months with expectation. It would be impolitic, perhaps disastrous, to ignore the people's wishes at this time. So they created a constitution, in many ways similar to that of the Girondins. The people voted to accept it in a nationwide plebiscite. Then, on the grounds of a national emergency, the constitution was set aside. The Constitution of 1793 (Montagnard) was to remain but an interesting document. A product of some of the most liberal ideals of all time, it actually seems to have been used as a step to appease the people and to make a smoother transition into what was believed to be a type of state that would better represent the interests of the majority. In effect, the First French Republic would cease to be a genuine republic. France would endure in succession the unrepresentative rule of Robespierre, the Directory, and Napoleon, and, finally, that of monarchy again.

Chapter VIII

France's Most Democratic Constitution:
Its Acceptance by the French People
in a Plebiscite

After their coup d'etat (on June 2, 1793) Robespierre and his men showed some signs of fear over their bold action. To silence the rumors, even in the capital itself, that they wanted to establish a dictatorship, they had to present the people of France with at least a token of good faith. They realized that they would have to prepare a constitution quickly in order to check the discontent that was becoming increasingly evident.[1] Every day petitions from the departments reminded the Convention that the long-promised charter was anxiously awaited. At the June 7 meeting of the General Council of the Paris Revolutionary Commune, some of the attendant "sovereign people" kept interrupting the session by shouting for a constitution. One of the members of the Council, Chaumette, was loudly cheered when he said that delegations from the forty-eight sections should petition the Convention every day for haste in finishing the charter.[2]

The Committee of Public Safety evidently did not need any reminders to make it hasten its constitutional work. Within ten days of its assigned task, it was able to announce to the Convention that it had finished a constitution. The committee's reporter and editor, Hérault de Séchelles,[3] read a charter to the Convention on

1. Cahen, Léon, and Goyot, Raymond, *L'Oeuvre legislative de la Révolution* (Paris, 1913), p. 71.
2. *Moniteur universel* (*Journal officiel de l'empire française*), (169 vols., Paris, 1789-1863), June 10, 1793.
   vols., Paris, 1789-1863), June 10, 1793.
3. Hérault de Séchelles seems to have been the principal editor of the project emanating from the Committee of Public Safety.

June 10, 1793. In many ways it was a simplification of Condorcet's.

In his introductory remarks Hérault de Séchelles said that from all parts of the republic were coming imperious demands for a frame of government. "Never had a greater necessity tormented a whole people."[4] The committee had worked fast so as to bring order out of the chaos threatening France. It believed that its constitution was probably the most democratic that had ever existed. Hérault de Séchelles, in his prefatory comments, explained how the project he was presenting differed from that of Condorcet. Actually, it seems to have been a modified form of the philosopher's project. In some respects it was more conservative. Séchelles apparently did not dare give credit to the famous associate of the ousted Girondin leaders, however. Moreover, Séchelles was correct in saying that there were some differences between the two plans.

The *status quo* of departments, districts, and municipalities, as established in 1789, was maintained in the plan of the second constitutional committee. Hérault de Séchelles explained that it was the committee's belief that the creation of large communes, as in Condorcet's project, would mean the destruction of thousands of small communes, the cradles of liberty. Moreover, the electoral assemblies were maintained, in antithesis to the plan of the first committee. There was to be one elector for every 200 citizens in the primary assemblies.[5] The electoral assemblies were to elect

4. *Moniteur universel*, June 12, 1793.

5. Hérault de Séchelles, Marie, *Projet de Constitution du Peuple français présenté à la Convention nationale au Nom du Comité de Salut public: précédé du Rapport fait par la même Citoyen au Nom du même Comité, et de la Déclaration des Droits déjà décrétée* (Paris, 1793), p. 16, Hereafter this work will be cited as Hérault, *Projet de Constitution.* Following the Committee of Public Safety's project there was to be one primary assembly for every section of territory containing between 400 and 600 citizens. The arrondissement of each primary assembly would form a canton. (*Ibid.,* p. 14).

all officials other than deputies or members of the National Jury,
who were to be chosen directly by the people in the primary
assemblies. The main reason for the electoral assemblies was to
simplify the electoral process and prevent the constant summoning
of the citizenry to vote.[6] The electors were to be renewed every year.

In all respects but one, the Committee of Public Safety's
Executive Council would be the same as that in Condorcet's (the
Girondin) plan. The difference was that in the second committee's
project the twenty-four members of the Council would be elected
by the Legislative Corps from candidates (one per department)
chosen by the electoral assemblies of each department. As Séchelles
explained, to have the Council elected directly by all the people
would be to give it too much importance and authority. The
executive should be but an agency to carry out the people's will
as expressed through the Legislative Corps.[7]

Both committees provided for a National Jury in their plans.
The Girondin scheme, however, besides arranging for more jurors,
was more explicit as to the duties of the jurors. In the Committee
of Public Safety's plan, there were to be as many jurors as there
were departments. They were elected directly by the people every
year, along with the Legislative Corps deputies.[8] The function of
the National Jury was to protect the citizens from arbitrary actions
either by the Legislative Corps or by the Executive Council.[9] In
the opinion of the committee, the idea that representatives were
inviolable was tyranny, commented Séchelles.[10]

Aside from the addition of districts and electoral assemblies
found in the second committee's project plus the selection of the

The constitution as amended and passed by the Convention
(June 24, 1793) made the provision that there were to be
between 200 and 600 citizens in each primary assembly.

6. Hérault, *Project de Constitution . . .*, p. 6.
7. *Ibid.*, pp. 7-8.
8. *Ibid.*, p. 20.
9. *Moniteur universel*, June 13, 1793.
10. Hérault, *Project de Constitution . . .*, p. 7.

Executive Council by the Legislative Corps, the two committees' projects were rather similar. They both permitted the people to elect certain officials directly. However, in its system of election the plan of the first committee was much more liberal. They both had arrangements for the exercise of the referendum. Their Conventional systems were somewhat alike, as were their Declarations of Rights.

Once the Committee of Public Safety had completed its charter, the Montagnards felt infinitely relieved. As yet they did not feel very secure about their usurpation of power. Robespierre said that as soon as the Convention decreed the constitution, copies of the constitution would be sent immediately to the administrations of all the departments as well as to all the popular societies and to the armies.[11] The Montagnard constitution would be the reply of the patriotic deputies to those who said that they wanted anarchy. Now that the people were sure that they were to have a charter, they could have faith in their government. They would not have to fear any new despotic chains, stated the Montagnard chief. Moreover, they could depend on the Mountain to sustain them in their constitutional rights.[12]

There were a few changes, however, that Robespierre thought necessary in the project presented by the Committee of Public Safety. In so far as the Convention was firmly controlled by the Montagnard leader, the desired changes were made. It is interesting to note that the man who suggested such socialistic amendments to the Girondin constitution was now rather conservative in his opinions. This would seem to indicate that the reason for his earlier socialistic professions was simply to appear more liberal than the Girondins. Now that the Girondin leadership was annihilated, he could be more frank. At one of the Conventional sessions in which the constitution was debated, there were some differences

11. *Moniteur universel,* June 12, 1793.
12. Aulard, François V. Alphonse, ed., *La Société des Jacobins: Recueil de Documents pour l'Histoire du Club des Jacobins de Paris* (6 vols., Paris, 1891-1892), V, 246-247.

of opinion over the institution of a National Jury. One deputy, Bazire, praised such a body. It would serve to check any dictatorially minded individuals, he remarked. Robespierre criticized the National Jury, however. He said that it might become corrupt. Good deputies, through intrigue, might be brought before it. Because of his comments it was decided to set aside an institution that had been proposed for the purpose of protecting the people against their own representatives.[13]

A number of deputies spoke against the article of the Committee of Public Safety's plan which stated that no citizen was excused from the honorable burden of paying taxes. They remarked that an obligation to pay taxes would be hard for an individual who earned only enough to pay for bare necessities. Robespierre favored the article. If the poor did not have to pay taxes, the government would soon fall into the hands of the rich. The rich would then say that the poor had no rights under the government, as they did not pay for its support. The best thing would be for the country to furnish an income to the poor so that they could give it back to the treasury.[14] Robespierre was listened to again. The Convention voted to leave the article in the constitution.

Following the recommendation of Robespierre, some changes were also made in the Declaration of Rights.[15] These changes largely pertained to the articles relating to resistance to oppression. The Committee of Public Safety's plan had simply stated that men ought to have a legal method of resisting oppression. When legal methods failed, then insurrection was a sacred duty. The declaration, as now passed by the Convention, said nothing about legal methods of combatting government tyranny. Insurrection was a natural right which could not be bound by laws. Perhaps when the Robespierrists removed the clause relating to legality, they had in mind their own recent coup (on June 2, 1793) against a group of the people's representatives. The articles relating to the

13. *Moniteur universel,* June 17, 1793.
14. *Ibid.,* June 20, 1793.
15. *Loc. cit.*

sanctity of property rights were allowed to remain as they were. It will be remembered that Robespierre had criticized the Girondin plan because it had placed no restriction on property.[16] His acceptance of the Committee of Public Safety's plan, whose articles relating to property were almost an exact replica of those in the Girondin plan, would seem to show that the Montagnard chief's criticisms before the coup d'état of June 2 were made mainly to embarrass his political opponents.

The Committee of Public Safety had offered its plan to the Convention on June 10, 1793. After a short debate of two weeks, it was adopted on June 24, 1793. Aside from the few amendments demanded by Robespierre, it was decreed by acclamation substantially as it had emerged from the committee.

June 24, 1793, was a gala day for the rump Convention composed chiefly of Montagnard deputies and some members of the Plain.[17] Completion of the Montagnard constitution was greeted with shouts of joy by the many people crowding the spectators' benches in the assembly hall. That afternoon, as the deputies filed out, they heard shouts of "Long live the Mountain!" and, significantly, "Long live the republic!" They also heard the cannon salvos fired by the cannoneers in the near vicinity of the hall.[18] Perhaps many of the deputies sincerely believed that their work was finished. Now they

16. Refer to p. 281.

17. After the proscription of their leaders, many of the less important members of the Girondin group refused to attend further meetings of the Convention. Quite a few members of the Plain also began to absent themselves. According to Meillan, for several months, sessions of the Convention were attended by fewer than one hundred deputies. (Meillan, *Mémoires* [Paris, 1823], p. 85.)

18. *Archives parlementaires, 1787-1860: Recueil complèt des Débats des Chambres françaises* (ed. by Mavidal, Jérôme; Laurent, Émile and others, series I, 1787-1799, 82 vols., Paris, 1879-1913; series II, 1800-1860, 137 vols., Paris, 1862-1913), series I, vol. LXVII, p. 150.

only had to wait until the people, through a national plebiscite, voted their acceptance of the constitution.

Bertrand Barère, who had been a member of both constitutional committees, drew up the decree relative to the convocation of the primary assemblies. The man who had praised the Girondin constitution found it just as easy to laud that of the Mountain. Barère was a shrewd politician who always managed to stay on the winning side. He introduced his decree by predicting a great future for the Montagnard frame of government. Being sanctioned by all the French citizenry, it would have an immense prestige. Barère, in his enthusiasm, became quite rhetorical. Speaking in metaphors, he compared the Montagnard charter to the tables of Moses. Like them, it sprang from the holy mountain (Mountain) in the midst of thunder and lightening. In a few days a document had been prepared that contained all the best governmental principles of the century.

To assure all property-holders, Barère declared that one of the most important principles of the Montagnard constitution was the recognition of the sacredness of property rights: "Property is solemnly recognized and assured here. In a wise republic it is a just recompense for work, economy or virtue."[19] Moreover, freedom of religion was guaranteed. He hoped that the guarantees of property and religion found in the constitution would stop any incipient rebellions that the priests and federalists might have stirred up in the departments. Besides, as a copy of the new republican frame of government was being sent to every soldier and sailor, they would soon know more clearly what they were fighting for.[20]

By the decree of June 27, 1793, relative to the national plebiscite on the constitution, all primary assemblies would be convoked for voting within eight days of their receipt of the convocation decree. Soldiers and sailors serving on various fronts and at sea would have the right to vote too. Envoys from all the primary

19. *Archives parlementaires* . . . , LXVII, 555-556.
20. *Loc. cit.*

assemblies and from army and navy commands would bring the voting results to Paris some time before August 10, 1793. August 10 would be a national holiday. On that day the votes would be officially tabulated by the National Convention.[21]

For the first time in its history all France was going to have the privilege of voicing its adherence to a republican frame of government. The Montagnards, by submitting their constitutional work to the French citizenry in record time, gave the appearance that they really were ready to follow the dictates of the sovereign people. They believed that the holding of a national plebiscite on the constitution would dispel any rumors about dictatorship.[22] They wanted the plebiscite to prove that the French citizenry accepted their constitution without any reservations. Moreover, they did not want any unfavorable propaganda against it to reach the departments. Needless to say, the Montagnards were greatly excited when one of their colleagues, Chabot, read (on July 8, 1793) a pamphlet to the Convention written by none other than the great *philosophe,* Condorcet.

Condorcet, who had not been indicted along with the Girondin leaders,[23] courageously wrote a pamphlet in order to criticize the Montagnard constitution as well as to condemn the illegal usurpation of power by the Robespierrists on June 2. The Robespierrists knew that it would be dangerous to allow such a brochure to reach the departments. Condorcet was too well known and liked as a liberal philosopher. Besides, it was known that he was the editor of the constitution emanating from the first constitutional committee. His opinions might influence many of the citizens to vote against the Montagnard frame of government.

21. Barère, B., *Rapport sur la Convocation des Assemblées prim-aires fait au Nom du Comité de Salut Public dans la Séance du Jeudi 27 Juin 1793 l'An II de la République française* (Paris, 1793), *passim.*

22. This had already been decreed as far back as September, 1792. Refer to p. 165.

23. Refer to p. 287.

Chabot accused Condorcet of trying to stir up the departments against Paris. He also accused him of attempting to win favor for the Girondin charter. Finally, charged Chabot, Condorcet wished to influence the people to vote against the Montagnard constitution. On the motion of Collot d'Herbois, a warrant of arrest was issued against Condorcet. In addition, an order was passed placing seals on all his papers.[24]

Apparently Condorcet's pamphlet had no great effect in the departments. In understanding the similarities as well as the differences between the two constitutions of 1793, however, the philosopher's analysis is noteworthy.

One constitution, that of the first constitutional committee, said Condorcet, had been prepared when the Convention was still free and not dominated by a faction. The second constitution, that of the Committee of Public Safety, had been hastily prepared and hastily voted on by a mutilated, subservient Convention with half the deputies absent. It was obvious that only the first frame of government would really represent the will of the majority of the Conventionals.[25]

Condorcet observed that there were many similarities between the two plans. They were similar in that they both granted equality of political rights to all, had the same requirements for citizenship, stressed the importance of the primary assemblies where the people exercised their sovereignty, provided for a single legislative body, guaranteed the frequent renewal of public functionaries, had requirements for public office common to all, took precautions against misuse of the armed forces, and made a distinction between laws and decrees.[26]

In the first plan, however, a more careful distinction was made between laws and decrees. Only those matters that it was believed the people were capable of understanding, and intelligently voting on through the referendum, were grouped as laws, said Condorcet.

24. *Archives parlementaires*, LXVIII, 438-440.
25. *Ibid.*, LXVIII, 445.
26. *Ibid.*, LXVIII, 445.

Decrees, relating to specialized matters beyond ordinary public comprehension, were to be issued by the Legislative Corps. They did not require the people's sanction, as did laws. The second plan was in error to link the matter of declaring war with other kinds of laws. The people were liable to be incited into declaring war foolishly. Declarations of war should be decreed by the Legislative Corps.[27]

It was Condorcet's opinion that the method of referring laws to the people was simpler in the Girondin project. This method has already been explained.[28] The method of referral as outlined in the Montagnard constitution was as follows: Each law was sent to all the primary assemblies. If, within forty days, the law was not rejected by one-tenth of the primary assemblies in one-half of the departments plus one, then it automatically went into effect.[29]

The system of voting established by the Montagnard constitution seemed undemocratic to Condorcet. The maintenance of electoral assemblies was sure to mean the continuance of intrigue and corruption in elections. It was not right that a select body of men, electors, should have the sole privilege of electing certain officials. The electoral system of the Girondin constitution was not as complicated as some people seemed to believe.[30] At least, all important officials were elected directly by the people. Moreover, in contrast to the second project, it stated that all elections would be by secret ballot. Thus, there would be no chance for coercion of voters.[31]

Condorcet's main criticism of the Montagnard constitution was that it did not really give the people enough of a direct voice in

27. *Ibid.*, LXVIII, 446.
28. Refer to p. 266.
29. *Acte constitutionnel précédé de la Déclaration des Droits de l'Homme et du Citoyen, présenté au Peuple français par la Convention nationale, le 24 Juin 1793, l'An deuxième de la République* (Paris, 1793), p. 21.
30. Refer to pp. 261-262.
31. *Archives parlementaires*, LXVIII, 446-447.

the government. The Executive Council was selected by the Legislative Corps from a list of nominees named by the electoral assemblies. The administrators of the Treasury and the Bureau of Accounts were named by the Executive Council. For civil justice, public arbiters were chosen by the electoral assemblies. On the other hand, in the Girondin constitution all these officials were selected directly by the people in their primary assemblies.

Condorcet's two final criticism of the Montagnard frame of government were: 1. There was no means of censuring officials. 2. The method of amending the constitution was inefficient.[32] As has already been seen, Robespierre had had the institution of a National Jury left out of the Constitution.[33] The National Jury would have had as its function the censoring of all officials. To amend the constitution, the following method was outlined: In one-half of the departments plus one, one-tenth of the primary assemblies in each department had to demand a revision of the constitution before the Legislative Corps would summon all the primary assemblies of the republic for a vote.[34]

Although, as Condorcet explained, the Montagnard Constitution of 1793 was in many respects not as democratic as that of the Girondins, it was nevertheless received with the greatest enthusiasm by all France. Certainly the Montagnards had worked hard to cultivate this enthusiasm. For weeks they had been sending pamphlets to all the departments, announcing near-completion of a republican charter. Hérault de Séchelles, by a report he made to the Convention in the name of the Committee of Public Safety, had probably encouraged a great flow of propaganda pamphlets from the capital. In the report Séchelles emphasized the importance of the press in counteracting unfavorable public opinion and its power to create a favorable public mood.[35] As soon as the Mon-

32. *Ibid.*, LXVIII, 448-450.
33. Refer to p. 294.
34. *Acte constitutionnel précédé de la Déclaration des Droits*, pp. 30-31.
35. *Archives parlementaires*, LXVIII, 27.

tagnard constitution was completed, thousands of copies of it were sent to all sections of France. The Paris presses turned out copies at the rate of 15,000 a day.[36] Illustrative of the enthusiasm with which the new constitution was received was an incident at Lille. When the package containing many copies of the charter finally arrived from Paris, all the city clerks danced around it and then, with great ceremony, escorted the welcome parcel to the town hall.[37]

Evidently Montagnard propaganda was very effective in many sections of France. The municipal officials of Excideuil drew up an address to their fellow citizens in which they said that the constitution would bring about a new social order based on complete equality. This marvelous document, they said, embodied the true democratic principles of the philosophers. It would put an end to all dissension in France. They asked their townsmen not to amend it, but rather to accept it exactly as it was. This constitution had been framed by "the healthiest part of the Convention, the arch-saint of liberty, the Mountain."[38]

Perhaps some communes were to approve the Montagnard constitution because they believed that it would mean the end of the Convention and the beginning of real republican government. According to Meillan, many communes were willing to receive a constitution from the Mountain only on the condition that the Convention would immediately dissolve and make way for new deputies having the confidence of the people.[39]

The decree relative to the convocation of the primary assemblies (issued on June 27, 1793)[40] had not stated any fixed date or dates on which the primary assemblies would vote. The reason for this was that certain sections of France were occupied by foreign troops. Other sections, the department of La Vendée and

36. *Ibid.*, LXVIII, 493.
37. *Loc. cit.*
38. Herman, Gustave, "La Constitution à Excideuil (Dordogne)," in *La Révolution française* (April, 1904), XLVI, 346-354, *passim.*
39. Meillan, *op. cit.*, pp. 84-85.
40. Refer to p. 296.

the cities of Marseilles and Bordeaux, were in revolt against the Convention.[41] There was no telling when these parts of France would be free. Most of the primary assemblies, however, voted their acceptance of the Montagnard charter some time in July. In a few isolated cases, voting did not take place until November and December, 1793.[42]

Adherence to the principle of universal manhood suffrage was followed in practically all the assemblies. In some rare cases, even women and children voted.[43] The great majority of assemblies accepted the Montagnard constitution without amendment. They felt the urgent need of a republican constitution, regardless of its point of origin.[44]

Possibly the greatest enthusiasm for the constitution was manifested by the soldiers of the many French armies. It may be that a little of this enthusiasm was somewhat artificial. A deputy on a mission to one of the northern armies, a Louis Beffroy, honestly admitted that cheers for the Montagnard charter increased considerably after each soldier had been given clothes and ten sous in order to drink a bumper to the glory of the republic.[45] Another

41. The Vendeans were royalists in sympathy. They generally condemned the Convention for killing the king. Moreover, religious feeling was strong in this part of France and there was resentment towards the Convention for measures passed against the clergy.

   Marseilles and Bordeaux were indignant over the treatment of their deputies (Girondin) on June 2, 1793. The revolt in Marseilles and Bordeaux, ineffectually organized, was of short duration.

42. Baticle, René, "Le Plébiscite sur la Constitution de 1793," in *La Révolution française* (December, 1909), LVII, 497-499.

43. Baticle, *op. cit.* (December, 1909), LVII, 510.

44. *Ibid.*, (May, 1910) LVIII, 409.

45. Aulard, François V. Alphonse, ed., *Recueil des Actes du Comité de Sàlut public avec la Correspondance officielle des Réprésentants en mission et le Registre du Conseil executif provisoire* (12 vols., Paris, 1889-1899), V, 226-227.

deputy, on mission to the Army of the Rhine, told how the soldiers, after hearing the reading of their new frame of government, loudly cheered and fired off their muskets in continuous salvos.[46] The Army of the Pyrenees was the most spectacular in its acceptance. One company of soldiers placed the constitution on a litter, covered it with flowers, and paraded up and down in sight of the Spanish lines. During a lull in the fighting, when parleying was going on between the French and Spanish, a proselytizing French officer gave a copy of the constitution to the Spanish. It was read with such avidity that one deputy on mission assigned to the army wrote the Convention to send thousands more copies to be distributed to the Spanish soldiers.[47]

Apparently the army and navy accepted the Montagnard constitution with unanimity.[48] Unanimity also characterized the vote of almost all the communes.[49] According to a report of August 9, 1793, out of all the French communes voting to date,[50] only that

46. *Ibid.*, V, 317.
47. *Ibid.*, V, 297-298, 348-349.
48. Baticle examined the various *procès-verbaux* of the army and navy. He stated that he found no negative votes. Methods of voting varied. Sometimes the commanding officers would read the constitutional act to their men, who would accept it by acclamation. At other times an oath to accept the constitution would be drawn up. Then delegations from either the army battalions or ships' crews, as the case might be, would sign the oath. Records are extant showing the votes of the crews of twenty-three ships. (Baticle, *op. cit.* [February, 1910], LVIII, 117-126.)
    Réprésentants en mission et le Registre du Conseil exécutif provisoire (12 vols., Paris, 1889-1899), V, 226-227.
49. In order to tabulate the votes, the Convention had appointed a commission of six. This commission gave its first report on August 9, 1793. (*Archives parlementaires*, LXX, 547-548.)
50. The number of communes voting was not given. There were 44,000 communes altogether in France. The communes were not of Revolutionary origin; these units had existed prior to

of Saint-Donan, forming part of the primary assembly of the canton of Plouvara, refused to accept the constitution and asked for a king.[51] Out of a total number of 1,869,004 people voting in the plebiscite, there were only 12,766 negative votes cast.[52] Some of the primary assemblies (especially in the department Du Nord) could not vote, as their territories were occupied by foreign troops.[53] Other assemblies, being located in sections in the throes of civil war, were not able to participate in the plebiscite either. However, as the foreign troops were driven back and civil war subsided, some of these assemblies were also to acknowledge their adherence to the constitution.[54]

> 1789. They varied greatly in size — all the way from small villages to huge cities. Ordinarily, prior to 1789, the word "commune" referred to the administration of any village, town, or city. With the coming of the Revolution and the creation of primary assemblies (based on population), the commune had rather a complicated relationship with other administrative units. For example, it might take several small communes (with slight populations)to make one primary assembly. On the other hand, one large commune (say, Bordeaux) might have a number of primary assemblies.
>
> Another administrative unit was the "canton." This term generally referred to a town of a fair size. As a rule, every canton had several primary assemblies. In 1793 there were 4,944 cantons in France.

51. Buchez, P. and Roux, P., *Histoire parlementaire de la Révolution française ou Journal des Assemblées nationales depuis 1789 jusqu'en 1815* (40 vols., Paris, 1834-1838), XXVIII, 426.

52. Baticle, *op. cit.* (February, 1910), LVIII, 144.

53. *Archives parlementaires*, LXX, 548.

54. Records regarding the final results of the plebiscite on the Constitution of 1793 are scarce. Buonarroti, the French socialist, writing in 1800, said that 4,800,000 people voted to accept the constitution. (Robiquet, Paul, *Buonarroti et la Secte des Égaux: d'après des Documents inédits* [Paris, 1910], p. 309.)

August 10, 1793 had been set aside as a special holiday.[55] On that date the official tabulation of the results of the plebiscite took place at Paris. More than that, the capital was the scene of a magnificent pageant staged in order to inaugurate France's first republican constitution. The arrangements for the pageant were made by the famous painter, David. There were five main settings constructed in various parts of the city and symbolic of different great events of the Revolution. The parade of the fête started at dawn and went from setting to setting, finally ending at the Champ de Mars, where the President of the Convention proclaimed the result of the plebiscite to thousands of cheering people. They all took an oath to defend the constitution even unto death.[56] The president in a short speech said that there never had been a more unanimous desire expressed for a republic. The Convention had now completed its task and the deputies, content with their splendid work, could make way for a legislative assembly.[57]

As the Robespierrists had hoped, the completion of a constitution and its submission to the people had brought comparative order to France. Moreover, it gave them time to obtain a firmer hold on the government. The majority of the French people had accepted the repeated announcements of Robespierre and his men that they, too, were anxious for the republican frame of government to go into effect. There were a few individuals, however,

55. Refer to p. 297.
56. Henderson, Ernest, *Symbol and Satire in the French Revolution* (New York, 19912), pp. 354-370.
57. *Constitution républicaine décrétée par la Convention nationale de France in 1793 et présentée a l'Acception du peuple français précédée du Rapport fait sur ce Sujet par Hérault-Séchelles, Membre de la Convention nationale; suivie du Procés-verbal des Monuments de la Marche, et des Discours de la Fête consacrée a l'Inauguration de la Constitution de la République française, le 10 Août 1793; de la Loi sur le Gouvernement provisoire et révolutionnaire et de la Réponse de la Convention nationale aux Manifestes des Rois ligués contre la République français* (Paris, 1793), pp. 90-97.

who were suspect of a faction having some members that appeared to favor dictatorship.

During the plebiscite some citizens were bold enough to say that the rump Convention would try to perpetuate its power.[58] Certain Girondin deputies and associates, some of them in prison, wrote that the Montagnard constitution was but a ruse to deceive the people. It had been used by Robespierre to enable him to overcome his Girondin opponents more easily and thus prepare the way for dictatorship.[59] Madame Roland laughed at those naive people who believed that Robespierre would really allow constitutional government to operate in France.[60]

Madame Roland and other sceptics appear to have been right. It seems that the Montagnard chief had no intention of ever allowing a legislative assembly to meet, Perhaps this is why the constitution that he had presented to the French people was only an abridgment of the Girondin constitution. He undoubtedly knew that it would never have to operate. The day following the great fête in celebration of the end of the plebiscite, Robespierre, in an address to the Paris Jacobins, said that a national emergency existed. The republic would be lost if the Convention dissolved and a new assembly took its place.[61] The chameleon-like Barère was not long in echoing the voice of the chief. Speaking in the name of the Committee of Public Safety on August 28, 1793, he said that there was danger of a counter-revolution. A constitution that was constructed to be used in time of peace could not successfully operate during a national emergency. The Convention was given about two weeks to ponder Barère's statements. It was then asked (on October 10, 1793) to decree the suspension of cons-

58. Aulard, ed., *Recueil des Actes du Comité de Salut public,* V, 175.
59. Durand-Maillane, Pierre, *Mémoires* (Paris, 1825), pp. 143-145; Meillan, *op. cit.,* p. 83.
60. *Mémoires de Madame Roland* (2 vols., Paris, 1905), I, 327-328.
61. Buchez and Roux, *op. cit.,* XXVIII, 453-459.

titutional government for an unstated period. Obligingly the Convention, composed of some 60 deputies[62] (out of the original 749 members) decreed that the provisional government of France would remain in power until the conclusion of peace. Thus, the application of the Constitution of 1793 was postponed indefinitely. In fact, the Constitution of 1793 would never have the opportunity of functioning.

Still, France's first republican constitution, and its most democratic, would live on in the memory of some French liberals. It became a sacred ideal, representative of something hoped for but never completely attained. During the hard times of 1794 and 1795, men such as Babeuf and Buonarroti — who were radically socialist, it is true — were to remind the French people that they had voted for a democratic charter in 1793. If this was put into operation, there would be less oppression and more to eat, said they. Babeuf and Buonarroti, however, were put away and the people were pacified by more promises.[63] The Constitution of 1793 was remembered when the revolutionaries of 1848, after dethroning Louis Philippe, sought a democratic pattern of government. The constituents of that year borrowed many of the principles of the first republican constitution.[64]

Perhaps even today there are some French constitutional scholars who reflect on the most democratic constitution that their country has ever had. A student of French constitutional law, André

62. Meillan, *op. cit.*, p. 85.
63. Robiquet, *op. cit.*, pp. 54-58; Claretie, Jules, *Les derniers Montagnards: Histoire de l'Insurrection de Prairial An III d'après le Documents originaux inédits* (ed., Paris, 1868), pp. 11-87.
64. Prat, J. G., ed., *La Constitution de 1793 précédée de la Déclaration des Droits de l'Homme présenté au Peuple français le 24 Juin 1793, publiée, annotée, comparée avec la Constitution des États-Unis d'Amérique* (Paris, 1884), *passim*. The Constitution of 1848, after being accepted by the people of France through a national plebiscite, was set aside by Louis Napoleon, who had been elected president of the Second French Republic.

Decencière-Ferrandière, wrote an article in 1936 in which he referred to the 1793 frame of government as the best that France had ever produced. It was to be especially admired, said he, because it placed government so directly in the hands of the people. With such a constitution, said Decencière-Ferrandière, the people would have adequate checks against their own representatives. It would prevent them from being misused eiher by a parliament or by a dictator. "Democracy is menaced with caesarism," warned he, "when it is refused legitimate satisfaction in its demands." Real democracy, commented Decencière-Ferrandière, signified that the people governed themselves to the greatest extent possible.[65]

Since Robespierre's coup d'état in 1793, there have been instances, not only in France but also in many other countries, when constitutional government has been set aside on one ground or another. Perhaps in some cases, in the face of severe national emergencies, this has been necessary. However, on many occasions rule without constitutional limitation has been questionable and, it would seem, maintained for the purpose of advancing the ambitions of a man or a clique. Undoubtedly Robespierre was an idealist, even though fanatical, who wanted to better the lot of the majority of French people. Furthermore, he was a man in a hurry. Idealists of a less efficient breed, such as Condorcet, Tom Paine, and Brissot, had to be pushed aside when they interfered with the construction of what was to be the ideal state. Considering the times and considering the opposition's forces, Robespierre did not believe that he could afford the luxury of a constitutional republic. Historians still argue as to the rightness or wrongness of his position.

Modern history is replete with instances where strong men, with far less justification than Robespierre, have done away with representative rule. Perhaps the Conventional Monsieur Robert came near the truth when he remarked that the *world* was far

65. Decencière-Ferrandière, André, "La Constitution de 1793," in *La Révolution française* (New Series, Third Quarter, 1936), No. 7, pp. 237-254.

from its infancy but the *social art* was still in that state.[66] Practically every century produces great thinkers whose liberal principles, enclosed in numerous volumes, are handed down for the edification of future generations. Yet man, in a social sense, appears unable to profit from the wisdom of the past. The plaint of St. John de Crèvecoeur seems *à propos*: "To what purpose, then, have so many useful books and divine maxims been transmitted to us from preceding ages? Are they all in vain, all useless? Must human nature ever be the sport of the few and its wounds remain unhealed?"[67]

66. *Moniteur universel*, April 27, 1793.
67. Crèvecoeur, St. John, *Letters from an American Farmer* (Reprint from the original edition, New York, 1909), p. 120.

BIBLIOGRAPHY

I. Bibliographies, Guides, Dictionaires, and Catalogues.

Caron, Pierre, ed. *Bibliographie des Travaux publiées de 1866 à 1897 sur l'Histoire de la France depuis 1789.* I vol. in 6 pts., Paris, 1907-1912. (Société d'Histoire moderne.)

—,—, ed. *Manuel pratique pour l'Étude de la Revolution française.* Paris, 1912. (Manuels de Bibliographie historique.)

Catalogue de l'Histoire de France. 12 vols., Paris, 1855-1895. (Bibliothèque nationale.)

Franklin, Alfred, ed. *Les Sources de l'Histoire de France, Notices bibliographiques et analytiques des Inventaires et des Recueils de Documents relatifs a l'Histoire de France.* Paris, 1877.

Guiffrey, Jules, ed. *Les Conventionnels: Listes par Départements et par Ordre alphabetique des Deputés et des Suppleants a la Convention nationale, dressées d'après les Documents originaux des Archives nationales avec nombreux Détails biographiques inédits.* Paris, 1889. Sociéte de l'Histoire de la Revolution française.)

Hatin, Louis Eugene, ed. *Bibliographie de la Presse periodique française.* Paris, 1866.

Havens, George R. and Bond, Donald F., eds. *The Eighteenth Century.* Syracuse, Syracuse University Press, 1951. (Vol. IV of *A Critical Bibliography of French Literature.* Ed. by David Clark Cabeen, Syracuse, Syracuse University Press, 1947–   .)

Hyslop, B. *Guide to the General Cahiers of 1789.* New York, 1936.

Kuscinski, A., ed. *Dictionnaire des Conventionnels.* Paris, 1916-1918. (Société de l'Histoire des Conventionnels.)

Langlois, Charles V. and Stein, Henri, eds. *Les Archives de l'Histoire de France*. 3 pts. in I vol., Paris, 1891-1893.

Lasteyrie du Saillant, Robert C., Comte de, and others, eds. *Bibliographie générale des Travaux historiques et archéologiques publiés par les Sociétés savantes, dressée sous les Auspices du Ministère de l'Instruction publique*. 6 vols., Paris, 1888-1918.

Martin, André and Walter Gérard, eds. *Catalogue de l'Histoire de la Révolution française*. 2 vols.

Robert, Adolphe, ed. *Dictionnaire des Parlementaires français*. 5 vols., 1889-1891.

Schmidt, Charles, ed. *Les Sources de l'Histoire de France depuis 1789 aux Archives nationales*, Paris, 1907.

Senelier, *Bibliographie des Oeuvres de Jean-Jacques Rousseau*. Paris, 1949.

Tourneux, Maurice, ed. *Bibliographie de l'Histoire de Paris pendant la Révolution française*. 4 vols., Paris, 1890-1906.

Tuetey, Alexandre, ed. *Les Papiers des Assemblées de la Révolution aux Archives nationales: Inventaire de la Série C (Constituante, Legislative, Convention)*. Paris, 1908. (Société de l'Histoire de la Révolution française.)

——, ——, *Repértoire général des Sources Manuscrites de l'Histoire de Paris pendant la Révolution française*. 9 vols. Paris, 1890-1910.

II. PUBLISHED DOCUMENTS.

Anderson, F. M. ed. *Constitutions and other Select Documents Illustrative of the History of France, 1789-1907*. Minneapolis, 1908.

Aulard, François V. Alphonse, ed. *La Société des Jacobins: Recueil de Documents pour l'Histoire du Club des Jacobins de Paris*. 6 vols., Paris, 1891-1892.

——, ——, ——, ——, *Recueil des Actes du Comité de Salut public avec la Correspondance Officielle des Représentants en mission et le Registre du Conseil executif provisoire*. 12 vols., Paris, 1889-1899.

Bourgin, Georges, ed., *Le Partage des Biens communaux*. Paris, 1908.

Braesch, F., ed., *Papiers de Chaumette*. Paris, 1908.

Buchez, P. J. and Roux, P. C., eds. *Histoire parlementaire de la Révolution française ou Journal des Assemblées nationales depuis 1789 jusqu'en 1815*. 40 vols., Paris, 1834-1838.

Chassin, Charles, ed., *Les Élections et les Cahiers de Paris en 1789*. 3 vols., Paris, 1888-1889.

Collection de Documents inédits sur l'Histoire de France. 280 vols., Paris, 1836 ff.

Collection de Documents inédits sur l'Histoire economique de la Révolution française. 100 vols., Paris, 1906 ff.

Dareste, F. R. and Dareste, P., eds. *Les Constitutions modernes*. 5 vols. and supplement, 4th. ed., Paris, 1928-1933.

Dauban, C. A. *La Démagogie en 1793 à Paris ou Histoire Jour par Jour de l'Année 1793 accompagnée de Documents contemporains rares ou inédits*. Paris, 1868.

Débats de la Convention nationale ou Analyse complète des Séances avec les Noms de Tous les Membres, Pétitionnaires ou Pérsonnages qui ont figuré dans cette Assemblée, précédée d'une Introduction par Leon Thiessé. 4 vols. Paris, 1828.

Décrets de la Convention nationale: Des 25 Octobre et 14 November 1792 l'An premier de la République française—4 Juin 1793, l'An 2ᵉ de la République française. Paris, 1792-1793.

Dufau, Pierre and Duvergier Jean, eds. *Collection des Constitutions, Chartes et Lois fondamentales des Peuples de l'Europe et des deux Amériques*. 7 vols., Paris, 1830.

Duvergier, Jean and others, eds. *Collection complète des Lois, Décrets, Ordonnances, Règlements, et Avis du Conseil d'État, publiée sur les Editions officielles du Louvre: de l'Imprimerie nationale par Baudoin; et du Bulletin des Lois (de 1788 à 1824)*. 24 vols., to date, Paris, 1824 ff.

Duguit, Léon and Monnier, Henri, eds. *Les Constitutions et les principales Lois politiques de la France depuis 1789*. 5th ed., Paris, 1932.

Gerbaux, Fernand, ed. *Procès-verbaux des Comités d'Agriculture de la Convention*.

Guillaume, James, ed. *Procès-verbaux du Comité d'Instruc-*

tion publique de la Convention nationale. 6 vols., Paris, 1891-1907.

Hawgood, John A., ed. *Modern Constitutions since 1787.* New York, 1939.

Mavidal, Jérôme, Laurent, Émile, and others, eds. *Archives parlementaires, 1787-1860: Recueil complet des Débats des Chambres françaises.* (Series I, 1787-1799, vols. I-82, Paris, 1879-1913.) (Series II, 1800-1860, vols. I-137, Paris, 1862-1913.)

Procès-verbal de la Convention nationale. 72 vols., Paris, 1792-An IV.

Recueil des Loix constitutives des Colonies Anglaises, confédérées sous la Denomination d'États-Unis de l'Amerique Septentrionale. Paris, 1778. (Dédié à M. le Docteur Franklin à Philadelphie et se vend a Paris, 1778.)

Stewart, J. H., *A Documentary Survey of the French Revolution.* New York, 1951.

Tourneaux, Maurice, ed. *Procès-verbaux de la Commune de Paris (10 Août 1792—1 Juin 1793).* Paris, 1894.

III. FRENCH REVOLUTIONARY PAMPHLETS (CONTEMPORARY)

Acte constitutionnel précédé de la Déclaration des Droits de l'Homme et du Citoyen, présenté au Peuple français par la Convention nationale de 24 Juin 1793, l'An deuxième de la République Paris, 1793.

(   ), (   )[1]. *Adresse aux vrais Impartiaux.* Paris, (   ).

Albouys, Barthélemy. *Principes constitutionnels, présentés à la Convention nationale.* Paris, 1793.

Audouin, J. P. *Quelques Idées preliminaires, soumises à l'Examen de ses Collègues par J. P. Aodouin.* (   ), (   ).

Bacon, Citoyen. *Examen impartial des Bases de la nouvelle Constitution présentée le 15 Février 1793.* (   ), (   ).

Baraly, (   ). *L'Agonie des Jacobins: Suite aux Jacobins demasqués.* (   ), (   ).

Barère, Bertrand. *Défense: Appel à la Convention nationale et aux Républicains françois.* Paris, 1794.

———, ———. *De la Pensée du Gouvernement Républicain.* 2d. ed. Paris, l'An V de la Republique.

1. Some of the pamphets are anonymous. Some do not indicate date or place of publications.

———, ———. *Rapport sur la Convocation des Assemblées primaires fait au Nom du Comité de Salut public dans la Séance du Jeudi 27 Juin 1793, l'An II de la République française.* Paris, 1793.

———, ———. *Rapport et Décret du 23 Aôut l'An II de la République sur la Réquisition civique des jeunes Citoyens pour la Défense de la Patrie présentés au Nom du Comité de Salut public.* Paris, 1793.

Bergoeing, ( ). *La longue Conspiration des Jacobins pour dissoudre la Convention nationale.* ( ), ( ).

Billaud-Varennes, (Jacques Nicolas). *Adresse aux Français contre les Oppresseurs actuels du Peuple; et pour la Liberté de la Presse.* Paris, 1794.

—————, —————. *Décret du 14 Frimaire précéde du Rapport fait au Nom du Comité de Salut public sur un Mode de Gouvernement provisoire et revolutionnaire à la Séance du 28 Brumaire l'An second de la République une et indivisible.* Paris, 1793.

—————, —————. *Discours sur les Députés de la Convention mis en État d'Arrestation par son Décret du 2 Juin prononcé dans la Séance du 15 Juillet. Paris,* 1793.

—————, —————. *Les Éléments du Républicanisme.* Paris, 1792.

Blaviel, Citoyen. *Réflexions préliminaires sur la Constitution française et sur l'Organisation d'un Gouvernement populaire préséntée a la Convention nationale par le Citoyen Blaviel, Député du Departement du Lot le 13 Mai 1793 l'An deuxième de la République.* Paris, 1793.

B( ), M( ) L( ). *La France en Perspective ou Exposition Libre de ce que la France a été et de ce qu'elle pourrait être.* Londres, 1789.

Bonguyod, Marc-Francois. *Observations sur le Projet du Comité de Constitution, relatif à l'Ordre judiciare.* ( ), ( ).

Brissot, Jacques Pierre. *Député a la Convention nationale a Tous les Républicains de France; sur la Société des Jacobins de Paris.* Paris, 1792.

———, ———, ———. *Discours sur les Conventions pro-*

noncé a la Société des Amis de la Constitution, Seante aux Jacobins, le 8 Aôut 1791. ( ), ( ).

————, ————, ————. *Observations d'un Républicain sur les differents Systèmes d'Administrations provinciales, particulièrement sur ceux de Mm. Turgot et Necker et sur le Bien qu'on peut en espérer dans les Gouvernement monarchiques.* Lausanne, 1787.

Cambacérès, (Jean Jacques Regis de). *Opinion sur les Communes, prononcée dans la Séance du 21 Mai.* Paris, 1793.

Chabot, Francois. *Project d'Acte constitutif des Français* ( ), ( ).

Cloots, Anacharsis. *Bases constitutionnelles de la République du Genre humain.* Paris, 1793.

Constitution française telle qu'elle a été lue à la Convention nationale, lé Vendredi 15 Fevrier 1793. Paris, 1793.

Constitution républicaine décrétee par la Convention nationale de France en 1793, et presentée a l'Acceptation du Peuple français, précédée du Rapport fait sur ce Sujet, par Hérault-Séçhelles, Membre de la Convention nationale suivie du Procès-verbal des Monuments de la Marche et des Discours de la Fête consacrée a l'Inauguration de la Constitution de la République française de 10 Août 1793; de la Loi sur le Gouvernement provisoire et révolutionnaire, de la Réponse de la Convention nationale aux Manifestes des Rois ligués contre la République française. Paris, 1793.

Coupé, J. M. *A Ses Commettants sur le nouveau Project de Constitution.* ( ), ( ).

————, ————. *Idées simples de Constitution: No. 2.* ( ), ( ).

————, ————, *Idées simples de Constitution: No. 3.* ( ), ( ).

Crachet, Robert Francois. *Discours sur le Départ du Roi, prononcé dans l'Église de Nielles-lès-Blequin, le 24 Juin 1792, au Salut du Saint-Sacrement par Robert-François Crachet, Curé de la Paroisse St. Omer.* ( ), ( ).

Daunou, C., *Discours prononcê par le Cen Daunou, Presi-

dent de la Convention nationale dans la Séance du 23
Thermidor, Jour anniversaire du 10 Août. Paris, 1795.

————, ————. Motion d'Ordre sur le Travail de la Constitution prononcée par le C. Daunou, á la Tribune de la
Convention nationale dans la Séance du 26 Avril. Paris,
1793.

Debry, Jean Projet de Déclaration des Droits de l'Homme,
et de Constitution française, qui ordonne la Convocation
des Assemblées primaires pour la Présentation de la Déclaration des Droits de l'Homme et du Citoyen et de
l'Acte constitutionnel. Paris, 1793.

Defrance, Citoyen. Réflexions sur quelques Articles de la
Constitution projetée. (   ), (   ).

Delacroix, C. H. Bases constitutionnelles de l'Établissement
des Communes proposées par C. H. Delacroix. (   ),
(   ).

Desacy, (   ). Nouvelles Observations sur le Plan de
Constitution (   ), (   ).

Desmoulins, Camille. Discours au Conseil général de la
Commune dans la Séance du 24 Juillet l'An IV de Liberté
sur la Situation dans le Capital. Paris, 1792.

Dupont, P. C. F. Bases de la Constitution français. (   ),
(   ).

Durand-Maillane, (   ). Addition importante à l'Examen
critique du Plan de Constitution. (   ), (   ).

Dutrau, (   ). Peuple, Réveilles-Toi, Il est Temps. (   ),
(   ).

(   ), (   ). Éveil du Patriotisme sur la Révolution.
Paris, 1791.

Exposition des Motifs d'après lesquels l'Assemblée nationale
a proclamé la Convocation d'une Convention nationale,
et prononcé la Suspension du Pouvoir exécutif dans les
Mains du Roi. Paris, 1792.

Fauchet, Abbè. Éloge civique de Benjamin Franklin. Paris,
1790.

Grande Dispute au Panthéon entre Marat et Jean-Jacques
Rousseau. (   ), (   ).

Guadet (Marguerite Elie). Réponse de Guadet à Robespierre

prononcée dans la Séance du Avril 1793. 3d. ed., Paris, 1794.

Guy-Kersaint, A. *De la Constitution et du Gouvernement qui pourraient convenir à la République française*. Paris, 1792.

Harmand, J. B. *Préliminaires et Ordre de la Discussion sur la Constitution*. (   ), (   ).

Hérault (de Séchelles). *Projet de Constitution du Peuple français présenté à la Convention nationale au Nom du Comité de Salut public: précéde du Rapport fait par le même Citoyen au Nom du même Comité et de la Déclaration des Droits déjà décrétée*. Paris, 1793.

Hollier, C. *Parallele de la République avec la Monarchie ou Discours sur les Avantages de la République prononcé dans la Salle des Séances de la Société des Amis de la Liberté et de l'Egalité*. Bordeaux, 1792.

Lanjuinais, J. D. *Mémoire justificatif*. Paris, 1815.

————, ————, *Rapport présenté a la Convention nationale au Nom de la Commission des Six sur l'Ordre a suivre dans la Discussion de la Constitution*. (   ), (   ).

————, ————, *Rédaction des derniers Articles du Titre II de la Constitution concernant la Division du Territoire proposée 22 Mai 1793, l'An deuxième de la République*. Paris, 1793.

Lanthenas, F. *Motifs de faire du 10 Août un jubilé fraternal, une Époque solennelle de Réconciliation générale entre Tous les Républicains, en consacrant une Déclaration des Devoirs de l'Homme, des Principles et Maximes de la Morale universelle*. Paris, 1793.

Laurens, (   ). *Constitution française*. (   ), (   ).

Leveaux, F. C. *Discours sur les Vices de la Constitution anglaise*. Paris, 1793.

La Vicomterie (Louis-Thomas Hébert). *Du Peuple et des Rois*. Paris, 1791.

Lefebure, Louis. *Constitution de Gouvernement pour la Nation française*. (   ), (   ).

Les Synonimes Jabobites: Du Pain–Insurrection; Constitu-

tion de 1793—Prétexte; Jacobins—Massacre de la Convention; Succès—Pillage, Anarchie, Horreurs. (   ), (   ).

Marat, J. P. *Éloge de Montesquieu.* Libourne, 1783.

——, ——. *Les Chaines de l'Esclavage.* Paris, 1792.

Meynard, F. *Quelques Observations sur la Division du Territoire proposée par le Comité de Constitution, et sur les Administrations qu'il convient d'établir; exposées à la Tribune de la Convention.* (   ), (   ).

Mille, Bernard F. *Hommage Catholique a la République française ou Accord de la Religion avec la Constitution: Discours prononcé le 15 Août dans la Métropole de Paris, en Actions de Graces de l'Acceptation de la Constitution.* Paris, 1793.

Mont-Gilbert, Francois. *Avis au Peuple sur sa Liberté et l'Exercice de ses Droits contenu dans un Projet de Constitution républicaine.* Paris, 1793.

Montmorin, (   ) *Observations de M. Montmorin adressées à l'Assemblée nationale sur les Discours prononcés par M. Gensonné et Brissot dans la Séance du 23 Mai 1792.* (   ), (   ).

Morel, Charles. *La Déclaration des Droits de l'Homme et du Citoyen mise à la Portée de Tout le Monde, et comparée avec vrais Principes de Toute Société.* 3d. ed. Paris, 1790.

Notice sur la Vie de Siéyès, Membre de la première Assemblée nationale et de la Convention. Paris, 1794.

(   ), (   ). *Offrande a la Patrie ou Discours au Tiers État de France.* (   ), (   ).

Oudot, C. F. *Un Mot sur la Question constitutional de la Division des grandes Municipalités.* (   ), (   ).

Paine, Thomas. *Droits de l'Homme: en Réponse a l'Attaque de M. Burke sur la Révolution française.* Tr. from English by F. S., Paris, 1791.

——,——. *Le Sens commun.* Tr. from English by (   ), Paris, 1791.

(Par l'Auteur de la Guinguette-Patriotique). *Le grand Dénouement de la Constitution.* Bruxelles, (   ).

Pénières, J. A. *Plan et Projet de Constitution pour la Répub-*

lique française présentés a la Convention nationale. Paris, 1793.

Petion, J. *Discours sur les Conventions nationales prononcé a la Société des Amis de la Constitution séante aux Jacobins, le 7 Août 1791.* Paris, 1791.

Petit, Michael Edme. *Constitution: Suite de la Discussion sur la Division du Territoire français prononcée le 21 Mai 1793, l'An second de la République.* (   ), (   ).

Plan de Constitution présenté a la Convention nationale, les 15 et 16 Frévrier 1793, l'An II de la République, Paris, 1793.

Pottier, Charles. *Mes Réflexions sur la Nécessité d'etablir la Constitution, et sur l'Ordre de sa Discussion.* (   ), (   ).

Poultier, Francois. *Sur la Constitution présentée par le Comité Salut public.* (   ), (   ).

Pressavin, (   ). *Project de Constitution.* (   ), (   ).

Projet d'Adresse a la Convention nationale présenté a l'Assemblée primaire du Canton d' (   ). (   ), (   ).

Projet de Règlements pour la Société patriotique de la Section du Luxembourg lus dans son Assemblée provisoire du 28 Janvier de l'An IV de la Liberté: Paris, 1793 .

Raynal, Abbè. *Raynal aux États Généraux.* Marseille, 1789.

Robert, François. *Avantages de la Fuite de Louis XVI, et Nécessité d'un nouveau Gouvernement. Second Edition du Républicanisme adapté a la France.* Paris, 1791.

———, ———. *Discours sur les Bases de la Constitution.* (   ), (   ).

Robespierre, Maximilien. *Adresse aux Français.* Paris, 1791.

———, ———. *Discours sur la Constitution.* (   ), (   ).

———, ———. *Déclaration des Droits de l'Homme et du Citoyen.* Paris, 1793.

Romme, G. *Troisième partie du Rapport fait au Nom de la Commission des Six dur la Déclaration des Droits dans la Séance du 17 Avril 1793 l'An de la République.* Paris, 1793.

Saint-Just, (Louis de). *Rapport fait au Nom du Comité de Salut public dans la Seance du 9 Juillet, sur les trente-deux Membres de la Convention detenus en Vertu du Decret* de 2 Juin, par Saint-Just, Député de l'Aisne. Paris, 1793.

Thionville, Merlin de. *Portrait de Robespierre*. Paris, (   ).

Thirion, Didier. *La Pierre angulaire de l'Edifice constitution-nel*. (   ). (   ).

(Un vrai Républicain). *Examen d'un Point important de la Constitution soumise à la Discussion de la Convention nationale*. (   ), (   ).

Vergniaud (Pierre Victurnien). *Opinion prononcée a la Convention nationale le 8 Mai 1793, l'An deuxiéme de la République*. Paris, 1793.

————, ————. *Opinion sur la Situation actuelle de la France, prononcé le 3 Juillet 1792 l'An IV de la Liberté*. Paris, 1792.

————, ————. *Opinion sur le Jugement de Louis XVI*. Paris, 1793.

————, ————. *Réponse de Vergniaud, Député de la Gironde, aux Calomnies de Robespierre, Député de Paris, prononcée a la Convention nationale, le 10 Avril 1793, An II de la République française, suivie de sa Lettre à Barère et à Robert Lindet, Membres du Comité de Salut public de la Convention nationale*. Paris, 1794.

Véron, (   ). *Au Peuple: Des Vérités terribles, mais indispensables tirées de J. J. Rousseau, Mably, Raynal, etcetera, et de Tous les Philosophes Amis des principes de l'Égalité*. (   ), (   ).

Wandelaincourt, A. H. *Observations sur le Plan de Constitution présentées par A. H. Wandelaincourt, Député du Département de la Haute-Marne*. (   ), (   ).

————, ————. *Suite des Observations sur le Plan de Constitution*. (   ), (   ).

Williams, David. *Observations sur la dernière Constitution de la France, avec des Vues pour la Formation de la nouvelle Constitution*. Tr. from English by Citizen Maudru, Paris, 1793.

Wilriot, Citoyen. *Hommage a la Convention nationale, d'un Projet de Gouvernement républicain à donner à la France* (   ), (   ).

IV. NEWSPAPERS.

L'Ami du Peuple ou le Publiciste Parisien. Paris, September 12, 1789-July 14, 1793.

La Chronique du Mois ou les Cahiers patriotiques de E. Clavière, C. Condorcet, Th. Paine, *etcetera*. Paris, 1792. Bibliothèque nationale. Le 2 649.

Le Journal des Débats et Décrets. Paris, August 29, 1789-Floréal An 5.

Le Moniteur universel (Journal officiel de l'Empire français). 196 vols. Paris, 1789-1863.

Le Patriote français ou Journal libre, impartial et national, par une Société de Citoyens. Paris, July 28, 1789 — June 2, 1793.

Le Républicain ou le Dèfenseur du Gouvernement représentatif par une Société de Républicains (Condorcet, Paine, Duchâtelet). Paris, 1791. There were only four numbers of this short-lived newspaper. Two numbers appeared on July 10, 1791, one on July 16, 1791, and the final number on July 24, 1791. Condorcet, Brissot, and Tom Paine, along with Duchâtelet, all collaborated on this journal, which might be termed France's first republican newspaper.

V. DIARIES AND CORRESPONDENCE.

Archenholtz, J. W. von. *Die Pariser Jacobiner in Ihren Sitzungen. Ein Auszug aus Ihren Tagebuch, veranstaltet und mit Anmerkungen versehen.* Hamburg, 1793.

Chinard, Gilbert, ed. *Les Amitiés américaines de Madame d'Houdetot d'après sa Correspondance inédite avec Benjamin Franklin et Thomas Jefferson.* Paris, 1924.

Davenport, Beatrix Cary, ed. *A Diary of the French Revolution by Gouverneur Morris, 1752-1816, Minister to France during the Terror.* 2 vols, Boston, 1939.

J. P. Brissot: Correspondance et Papiers. Ed. by Claude Perroud, Paris, 1912.

Lettres de Madame Roland. Ed. by Claude Perroud, 2 vols, Paris, 1900-1902.

VI.   MEMOIRS, TRAVELERS' ACCOUNTS, AND COLLECTED WORKS.

Argenson, Marquis d' (René de Voyer de Paulmy). *Journal et Mémoires.* 9 vols., Paris, 1859-1867.

Beiträge zur Geschichte der Französischen Revolution von 1789: St. Justs Gesammelte Schriften. 2 vols, Leipzig, 1851.

Brissot, J. P. *New Travels in the United States of America.* Tr. from the French by (   ). Dublin, 1792.

Chastellux, Marquis de. *Travels in North America in the Years 1780, 1781 and 1782.* Tr. from the French by (   ). 2 vols., London, 1787.

Claretie, Jules, ed. *Oeuvres de Camille Desmoulins, recueillis et publiées d'après les Textes originaux.* 2 vols., Paris, 1874.

Clavière, Étienne, and Brissot, J. P. *De la France et des États-Unis ou de l'Importance de la Révolution de l'Amérique pour le Bonheur de la France, des Rapports de ce Royaume et des États-Unis, des Avantages reciproques qu'ils peuvent retirer de leurs Liaisons de Commerce et enfin de la Situation actuelle des États-Unis.* London, 1787.

Condorcet, Marquis de. *Oeuvres complètes.* 21 vols., Paris, 1801-1804. It was this edition that was used in the preparation of the monograph. Madame Condorcet, the brilliant wife of the great *philosophe,* collaborated with the famous French Revolutionary publisher Garat and Dr. Cabanis in its publication.

Dauban, C. A. ed. *Mémoires de Pétion, Buzot et Barbaroux.* Paris, 1865.

Dumont, Étienne. *Souvenirs sur Mirabeau et sur les deux premières Assemblées législatives; Ouvrage posthume publiée par J. L. Duval.* Paris, 1832.

Durand-Maillane, Pierre. *Mémoires.* Paris, 1825.

J. P. Brissot: Mémoires, 1754-1793. Ed. by Claude Perroud, 2 vols., Paris, 1911.

La Rochefoucould-Liancourt, Marquis de. Mémoires de Condorcet sur la Révolution français, extraits de sa Correspondance et celle des ses Amis. 2 vols., Paris, 1824.

Mably, L'Abbè de. *Collection complète des Oeuvres de l'Abbè de Mably.* 15 vols., Paris, 1794-1795.

Meillan, Arnaud. *Mémoires.* Paris, 1823.

Mémoires de Madame Roland. Ed. by Claude Perroud, 2 vols., Paris, 1905.

Rousseau, Jean-Jacques. *Oeuvres de J. J. Rousseau de Genève. Nouvelle Édition, revue, corrigée et augmentée de plusieurs Morceaux qui n'avaient point encore paru.* 11 vols., Amsterdam, 1769.

The Writings of Thomas Paine. Ed. by Daniel Moncure Conway. 4 vols., New York, 1894-1908.

Vellay, Charles, ed. *Oeuvres complètes de Saint-Just.* 2 vols., Paris, 1908.

Voltaire, Francois Marie Arouet de. *Oeuvres complètes.* Edited by Beaumarchais and Condorcet. 70 vols., Paris, 1784-1789. Note the names of the two famous personages, both important in the evolution of a republican spirit in France, who edited this edition of the works of the great philosopher. This particular edition, used by many of the French Revolutionary generation, was the one consulted in the preparation of the monograph.

Williams, Helen Maria. *Memoirs of the Reign of Robespierre.* London, 1929.

VII. HISTORIES BY CONTEMPORARIES.

Mazzei, Filippo. *Recherches historiques et politiques sur les États-Units de l'Amérique septentrionale.* 4 vols., Paris, 1788. One edition of this work was edited by the Marquis de Condorcet.

Raynal, Abbé. *Histoire philosophique et politique des Établissements et du Commerce des Européens dans les deux Indies.* 4 vols., Génève, 1780.

VIII. SPECIAL STUDIES AND MONOGRAPHS.

Allain, Abbé. *L'Instruction primaire en France avant la Révolution.* Paris, 1880.

Andrews, G. G. *The Constitution in the Early French Revolution.* New York, 1917.

Auerbach, R. von. *Montesquieu et son Influence sur le Mouvement intellectual du XVIIIe Siècle*. Paris, 1876.

Aulard, Francois V. Alphonse. *L'Éloquence parlementaire pendant la Révolution française: Les Orateurs de la Législative et de la Convention*. 2 vols., Paris, 1885-1886.

———, ———, ———, and Mirkine-Guetzevitch. *Les Declarations des Droits de l'Homme, Textes constitutionnels, concernant les Droits de l'Homme et les Garanties des Libertés individuelles dans Tous les Pays*. Paris, 1929.

———, ———, ———. *Mémoires de Chaumette sur la Révolution du 10 Août 1792*. Paris, 1893.

Babeau, Albert. *L'Instruction primaire dans les Campagnes avant 1789*. Troyes, 1875.

Barber, Elinor G. *The Bourgeoisie in Eighteenth-Century France*. Princeton, New Jersey, 1955.

Barère, Bertrand. *Montesquieu peint d'après ses Ouvrages*. Paris, 1796.

Bastid, P. *Siéyès et sa Pensée*. Paris, 1939.

Bastide, Charles. *John Locke: Ses Théories politiques et leur Influence en Angleterre*. Paris, 1907.

Biré, Edmond. *La Légende des Girondins*. Paris, 1881.

Bonno, G. *La Constitution britannique devant l'Opinion française de Montesquieu à Bonaparte*. Paris, 1931.

Bossuet, Monsieur. *Juste Idée d'un bon Governement*. ( ), 1756.

Bouglé, C. *Socialisme français*. Paris, 1932.

Bouzinac, J. *Les Doctrines économiques au 18e Siècle: Jean-Francois Melon, Économiste*. Toulouse, 1906.

Brinton, Clarence Crane. *The Jacobins: An Essay in the New History*. New York, 1930.

———, ———, ———. *The Portable Age of Reason Reader*. New York, 1956.

Cahen, Leon and Gujot, Raymond. *L'Oeuvre législative de la Révolution*. Paris, 1913.

Carcassonne, E. *Montesquieu et le Problème de la Constitution française au XVIIIe Siècle*. Paris, 1926.

Cardenal, L. de *La Province pendant la Révolution: Histoire des Clubs Jacobins (1789-1795)*. Paris, 1929.

Cassirer, E. *The Philosophy of the Enlightenment.* (Tr. by Fritz C. A. Koelln and James P. Pettgrove, Boston, 1955.)

————, ————. *The Question of Jean-Jacques Rousseau.* Tr. by Peter Gay, New York, 1954.

Champion, Edme. *J.-J. Rousseau et la Revolution française.* Paris, 1909.

————, ————. *La France d'après les Cahiers de 1789.* Paris, 1897.

Claretie, Jules. *Les derniers Montagnards: Histoire de l'Insurrection de Prairial An III d'après les Documents originaux inédits.* 2d. ed., Paris, 1868.

Cochin, Augustin. *Les Sociétés de Pensée et la Démocratie: Études d'Histoire Révolutionnaire.* Paris, 1921.

Combes de Patris, Bernard. *L'Espirit financier des Girondins.* Paris, 1909.

Crèvecoeur, J. Hector Saint-John. *Letters from an American Farmer.* Ed. by Ludwig Lewissohn, New York, 1904.

Derathé, Robert. *Jean-Jacques Rousseau et la Science politique de son Temps.* Paris, 1950.

Des Opinions politiques du Citoyen Siéyès et de sa Vie comme Homme public. Paris, 1800.

Echeverria, D. *Mirage in the West: A History of the French Image of American Society to 1815.* Princeton, 1956.

Fabre, Auguste. *La Révolution de 1830 et le véritable Parti républicain.* 2 vols. in 8, Paris, 1833.

Fabre, Joseph. *Les Pères de la Révolution de Bayle à Condorcet.* Paris, 1900.

Faguet, Émile. *La Politique comparée de Montesquieu, Rousseau et Voltaire.* Paris, 1902.

Faÿ, Bernard. *L'Esprit révolutionnaire en France et aux États-Unis à la Fin du XVIIe Siècle.* Paris, 1924.

Frayssinet, Marc. *La République des Girondins.* Toulouse, 1904.

Funck-Brentano, Franz. *Die Bastille in der Legende und nach historischen Documenten.* Tr. from the French by Oscar von Bieberstein. Breslau, 1899.

Galy, François. *La Notion de Constitution dans les Projets de 1793*. Paris, 1932.

Gay, Peter J. *Voltaire's Politics; The Poet as a Realist*. Princeton, New Jersey, 1959.

Gidney, Lucy M. *L'Influence des États-Unis d'Amérique sur Brissot, Condorcet, and Mme. Roland*. Paris, 1930.

Goetz-Bernstein, H. A. *La Diplomatie de la Gironde et de Jacques Pierre Brissot*. Paris, 1912.

Gooch, R. K. *Parliamentary Government in France: Revolutionary Origins, 1789-1791*. Ithaca, New York, 1960.

Gottschalk, L. R. *Lafayette between the American and the French Revolution*. Chicago, 1950.

Grouvelle, ( ). *De l'Autorité de Montesquieu dans la Révolution présente*. Paris, 1789.

Guadet, J. *Les Girondins: leur Vie privée, leur Vie publique, leur Proscription et leur Mort*. Paris, 1889.

Hale, Edward E., and Hale, Edward E., Jr. *Franklin in France*. 2 vols., Boston, 1887-1888.

Hansen, Harold A. *Guadet, Girondin Orator: A Study of the French Revolution*. Unpublished M. A. thesis, University of California, Berkeley, California, 1930.

Havens, G. R. *The Age of Ideas: From Reaction to Revolution in Eighteenth-century France*. New York, 1955.

Hazen, Charles Downer. *Contemporary American Opinion of the French Revolution*. Baltimore, 1897.

Hendel, Charles William. *Jean-Jacques Rousseau, Moralist*. London, 1934.

Hendel, Hazard P. *European Thought in the Eighteenth Century*. London, 1954.

Henderson, Ernest F. *Symbol and Satire in the French Revolution*. New York, 1912.

Herriot, Edouard. *The Wellsprings of Liberty*. Tr. from the French by Richard Duffy. New York, 1939.

Hyslop, Beatrice Fay. *French Nationalism in 1789 According to the General Cahiers*. New York, 1934.

Jellineck, G. *La Déclaration des Droits de l'Homme*. Paris, 1901.

La Forge, Anatole de. *La Liberté de la Presse pendant la Révolution française*. Paris, 1881.

Lavaux, Briquet de. *Éloge de Montesquieu*. (   ), 1783.

Lefebvre, G. *Coming of the French Revolution*. Tr. by R. J. Palmer, Princeton, New Jersey, 1947.

Levin, Laurence Meyer. *The Political Doctrine of Montesquieu's Esprit de Lois: Its Classical Background*. New York, 1936.

Locke, John. *Two Treatises on Civil Government*. London, 1884.

Marcaggi, V. *Les Origines de la Déclaration des Droits de l'Homme de 1789*. Paris, 1904.

Mathiez, Albert. *Girondins et Montagnards*. 6th. ed., Paris, 1930.

————, ————. *Le Club de Cordeliers*. Paris, 1910.

Mautouchet, Paul. *Le Gouvernement révolutionnarie 10 Août 1792—4 Brumaire An IV*. Paris, 1912.

McIlwain, Charles Howard. *Constitutionalism, Ancient and Modern*. New York, 1940.

McKee, George H. *Thomas Jefferson: Ami de la Revolution française*. Paris, 1928.

Michel, Henri. *L'Idée de l'État: Essai critique sur l'Histoire des Théories sociales et politiques en France depuis la Révolution*. Paris, 1896.

Michelet, J. *Les Femmes de la Révolution*. Paris, (   ).

Mornet, Daniel. *Les Origines intellectuelles de la Révolution française, 1715-1787*. Paris, 1933.

Osborn, Annie Marion. *Rousseau and Burke: A Study of the Idea of Liberty in Eighteenth-century Political Thought*. New York, 1940.

Palm, Franklin C. *The Middle Classes Then and Now*. New York, 1936.

Palmer, R. M. *Twelve Who Ruled*. Princeton, New Jersey, 1941.

————, ————, ————. *The Age of the Democratic Revolution: A Political History of Europe and America, 1760-1800*. Princeton, New Jersey, 1959.

Parker, Harold Talbot. *The Cult of Antiquity and the French*

Revolutionaries: A Study in the Development of the Revolutionary Spirit. Chicago, 1937.

Perroud, Claude. *La Proscription des Girondins.* Paris, 1917.

Prat, J. C. ed. *La Constitution of 1793, précédée de la Déclaration des Droits d l'Homme présentée au Peuple français le 24 Juin 1793, publiée, annotée, comparée avec la Constitution de 1884 et la Constitution des États-Unis d'Amérique.* Paris, 1884.

Read, Conyears, ed. *The Constitution Reconsidered.* New York. 1938.

Rice, Howard C. *Le Cultivateur américain: Étude sur l'Oeuvre de Saint-John de Crèvecoeur.* Paris, 1933.

Robiquet, Paul. *Buonarroti et la Secte des Égaux: d'après des Documents inédits.* Paris, 1910.

Sagnac, P. *La Fin de l'ancien Regime et la Revolution americaine 1763-1789.* Paris, 1947.

Schapiro, J. Salwyn. *Condorcet and the Rise of Liberalism.* New York, 1934.

Schatz, Richard. *J. J. Rousseaus Einflusz auf Robespierre.* Leipzig, 1905.

Sée, Henri. *Les Idées politiques en France au XVIIIe Siècle.* Paris, 1923.

Selsan, J. P. *The Pennsylvania Constitution of 1776: A Study in Revolutionary Democracy.* Philadelphia, 1936.

Sicard, A. *Les Études classiques avant la Révolution.* Paris, 1883.

Silvy, A. *Les Collèges en France avant la Révolution.* Paris, 1885.

Soltau, Roger. *French Political Thought in the Nineteenth Century.* New York, 1931.

Sydenham, M. J. *The Girondins.* London, University of London, Athlone Press, 1961.

Torrey, N. *The Spirit of Voltaire.* New York, 1938.

Thompson, J. M. *Robespierre and the French Revolution.* New York, 1953.

Vaughan, C. E. *The Political Writings of Rousseau.* 2 vols., Cambridge University Press, England, 1915.

Wadia, P. A. *The Philosophers and the French Revolution.* London, 1904.

Waldinger, Mrs. Renée. *Voltaire and Reform in the Light of the French Revolution.* Geneva, 1959.

Wallon, H. *La Révolution du 31 Mai et le Fédéralisme en 1793.* 2 vols. in 1, Paris, 1886.

Weil, G. *Histoire du Parti républicain en France de 1814 à 1870.* Paris, 1900.

IX. BIOGRAPHIES.

Alengry, Franck, *Condorcet: Guide de la Révolution française, Théoricien du Droit constitutionnel et Précurseur de la Science sociale.* Paris, 1904.

Bigeon, *A. Siéyès: L' Homme, le Constituant.* Paris, 1893.

Bougeart. A. *Marat, l'Ami du Peuple.* 2 vols., Paris.

Cheetham, James. *The Life of Thomas Paine, Author of Common Sense, The Crisis, Rights of Man, etcetera.* New York, 1809.

Conway, Moncure Daniel. *Thomas Paine (1737-1809) et la Révolution dans les deux Mondes.* Tr. from the English by Felix Rabbe. (   ),(   ).

Dard, Emile. *Hérault de Séchelles.* Paris, 1907.

Ellery, Eloise. *Brissot de Warville: A Study in the History of the French Revolution.* Boston, 1915.

Feugère, Anatole. *Un Précurseur de la Révolution: L'Abbé Raynal (1713-1796).* Angoulême, 1922.

Gershoy, Leo. *Bertrand Barère: A Reluctant Terrorist.* Princeton, New Jersey, 1962.

Gottschalk, L. R. *Lafayette between the American and the French Revolution.* Chicago, 1950.

Guerrier, M. W., *L'Abbé de Mably: Étude sur la Doctrine morale du Jacobinisme puritaine et sur le Développement de l'Esprit républicain au XVIIIᵉ Siècle.* Paris 1886.

Hamel, Ernest. *Histoire de Robespierre: d'après des Papiers de Famille, les Sources originales et des Documents entièrement inédits.* 3 vols., Paris, 1866.

————, ————, *Histoire de Saint-Just.* Paris, 1859.

Hérissay, Jacques. *Un Girondin: Francois Buzot, Député de l'Eure à l'Assemblée constituante et à la Convention 1760-1794.*

Levy, L. *Le Conventionnel Jeanbon Saint-André*. Paris, 1901.

Malone, Dumas. *Jefferson the Virginian* and *Jefferson and the Rights of Man*. Vols. I and II of *Jefferson and His Time*, Boston, 1948, 1951.

Mitchell, Julia Post. *Saint-Jean de Crèvecoeur*, New York, 1916.

Neton, A. *Siéyès (1748-1836) d'apres des Documents inédits*. Paris, 1900.

Pardee, M. A. *Thomas Paine (1737-1809)*, *d'après ses Écrits et les Archives*. Paris, 1938.

Schapiro, J. Salwyn. *Condorcet and the Rise of Liberalism*. New York, 1934.

Thompson, J. M. *Robespierre and the French Revolution*. New York, 1953.

Vallette, G. *Jean-Jacques Rousseau Génèvois*. Geneva, 1911.

Vatel, Charles. *Charlotte de Corday et les Girondins, Pièces classées et annotées*. 2 vols., Paris, 1864-1872.

Whitefield, Ernest A. *Gabriel Bonnet de Mably*. London, 1930.

X. GENERAL HISTORIES.

Aulard, Francois V. Alphonse. *Histoire politique de la Révolution Française: Origines et Développement de la Démocratie et de la République*. Paris, 1901.

Brinton, Crane. *A Decade of Revolution, 1789-1799*. New York, 1934. (Rise of Modern Europe series, edited by William L. Langer.)

Brunetière, Ferdinand and others. *Histoire de la Littérature française classique, 1915-1830*. 4 vols. in 6. Paris, 1904-1917.

Deslandres, M. *Histoire constitutionnelle de la France de 1789 à 1870*. 2 vols., Paris, 1932.

Gershoy, L. *The French Revolution and Napoleon*. New York, 1933.

Gottschalk, Louis R. *Era of the French Revolution, 1715-1815*. Boston, 1929.

Jaurès, Jean, ed. *Histoire socialiste, 1789-1900*. 12 vols., Paris, 1901-1909.

Sagnac, P. *La Révolution (1789-1792)*. (Volume I of

Histoire de France Contemporaine depuis la Révolution jusqu'à la Paix de 1919. Ed. by Ernest Lavisee. 10 vols., Paris, 1920-1922.)

XI.   PERIODIC AND ENCYCLOPAEDIC ARTICLES.

Aulard, Francois V. Alphonse. "La Constitution Girondine," *La Révolution française* (June, 1898), XXXIV, 503-554.

————, ————, ————. "La Révolution américaine et la Révolution française: Declaration d'Independence, Constitutions," *La Révolution française* (May-June, 1918), LXXI, 193-229.

————, ————, ————. "La Révolution américaine et la Révolution française: Franklin," *La Révolution française* (September-October, 1918), LXXI, 385-417.

————, ————, ————. "La Révolution américaine et la Révolution française: William Penn et Locke," *La Révolution française* (January-February, 1918), LXXI, 21-47.

————, ————, ————. " La Société des Nations et la Révolution française" *La Révolution Française* (March-April, 1918), LXXI, 104-122.

————, ————, ————. "L'Évolution de la Déclaration des Droits de l'Homme," *Livre d'Or des Droits de l'Homme*, Paris, 1927.

————, ————, ————. "Une Manifestation républicaine avant le 10 Août 1792," *La Révolution française* (September, 1905), XLIX, 266-267.

Baticle, Rene. "Le Plébiscite sur la Constitution de 1793," *La Révolution française* (December, 1909), LVII, 496-524; (January, 1910), LVIII, 5-30; (February, 1910), LVIII, 117-155; (March, 1910), LVIII, 193-238; (April, 1910), LVIII, 37-342; (May, 1910), LVIII, 385-411.

Baudouin, Ernest. "Le Suffrage universel et la Révolution," *Revue de la Révolution* (April, 1883), I, 294-301.

Bord, Gustavel. "La Proclamation de la République," *Revue de la Révolution* (January, 1883), I, 24-46; (February, 1883), I, 147-163; (April, 1883), I, 313-333; (July, 1883), II, 67-78; (August, 1883), II, 152-161; (January,

1884), III, 47-62; (May, 1884), III, 380-395; (August, 1884), IV, 131-141; (October, 1884), IV, 317-323; (November, 1884), IV, 334-341; (December, 1884), IV, 440-451.

Bourne, H. E. "American Constitutional Precedents in the French National Assembly," *American Historical Review* (April, 1903), VIII, 466-486.

Brinton, Crane. "Declaration of Rights of Man." *Encyclopedia of the Social Sciences* (ed. by Seligman, Edwin, and Johnson, A., 15 vols., New York, 1930-34), V, 49-51.

Buffenoir, Hippolyte. "L'Image de J.-J. Rousseau dans les Sociétés de la Révolution à Paris," *La Revolution française* (November-December, 1917), LXX, 504-518.

————, ————. "L'Image de J.-J. Rousseau dans les Sociétés de la Révolution en Provence," *La Révolution française* (January-February, 1918), LXXI, 47-57.

————, ————. "L'Image de J.-J. Rousseau dan les Sociétés de la Révolution à Genève," *La Révolution française* (May-June, 1918), LXXI, 193-229.

Cardenal, Le de. "A propos du Fédéralisme," *Annales historiques de la Révolution française* (May-June, 1937), no. 81, 234-240.

Caron, P. "Conseil exécutif provisoire et Pouvoir ministériel (1792- 1794)," *Annales historiques de la Révolution française* (February, 1937), no. 79, 4-16.

Carré, M. H. "Les Émigrés français en Amérique," *Revue de Paris* (May-June, 1898), III, 311-341.

Celeste, R. "Montesquieu, Légende-Histoire," *Archives historiques de la Gironde* (1907), XLII, 491-497.

Crocker, Lester G. "The Relation of Rousseau's Second Discourse and the *Contrat social*," *The Romantic Review* (February, 1960), 33-34.

Decencière-Ferrandière, André. "La Constitution de 1793," *La Révolution française* (New Series, Third Quarter), no. 7, 237-254.

"De l'Autorité de Montesquieu dans la Révolution," *Bibliothèque de l'Homme public* (ed. by L. S. Balestrier de Canilhac, 128 vols. in 14, Paris, 1790-1792), VII, 6-85.

Desjardins, Paul. "Thomas Paine, Républicain," *Revue bleue* (April 20, 1901), XV, 480-490; (April 27, 1901), XV, 518-524; (May 4, 1901), XV, 552-558; (June 1, 1901), XV, 684-688; (July 20, 1901), XVI, 79-82; (August 3, 1901), XVI, 132-138; (August 31, 1901), XVI, 275-280.

Greenlaw, R. W. "Pamphlet Literature in France during the Period of the Aristocratic Revolt," *Journal of Modern History* (1957), 349-54.

Hermann, Gustave. "La Constitution de 1893 à Excideuil (Dorgogne)," *La Révolution française* (April, 1904), XLVI, 346-354.

Hill, Henry Bertram. "Bibliographical Article: The Constitutions of Continental Europe, 1789-1813," *The Journal of Modern History* (March, 1936), VIII, 82-94.

"La Convention nationale et la Constitution de 1793: Une Lettre du Conventionnel Campanas," *La Révolution française* (July-August-September, 1920), LXXIII, 258-259.

Lion, Henri, "Les Ideés politiques et morales de d'Holbach," *Annales historiques de la Révolution française* (July-August, 1924), I, 356-370.

Mathiez, Albert. "La Constitution de 1793," *Revue de Paris* (July 15, 1928), XV, 298-322.

————, ————. "La Place de Montesquieu dans l'Histoire des Doctrines politiques du 18ᵉ Siècle," *Annales historiques de la Révolution française* (1930), VII, 97-112.

————, ————. "Le Gouvernement révolutionnaire," *Annales historiques de la Révolution française* (March-April, 1937), no. 80, 97-126.

Nicolle, P. "Le Mouvement fédéraliste dans l'Orme en 1793," *Annales historiques de la Révolution française* (November-December, 1936), no. 78, 481-512; (May-June, 1937), no. 81, 215-233; (January-February, 1938), no. 85, 12-53; (July-August, 1938), no. 86, 289-313; (September-October, 1938), no. 89, 385-410.

Palmer, R. R. "Recent Interpretations of the Influence of the French Revolution," *Journal of World History*, II (1954), 173-175.

————, ————. "Reflections on the French Revolution," *Political Science Quarterly, LXVII* (1952), 64-80.

————, ————. "The World Revolution of the West, 1763-1801," *Political Science Quarterly*, LXIX (1954), 1-14.

Pegg, Carl Hamilton. "Sentiments républicains dans la Presse Parisienne à partir du Retour de Louis XVI jusqu'au Rapport des sept Comités," *Annales historiques de la Révolution française* (July-August, 1936), no. 76, 342-356.

"Reimpression: Adresse de la Convention nationale aux Français 26 Juin 1793," *Ia Révolution française* (September-October, 1917), LXX, 462-466.

Robiquet, Paul. "Babeuf et Barras," *Revue de Paris* (March 1, 1896).

Sagnac, Phillippe. "L'Influence américaine sur la Révolution française," *Revue des Études Napoléoniennes* (January-February, 1924).

See, Henri. "La Doctrine politique et sociale de Mably," *Annales historiques de la Révolution française* (March-April, 1924) I, 135-148.

See, Henri. "La Doctrine politique et sociale de Turgot," *Annales historiques de la Révolution française* (September-October, 1924), I, 413-426.

Souquet, Paul. "Pierre Bayle, Libre-Penseur et Politique," *La Révolution française* (February, 1890), XVIII, 97-125; (March, 1890), XVIII, 210-232.

Tchernoff, J. "Montesquieu et J.-J. Rousseau; Contribution à l'Étude de la Philosophie politique du 18e Siècle," *Revue du Droit public* (1903), XIX, 477-514; (1904), XX, 49-97.

"Un Document inédit sur la Gironde: David Williams," *Annales historiques de la Révolution française* (September-October, 1938), no. 89, 411-431.

INDEX

A

Adams, John, 40, 73, 94, 109, 215—footnote 86

Alembert, Jean le Rond d', 55, 56, 144—footnote 52

Alengry, Franck, 131—footnote 38; 185—footnote 2; 195—footnote 28

Amar, 271

American Revolution, 64-81, 87-93
    effect on Brissot, 65
    effect on Condorcet, 64-65, 79
    effect on French officers serving in, 87-90
    effect on Lafayette, 91-92

Anthoine, François, 187—footnote 8

Antiquity,
    cult of and influence on French Revolutionary leaders, 32, 61—footnote 224

Archives parlementaires . . . , passim.

Argenson, Marquis d', 54-55

Assignats, 250—footnote 74

Aulard, François V. Alphonse, ed., *La Société des Jacobins...* *passim.*
    Recueil des Actes du Comité de Salut public . . . passim.

Austrian Netherlands, 246, 249

B

Babeuf, François Noel, 307

Barbaroux, Charles Jean Marie, as deputy to Convention, 169-172, 229-230
    as member of first French republican constitutional committee, 185, life, 169—footnote 52

Barbet, 23

Barère (de Vieuzac), Bertrand as member of first French republican constitutional committee, 185, 232, 253—footnote 4; 272, 279
    as member of the second constitutional committee (from the Committee of Public Safety), 296, 306
    influence of *philosophes,* 48
    life, 145—footnote 2

Barère (de Vieuzac), Bertrand on Montesquieu, 44-45, 48

Bastille,
    Brissot, inmate of, 118—footnote 12
    fall of, 118

Bayle, Pierre, 53-54
    influence on Revolutionary leaders, 53

Beaumarchais, Augustin Pierre de, 71

Bibliothèque de l'Homme public, 45-49

335

Date Due